MW00715535

Missing
411
Canada

•UNEXPLAINED DISAPPEARANCES•

BY

DAVID PAULIDES

www.canammissing.com

ISBN: 978-1-7923-2265-5

GLOSSARY OF TERMS

ATV	All Terrain Vehicle
CAP	Civil Air Patrol
DOI	Department of the Interior
FBI	Federal Bureau of Investigation
FLIR	Forward Looking Infrared Radar
FOIA	Freedom of Information Act
NPS	National Park Service
PLS	Point Last Seen
RCMP	Royal Canadian Mounted Police
SAR	Search and Rescue
USFS	United States Forest Service

TABLE OF CONTENTS

INTRODUCTION

I have always thought of Canadians as brothers and sisters to us in the United States. I have traveled there extensively and always enjoyed the people, landscape, and recreation offered by their great country.

This is the first Missing 411 book dedicated to one country. The parallels between the United States and Canadian missing person cases are apparent and only differentiated by an imaginary line between the two countries.

The research into the Missing 411 cases started when I was visiting a United States national park and was approached off park property by two off duty national park rangers. They told me a story that they had worked at different parks and became concerned over missing people. They thought the location in the parks where people were vanishing was odd, and they quickly realized that there was a lot of publicity and SAR activity during the first 7-10 days, then nothing. When each attempted to research the disappearances and obtain documents, their agency thwarted them. When they both arrived at this park, they started to compare notes and realized there were too many missing people, and nobody was investigating the cases. Each ranger told me that they believed that I was the person that should be looking into this issue.

As I was driving home the day after meeting the rangers, I called a friend in law enforcement and asked them to search national parks and understand if there were an abnormal number of missing people. Inside an hour of my call, my friend called me back and said that there were high numbers of missing people in parks that had never been found and that there was very little information available on the cases.

Once I arrived home, I filed a series of Freedom of Information Act (FOIA) Requests against the National Park Service Police for a list of missing people in their jurisdiction. The National Park Service Police are a group of highly trained law enforcement officers that are trained at the federal law enforcement training center. Their law enforcement training is better than the majority of training police get in other parts of the United States.

Approximately six weeks after filing the FOIA, I received a call from an attorney from the National Park Service (NPS) asking why I wanted a list of the missing? This was a very odd inquiry. According to the FOIA law in the United States, a government agency cannot use the reason for your request as a determining factor if you get the information, which I told the attorney. He quickly stated that they would not use the answer in that manner; they were just interested. I told them I was doing research on missing people and wanted to see the names. The attorney said that they did not have a list of missing people. As someone who was a police officer and detective in a sizeable metropolitan police force in California (San Jose), I understand the need for lists to be kept by police. I re-phrased the question to the attorney; he again said that their agency does not have any list of any missing people.

Once the call terminated with the NPS attorney, I called several law enforcement friends and told them what I was told, nobody believed it. One investigative journalist told me it must be a semantics issue in the way I wrote the request. I re-wrote another FOIOA and submitted it again. Six weeks after the second submittal, another NPS attorney called and stated that they received my request and again informed me that NPS did not have any lists of missing people in their jurisdiction. I knew that this might be their answer, so I had a backup plan. There is an exemption in FOIA that if you are a published author (which I am), you can request the government agency to go out and get your information for free under the belief you will write about it and inform the public. I requested that NPS obtain a list of missing people from their jurisdiction under the author's exemption. Six weeks later, I received notification that my request was denied. NPS stated that they did an online check and my books were not in enough libraries to qualify for the exemption, Ha! There is no such section in the FOIA that defines how many libraries your books need to be in. I then asked how much they would charge me for a list of missing people inside the NPS and Yosemite National park?

Eight weeks after requesting a price quote from NPS, I got an email from the western regional director of FOIA for NPS. The email stated that the list of missing people for Yosemite National Park would cost $36,000, and the cost for a list from the entire NPS system was 1.4 million dollars. Nine years after I first requested these lists, the NPS released their list of missing from Yosemite, why? Everyone on the Yosemite list of missing was someone I had documented or written about in some way. They still have not released a list of missing from their entire jurisdiction; I guess I have not identified all of them.

I have had friends in Canada request case filed for me on certain Parks Canada cases. The majority of the time where a case has been requested, the request was denied. We have been successful in many instances in getting details. Our organization (www.canammissing.com) does not research every case of a missing person that vanishes in the wild. The case must fit a narrowly defined profile which has been refined after years of research, see profile points. If the disappearance doesn't match our profile, we won't look into it. We are not implying that all of the cases in this book are all of the cases in Canada that match our profile, quite the contrary. This book does constitute nine years of exhaustive research. Sixty plus cases in this book are new and do not appear in any Missing 411 book.

When you read the stories, think about the SAR workers that have volunteered their time to search for others. The vast majority of search and rescue workers are volunteers, and they get their credentials on their own time with their own money. Without search and rescue volunteers, the vast majority of missing people would never be found. I want to personally thank every SAR worker for dedicating their time and helping others, and you have my gratitude.

Profile Points

If someone read one hundred search and rescue reports, you'd have a general understanding of a handful of disappearances. If you have read five thousand cases, your view of the topic is much more thorough. There was a time that I was reading these cases when

I started to remember recurring facts. I put these reports in in my living room until I had many large stacks. After combing through the stories, I decided to call these facts, profile points. In much the same way a criminal profiler profiles crimes, these disappearances are now categorized and identified through a series of common denominators, profile points.

Canine Cannot Find a Scent

In nearly 99% of the cases I have documented, Bloodhounds brought to the point where the victim was last seen cannot find a scent, aren't interested in tracking, or seem oblivious to the smell. As a former member of a law enforcement SWAT team that had the canine unit attached to our division, I can guarantee that these dogs love their job and relish tracking people. When I first came across the anomaly of dogs not finding a scent or not willing to follow, I thought it might be an isolated issue. This is one of the most prevalent profile points in the cases we have identified.

Weather

In the vast majority of the cases highlighted in the eight books, the weather has a significant impact on the rescue or recovery of the victim. The weather seems to take a turn for the worse just as the person is going missing or just after they disappeared. Weather issues include blizzards, fog, rain, snow, hail, dust storms, freezing cold and hot temperatures. When you first start to read about this, your natural reaction is that its bad luck. After reading eight books and seeing the scenario replicate itself time after time, you'll be stunned.

Victims Found in an Area Previously Searched

In *Missing 411: The Devil's in the Detail*, I present a table showing dozens of cases where the missing person was found in an area that was previously searched. Sometimes the location of the recovery had been searched dozens of times. In one instance, the searchers had taken the same trail hundreds of times over the week hiking to where they believed the victim was located. On one day of the search, a tree had fallen across the path, and the young victim was found lying on it. Nobody could explain the perplexing scenario. In *Missing 411: A Sobering Coincidence*, I presented several cases where remote vehicles, divers, etc, searched a body of water. The victim was then found precisely where searchers had just left. Many readers have stated that it appears the victim has been placed there to be located. In the past few years, we have been told by other researchers that they think the people were dropped into place to be found. Nobody ever observes the victims arriving into the area. How the victims got to the space where they are eventually located is one of the most perplexing issues.

Missing Clothes or Shoes

Often the victims are found without shoes or missing pieces of clothing. It doesn't matter the type of climate; this has been documented in all kinds of weather. There have been people who have never read the books that make claims that this is due to hypothermia. The issue with that is that many small children are located missing clothing and their parents state that they could not remove their clothes. In other instances, on a warm afternoon, a person disappears. Hundreds of yards from the location he or she was last seen, searchers find a pile of clothing: The victim didn't have the time to get to the hypothermia state, yet all of their clothes had been removed. You will read stories in this book where clothing and shoes had been removed under highly unusual circumstances.

Time of Disappearance

The vast majority of disappearances occur in the late afternoon or early evening. In *Missing 411: Off the Grid*, there is a table on page 358 that shows cumulative data from seven books. The predominant time disappearances occur is just before it gets dark; that fact hasn't changed.

Disability or Illness

An abnormal number of the missing has some disability or illness. This fact only shows itself after vetting thousands of cases. Many readers have stated that it appears to them as though someone or something is closely monitoring these people and wants to understand more about their genetic markers.

Lack of Memory

In the instances where a victim can talk and be questioned, the vast majority cannot remember how they got lost or what happened while they were missing. In almost every instance where a victim is found alive, searchers and law enforcement rarely sit with them and debrief about the experience. The effort may be futile as the victim's memory may be blank.

Missing Are Often Found Near Creeks, Rivers, Ponds, Lakes, and Streams

In my book, *Missing 411: A Sobering Coincidence*, I documented over 100 cases where young men vanished, sometimes in a large crowd of friends. Nobody can explain where the person went or how they left. Days, sometimes weeks, later he is found in a body of water, deceased. Just as in previous books, there is a geographical clustering of the missing. I would refer readers to our Geographical Cluster Map of North America for details on this portion of the research.

In my first four *Missing 411* books, many victims were found near creeks, rivers, and ponds, and many times the victims would've had to travel unusual and difficult terrain to get to those places.

In many instances, the victim is located amongst rocks and boulders adjacent to the body of water.

Boulders and Granite

The most significant cluster of missing people anywhere in the world that matches our criteria is Yosemite National Park. Yosemite happens to be one of those locations in the world that has a high concentration of granite. There are many people documented in our books that are found in boulder fields, amongst boulders and large rocks.

Swamps and Bogs

Some readers will find the fact that many missing people are located in the middle of swamps and bogs a highly unusual place to discover people. I have lost count of the number of times this fact has proven itself to be true. Marshes are one of those places that the general public won't casually wander. It could be considered one of those locations where few people ever trek. It is also a place discounted by many SAR personnel as too difficult for the victim to travel.

Point of Separation

I want readers to have an awareness of when two people decide to part company. I've always claimed that a hiker traveling alone in the mountains is probably going to be more safety-conscious than someone traveling with a group. I can attest that when I am alone, I am much more aware of my surroundings and the inherent danger of what I might be doing. I know that if I break my leg in the wild, I'm alone against the elements with nobody to seek assistance on my behalf. Hundreds have written to me about this point and that it appears as though the victim was being watched—and at the time they were vulnerable and isolated, the unusual happened.

Equipment Malfunction

In documenting hundreds of missing people, you will eventually read about the air support that goes along with all SARs. There are a high number of engine and equipment issues associated with the SAR of the victims. In my book «Missing 411: Hunters, I included a story about a hunter. I think the facts surrounding an equipment issue is essential and I add it again below.

When I was writing *Missing 411: Hunters*, I came across a cluster of missing outdoorsmen in an area within 5 miles from Lake Superior on the Wisconsin–Michigan border. On November 21, 1948, Frank Naslund went hunting with three other friends in this exact area. Sometime in the early morning hours, the men separated to hunt. Three of the four hunters made it back to their vehicles at lunch. Frank didn't arrive, and a search was initiated.

Late in the afternoon on November 22, Frank found a fire cut and followed it until he came to a roadway and got assistance. The reason this story is relevant is for what Frank told a reporter in a

November 23, 1948, article in the *Rhinelander Daily News*: "He said his compass was not functioning properly and he built a fire alongside a creek and spent a night there."

A malfunctioning compass is a factor in disappearances that nobody has addressed. Anomalies in the environment that would cause a compass to malfunction are a fascinating topic to explore. In Frank's case, we don't know if he had a broken compass or if there was something in the environment that caused Frank's instrument to malfunction. If it was something in the atmosphere, could this be a contributing factor in many of the disappearances? With the advancements made in GPS technology, people are carrying trail guides and other items based on this technology. The compass has taken a backseat to GPS in need to determine location, direction, and route.

I realize that various types of rocks can affect the materials used in the manufacture of a compass. Could boulders have had an impact on how the compass operated? Could something else have been happening in Frank's location that impacted how it functioned? This is good food for thought. Now take the issue of the compass and transfer that to instruments on airplanes. Could the crashes in the triangles be related to some atmospheric anomaly that effects engines and devices? If a compass is malfunctioning on the ground, could the same be happening above?

Notes

Many of you will mark this book up extensively with notes and thoughts on cases; I encourage this. I've had readers tell me that they've read each book three or four times to absorb raw facts better. In each case, I have attempted to leave several notes to identify source material. Many of the case facts came directly from SAR and law enforcement reports.

The NPS has given me the designation of a "Commercial Requestor" for all FOIA requests. This essentially means they can charge me up to four times what they charge the average citizen for documents and materials. This is a blatant attempt to detract us from requesting and obtaining missing person reports, as they know we can't afford those outrageous prices. Many of you have stepped forward and offered to seek case files on our behalf and allow our research to continue; this is sincerely appreciated. Your continued and ongoing support is needed for us to further our work. My contact information is on the last page of this book.

Vetting Cases

After reading thousands of SAR and law enforcement reports on missing people, we developed a series of vetting points. These items determine if we exclude a case from the study. The facts that we rely upon come directly from SAR members, reports, news archives, and witness statements.

Voluntary Disappearance: if evidence is presented that the person planned to disappear and wanted to fall out of society, this is an exclusionary point.

Mental Health: If the individual has a history of mental health issues, we will not include the case in studies.

Animal Predation: Some in the public think that animal attacks are difficult to located and understand. When a mountain lion or bear attacks a person in the wild, the victim will fight for their life. The scene will include, blood, skin tissue, drag marks, the ground will be torn up and bits of clothing will be located. SAR teams are trained to look for and find predation areas. In conferences, I routinely ask attendees how many fatal mountain lion attacks have happened in North America in the last 100 years? Nobody gets this question correct. The answer is 16, that's it. Mountain Lion attacks are not that unusual, fatal attacks are rare. If you happen to see Jaryd Ataderos name on a list of deadly mountain lion attacks, it's a lie. Watch our first documentary, Missing 411; four different mountain lion experts wrote that it was not a mountain lion that attacked Jaryd.

I've read many online forums where people who have never read my books or just watched a few videos are convinced that the majority of the disappearances we've documented are caused by predation, no.

Criminal Activity: Crime on a mountain trail is rare, but it does happen. If there is any evidence that a crime occurred in conjunction with a disappearance, we will exclude that case from our study.

Maps

Maps are an expensive item for authors to include in books. Since 40% of this book is about disappearances in British Columbia, I thought it would be prudent to include a map that showed the location of these cases. Study the map and you will quickly realize that there is something very unusual happening in the great Vancouver area.

Geographical Clusters

After reviewing thousands of cases and finding the ones that match our profile, we plotted those incidents on a map. We have produced the North America Cluster Map that is available on our website (www.canammissing.com). The map shows dozens of clusters in North America and southern Canada. Conducting the research for this book uncovered a new cluster in the Vancouver area. We refer you to the map that is included with this book and studies the areas where these people have gone missing. There is one large cluster in the Vancouver region and several smaller groups inside the area. This is one of the most significant clusters we have ever identified.

Alberta

Population: 4,362,000
Capital City: Edmonton
    Alberta is considered the westernmost prairie province of the three. It is 250,000 square miles in size with 6500 square miles of freshwater. It is 750 miles from its southern to the northern border and 400 miles wide. The far western portion of the region has the Rocky Mountains and three gorgeous national parks, Banff, Jasper, and Waterton Lakes. The central portion of Alberta has Elk Island National Park, and Wood Buffalo National Park is at the far northeastern part of the province.

The largest cities in Alberta are:
Edmonton (Capital): 972,223
Calgary: 1,246,000
Red Deer: 100,000
Lethbridge: 98,198
St. Albert: 68,000
    The tallest mountain in the province is Mount Columbia at 12,294 feet tall. There are many mountains in the Canadian Rocky Mountain range over 11,000' with the plains having an elevation from 1,000-3000' in elevation.
    If you are ever in the Canadian Rockies, take a trip to the Columbia Icefield. This is a giant glacier that is the headwaters for two different rivers. There is a Canadian business that has large glacier vehicles that take tourists far up into the ice landscape; it is epic.
    Farming and ranching have a significant hold on the Alberta economy. Farmers tend to grow rapeseed, hay, grains, barley, and wheat, along with sugar beets, potatoes, and peas. Ranchers raise cattle, pig, poultry, sheep and even deer. Forest covers just a little under half the province.
    Mining of several different types is also a significant employer in the province. Oil, natural gas, crude oil, and coal are all mining staples in the westernmost prairie province.
    When my kids were much younger and playing hockey, I can remember several trips we made to the north to play Canadian teams.

I remember one specific game our group of 12-year olds stepped onto the ice against a team from Calgary's oil fields. The boys on that team looked like giants compared to our California kids. My son came off the ice at the end of that game and said the boys on the other team were, "giants." Needless to say, our California team was crushed. The area of Calgary, Red Deer, Rocky Mountain House, and a few other small communities are known as ice hockey strongholds of Canada.

The Canadian Rockies on the western side of Alberta are worth a family trip. Go north from Idaho or Montana and take the road through the middle of the mountains. You will see bears, goats, Bighorn Sheep, and nature that will take your breath away. A stop at Lake Louise will have you sitting lakeside mesmerized by the natural beauty that surrounds you.

Alberta Missing Person List by Date

Missing Person	Date Missing• Age• Sex
Evelyn Rauch	07/15/34–9 a.m. •2 •F
Edward Schnaknacht	09/01/37–PM •4 •M
Cathleen Whitlock	07/22/49-P.M.• 62• F
Helen Bogen	08/07/50-10:00 A.M.• 2½ •F
Lorraine Smith	09/02/50•2•F
Paul Schroeder	07/06/72- 6:30 P.M.• 72• M
Kevin Reimer	06/29/79–Noon •9•M
James Caraley	07/18/79•22•M
Steve Maclaren	06/30/81•25•M
Shelly Bacsu	05/03/83•16•F
Sharel Haresym	09/04/84•35•F
Jesse Rinker	05/04/87–4:30 p.m.•2•M
Brian Adrian	02/04/91• 37•M
Lillian Owens	06/28/91•46•F
Donald Belliveau	01/27/95•28•M
Rhonda Runningbird	03/26/95•25•F
Knut Thielemann	08/04/95•22•M
Melvin Hoel	03/12/97•64•M
Tom Howell	09/12/05•46•M
Wai Fan	09/28/05•43•M

Robert Leigh	08/13/06•20•M
Stephanie Stewart	08/26/06•70•F
Robert Neale	05/02/07•77•M
Kevin Kennedy	08/21/11•59•M
Rhonda Cardinal	07/13/12•42•F

Evelyn Rauch
Missing 7/15/34–9 a.m., Rocky Mountain House, AB
Age at Disappearance: 2 years

Rocky Mountain House is a small town at the base of the Rocky Mountains, fifty miles northeast of Banff National Park. Once you leave the outskirts of town, the area gets very wild quite quickly. The region is dotted with farms, ranches, and large wild mammals. The location of this incident was twelve miles south of Rocky Mountain House, in a very wet region with many lakes, creeks, and rivers.

On July 15, 1934, at approximately 8 a.m., John Rauch was on his farm with his two-year-old daughter, Evelyn. The pair was outside near their barn when John told his daughter to stay at that location while he went into his pasture to tend to the cows. After tending to his animals, John returned to the barn and could not locate Evelyn. He and friends searched the entire farm, barn, and personal residence throughout the night and couldn't find a trace of the girl. Late that first night, John contacted the local Royal Canadian Mounted Police, and they took charge of the search.

On July 16, the search for Evelyn started at dawn with 150 local volunteers. The area around the Rauch farm was covered by searchers, as well as local sloughs, rivers, creeks, and pastures. On July 17, the search gathered more steam, and over one thousand volunteers and RCMP from local cities responded. Now the entire area around John's property was completely covered with people.

At approximately 11 a.m. on July 17, fifty hours after Evelyn vanished, searchers were working a wet and damp bank near a local slough and found Evelyn. A July 17, 1934, article in the *Calgary Herald* had the following description of what searchers found: "Standing in tall grass beside a slough about a mile and a half from her home, she was crying bitterly when she was found by Joe Bertagnolli, a farmer who was one of the search party. She was hurried home and found to be suffering no ill effects except exhaustion and was put to bed. She was unable to explain where she had been and how she had lived through two hot days and two cold nights since she vanished early Sunday."

Summary

The area around Rocky Mountain House has been a region where people disappear under unusual circumstances. This region contains one of the clusters that extends into the Banff National Park area.

There are a few elements of Evelyn's case that strike me as unusual. The fact that searcher Joe Bertagnolli found her "crying bitterly" is unusual. Children cannot cry for days at a high pace. What Joe described was almost a fanatical crying, as though he just happened onto the girl as she started to break down, or just as her scenario changed and Evelyn had the opportunity to break down. If the situation had changed (possibly because Joe just happened onto the scene), and Evelyn was just left alone to her own emotions, maybe Joe just happened onto her at the optimal moment.

The fact that hundreds of searchers were just a mile and a half from Evelyn for two days and she was unable to call out to them seems unusual, especially in an area that is farmlands, where sounds travel for miles. Why didn't Evelyn call out to other volunteers?

The last important fact is the location where Evelyn was found, on the banks of a slough. This is a location next to water, a location where there is access to other locations via the water, rather than having to walk across land. There was never any mention of what Evelyn was wearing or how she was able to survive the two very cold nights she was supposedly out in the elements.

There are too many incidents in these three books that describe small children who disappear for a few days. If they are found, the majority cannot remember or will not admit they remember what happened to them. Evelyn Rauch appears to be another in a long line of victims.

Edward Schnaknacht
Missing: 9/01/37–PM, Tiger Lily, AB
Age at Disappearance: 4 years
Water•

Tiger Lily, Alberta, is located forty miles west of Westlock and seventy-five miles northwest of Edmonton. This is predominantly a farming area. Tiger Lily is a very, very small community, surrounded by hundreds of small bodies of water and a large river just to the north. The Holmes Crossing Sandhills Ecological Reserve is also to the north, and the Fort Assinboine Wildland Area lies to the northeast. The region is rich with water, wilderness, and open space.

On September 1, 1937, four-year-old Edward Schnaknacht was playing alone at the front of his farmhouse when he vanished. The farm is not located near any populated areas or major roadways. The parents initially felt that Edward had wandered away and asked local friends and other farmers to help scour the region looking for the boy. A September 7, 1937, *Lethbridge Herald* article highlighted the search efforts: "A posse of neighbors, farmers and residents in the tiny village of Tiger Lily joined Mounted Police at the weekend and again Monday in combing the district for traces of the lost youngster. They dragged many sloughs and swamps near the boy's home." Other articles indicated that the Schnaknachts' farmhouse was bordered on three sides by some type of water, including sloughs, swamps, a creek, and a deep lake.

The formal search for Edward lasted a week but informally, the family searched much longer. The Royal Canadian Mounted Police made a statement early in the search that the boy was "lost." One of the later articles about Edward indicated that it was the feeling of the police that Edward had drowned, even though days were spent dragging every body of water in the area, and his body never did surface.

There is something about the northern reaches of Canada that has always had me interested in disappearances in that region. A four-year-old farm boy is well versed on the dangers that surround his home. He has been counseled extensively about not walking away from the confines of his home, and he is well aware of the dangers that exist once he leaves. When a child raised on a farm, ranch, or in a rural environment disappears, it always bothers me that it may not have been voluntary. With the absence of human predators in an area like Tiger Lily, what could have taken Edward? He was never found.

Cathleen Whitlock
Missing: 07/22/49- P.M., Fawcett, AB
Age at disappearance: 62 years
Weather• Water• Canines

I've traveled extensively throughout Alberta. One of the main constants is the amount of open space, farm fields, and wilderness that still exists. This incident is centered on an area seventy-Five miles north of Edmonton. The community where the victim lived is Fawcett, located adjacent to the Athabasca River Slough and just eight miles east of the main river. The Hubert Lake Wildland area is just west of the city and has hundreds of small bodies of water and is thick with vegetation.

In July of 1949, Cathleen Whitlock and her husband lived on the outskirts of Fawcett, Alberta raising their cows. On July 22, Mr. Whitlock was twenty-five miles north of his home, working in Chisholm while his wife tended the ranch. In the afternoon hours, the sixty-two-year-old woman went out to herd her cattle and did not return.

On July 23, 1949, two boys living near the Whitlock property went to the home to see Mrs. Whitlock and could not locate her. The boys went back to their residence and notified their parents, who also went to look for Cathleen. After several hours of calling her name and searching the property, the RCMP was called.

In rural areas, such as Fawcett, the community supports themselves. Once a call goes out for anything critical, locals respond to the scene and assist in the effort, as happened here. The local police called for local ranchers and farmers to help in the search for Mrs. Whitlock. The search started almost immediately and is described in the July 27, 1949 edition of the *Edmonton Journal,* "Police dogs, an RCAF aircraft and a ground search of more than 100 civilians and RCMP Wednesday were combing the Fawcett area, 75 miles north of Edmonton for Mrs. Cathleen Whitlock, 62, who disappeared from her home Friday. The country in which the elderly woman is lost is rugged and heavy with brush. Following heavy rains, ground searchers are having much more difficulty in traveling the area."

The RCMP could tell that the effort to locate Cathleen was not leading to her discovery. The police called the Royal Canadian Air Force (RCAF)for assistance. The RCAF in Edmonton dispatched twenty-five airmen to search the ground and also sent a Canso aircraft that scoured the land from the sky. One article described how the plane flew 400-500 feet off the ground and dropped a walkie talkie to ground teams so they could communicate.

The formal search for Cathleen Whitlock lasted nine days. Searchers did find what they believed to be her tracks on the ranch, but they couldn't determine if they were old or new. Following her tracks did not lead to finding the lady.

Cathleen Whitlock was never located.

I have written several stories about ranchers going into the fields and woods to herd their cattle and never coming back. When you think about the situation, missing animals, why were they missing? Was there a predator in the area that scattered them? Was there something in the region that spooked the cows? What was the reason that the animals weren't in their usual location and be easily found? Was the reason that the cattle were gone the same reason searchers could not locate Cathleen?

If a predator had scattered the herd and even attacked Mrs. Whitlock, it's almost a guarantee that she would've been found. Predation attacks leave a scene of violence, blood, torn clothes, etc.

The land in the area of Fawcett is relatively flat. A plane in the sky can cover a lot of ground and see something that was not moving. It's difficult to understand why Mrs. Whitlock was never found in an area she knew like you know your backyard.

Helen Bogen
Missing: 08/07/50-10:00 a.m. • 2½ • Monitor, AB
Age at disappearance: 2½ years
Weather• Missing Clothing• Previously Searched• Water• Point of Separation

Monitor is an extremely small city nearly two hundred miles southeast of Edmonton. It's approximately ten miles southeast of

Gooseberry Lake Provincial Park and in an area of hundreds of small swamps and ponds. The Bogen farm was ten miles north of the small city.

On August 7, 1950, at 10:00 a.m., a few of the Bogen children were mounting horses for a ride to their grandparents' home. Helen asked to go on the trip and was told by her parents that she could not. The kids rode off, leaving Helen alone in the garden. Sometime after the kids left, Helen disappeared. Mr. and Mrs. Bogen searched the yard and surrounding farm and found her nightgown near a gate on their property. It was at this point that they made a call to neighbors to help in the search. It wasn't soon after that first call that 150 neighbors responded to the Bogen farm, yelling and calling for Helen.

The neighbors searched nonstop for that first twenty-four hours. They lit fires and yelled for the girl while not getting a response. Bloodhounds from Westlock were brought to the farm, and they couldn't pick up a scent. Two private planes from Provost also responded and flew the skies above the farm without finding anything of value. A total of 450 area residents responded to the Bogens' call for assistance.

Thirty hours after Helen had vanished, an abandoned farm was being searched when a severe thunderstorm hit the search area. All searches were stopped. Searchers found nothing on the farm. An hour after the rain stopped, Mrs. Douglas Tainsh was back at the same abandoned farm that was searched an hour earlier and found Helen. An August 9, 1950, article in the *Lethbridge Herald* explained what Mrs. Tainsh found: "Naked and splashing happily in an old tub of dirty water inside a shed on an abandoned farm, 30 month old Helen Bogen was found Tuesday night." She was hungry, weak, and happily, she was alive. She had scratches over her body.

An August 9, 1950, article in the *Edmonton Journal* reported the feelings of searchers about the discovery of Helen: "Observers termed it a miracle that she had survived the 30 hour period, unclothed, unfed, plagued by insects and exposed to a rain shower and overnight temperatures that dropped to about 40 degrees."

Helen was taken to the hospital for observation and an evaluation. Helen made only a few statements to her father the first morning after she was found. She stated that the night she was gone she spent on a hill and "rested and listened." She made no mention of the dozens of searchers that had to have been in the area or the fires that were built to attract her attention. She also said nothing about being cold, even though temperatures were in the low forties.

Summary

This case is important because of the details that emerged. Searchers had gone through the abandoned farm just before a major thunderstorm hit the region. They were calling Helen's name and looking in the area. Helen wasn't found, no tracks were located, and she didn't respond. The thunderstorm hits, the farm is searched again afterward, and Helen is found playing in a tub. We know that weather plays some role in disappearances. This case makes it even more obvious.

Helen was out in the elements naked, yet she never complained about being cold and did not suffer from hypothermia.

The region of the Bogen farm is literally covered with hundreds of small bodies of water.

Lorraine Smith
Missing: 09/02/50, 5:00 p.m., Lake Edith, Jasper National Park, Alberta
Age at disappearance: 2
Water• Canines•

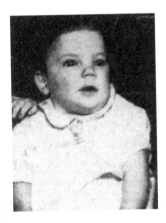

Lorraine Smith

Mr. and Mrs. Eric Smith left their Edmonton residence on Saturday, September 2, 1950, with their twins, Lorne and Lorraine, and headed for Edith Lake inside Jasper National Park. The ride was slightly over two hundred miles and covers some of the most beautiful terrain in the province. Highway 16 also bisects several of the areas between Edmonton and the park, where many of the missing people in this chapter have vanished.

The family arrived late in the afternoon and headed for the southern area of the lake to establish their camp. They were there to meet a church group that was going to spend the weekend together. Soon after the Smiths arrived, they noticed that Lorraine had disappeared. A frantic search started and the family enlisted the aid of others in the area. Everyone soon realized that two-year-old Lorraine was nowhere to be found, and the RCMP (Royal Canadian Mounted Police) were notified.

Edith Lake sits at the bottom of a valley that contains more than twenty small lakes and a river. The lake is a popular spot on the fringe of the wilderness approximately three miles from the Jasper Park Lodge. Heavy woods surround the valley and a 7,500-foot mountain looms just to the southeast with a ridgeline that starts near the water.

Within two days the RCMP had two hundred people searching for Lorraine. They also brought in canine search teams, airplanes, water rescue teams, and horseback mounted patrols.

On September 5 the RCMP received reports that blood was found on a ridge near Signal Mountain just southeast of the lake. They sent a team and a physician to check on the report, but details as to what they found were not available. It was on this day that an additional thirty trained searchers were brought into the park from the Canadian Northwest Air Command.

Searchers combed an area in thick woods five miles from Edith Lake. It wasn't clear why they were searching that location, but it was reported that game wardens shot a bear in the area; however, they confirmed that no remains of Lorraine were found in the bear.

A September 7 article in the *Calgary Herald* expressed the frustration of searchers: "A belief continued among some searchers that the child might not be in the area. Police are investigating the possibilities of abduction or an accidental death, where persons responsible may have removed the body."

After several days searchers did something quite intelligent: they brought Lorraine's twin brother into the forest to see how quickly and efficiently he could move on the ground. The article stated that they were surprised how easily he made his way through the forest. An RCAF helicopter flew the area in hopes of spotting Lorraine.

On September 8 the RCMP officially terminated the search. The police so strongly believed she was abducted that they were stopping vehicles at border crossings to search for the girl.

The search included over one thousand searchers who covered thirty-six square miles of forest. It was documented as the greatest civilian search in the history of Alberta. The search commander stated that he did not believe Lorraine had been consumed by an animal because no traces of clothing or blood were found. In fact, the search didn't find any evidence of Lorraine.

Case Summary

The response of SAR commanders is typical and understandable after an unsuccessful mission. If they cannot find evidence that the girl was in the area, they will immediately start to believe that the girl was abducted and taken from the area. A six-day search for a two-year-old girl seems too short for a search in this day and age, but maybe not for 1950. There are many people missing from this mountain range in Alberta. One last interesting note, Lorraine had a twin brother, Lorne. I've been casually keeping track of the number of twins thaq have vanished, no solid numbers yet, but it has tweaked my interest.

Paul Schroeder
Missing: 07/06/72- 6:30 P.M., 40 Miles west of Edmonton
Age at disappearance: 72 years
German• Water• Disability• Canines

Paul Schroeder was a German immigrant and had brought his family to Edmonton in 1954 and established their residence at 9837 83rd Avenue. He worked for Western Archrib Structures Limited in Edmonton until his retirement in 1965. Paul was a nonstop worker and found his only relaxation in the family cottage at Lac Saint Anne Lake forty miles west of Edmonton.

In early July of 1972, Paul and his wife were at their cottage, which was part of the German Pentecostal Complex near the lake. Mr. Schroeder was described in various articles as being extraordinarily religious and only speaking German. One report said that he also spoke Polish and very little English.

At approximately 6:30 p.m. on July 6, 1972, Paul just finished helping his wife ready their cottage for the summer when he vanished. He was not carrying any money or identification. The church camp and the cottage were located on Sunset Point adjacent to the lake. A July 13, 1972 article in the Edmonton Journal had this explanation of what happened, "Mr. Schroeder mowed the lawn in front of his cottage, part of the German Pentecostal Camp complex, and then went for water just before he disappeared. Alf (son) said: "My mother was going to make coffee before they came back to the city." He was spotted at 6:30 p.m. by two other campers on the east side of the camp and then vanished." Later in the same article was this, "Mr. Schroeder, who wears glasses, is almost blind in his left eye, and also walks in a stooped, shuffling manner." Paul has a visible disability in the way he walks, and his vision is compromised.

The landscape around the southern portion of the lake was predominantly farmlands in 1972 and still is much that way today. The area around the church camp has more homes and looks like a city in the twenty-first century.

Once Mrs. Schroeder could not find her husband, she called the RCMP. I can only imagine what the local officer thought when he took the report. The missing man walks bent over, has poor vision, and sometimes falls, it should be a quick and easy search to locate the 72-year-old retiree. The search was anything but quick and easy.

One of the last articles I could find on this disappearance was published in the December 23, 1975 edition of the Edmonton Journal and highlighted the effort to locate Paul, "Mr. Schroeder's disappearance was first reported to Stony Plain RCMP at 9 p.m., July 6, 1972. There was a major search on foot of the area around his cabin. No luck. Then a bulletin was prepared for distribution to all police units in Alberta and to RCMP divisions in the western provinces. A shoulder to shoulder search was conducted, and tracking dogs were used, as time went by, searches were held daily for several days, and people throughout the area were interviewed. Friends and relatives of Mr. Schroeder in other cities were contacted, and all trains, buses, and airports were checked. In the fall, after the leaves had fallen from the trees, an aircraft searched the area. Then another foot search was conducted. Again, no luck. His medical history was read for any possible clues, but to no avail."

When Paul was initially reported as a missing person, the RCMP focused on the area around the church camp. After a day, they moved out to focus on the lake and surrounding water and fields. After a week of searching, they started to talk about him hitchhiking, taking a bus, or train out of the area. There was never a report of Paul being seen anywhere after the 6:30 p.m. sighting at the church camp. He was last observed wearing an orange shirt, brown coat, and grey pants.

What happened to Paul Schroeder?

Kevin Reimer
Missing 6/29/79–Noon, the northern end of Elk Island National Park, AB
Age at Disappearance: 9 years

To understand the specifics of Kevin's disappearance, it's imperative to understand the location where this incident occurred. Elk Island National Park is located approximately twenty miles east of Edmonton. In the 1700 to 1800s, the area of the park was utilized as the point where the Blackfeet, Cree, and Sarcee First Nations People crossed into the hunting areas of Alberta. The park still maintains over two hundred campsites where these natives stayed, and they have been maintained as archaeological locations.

In July 1906, Elk Island received the status as a wildlife sanctuary. In 1930 the Canadian government passed the National Park act and applied that status to the island land and lakes.

Elk Island National Park is open year-round and is utilized for wildlife viewing, cross country skiing, and snow shoeing in the winter and kayaking, canoeing, hiking, and wildlife viewing in the summer. In earlier times, people used to be allowed to swim, but that is not recommended now because of bacteria in the water.

According to the Elk Island Park website, here is a partial list of mammals and their numbers that call the park home:

- Beaver (1,000)
- Elk (950)

- Bison (770)
- Moose (400)
- Coyote (100)

On Friday, June 29, 1979, Velma (age thirty-seven) and Peter (age forty-four) Reimer and their son, Kevin, traveled from their home in Edmonton and had established their camp at the northern end of Elk Island National Park. At 11 a.m., Peter and Velma realized that Kevin wasn't near their site, and they started to search for him. They were walking the local roadway, calling Kevin's name and not getting a response. As the Reimers were looking for Kevin, another female camper allegedly saw Kevin walking through the area. Kevin asked the woman for directions back to his camp, and she gave them. That was the last time Kevin was supposedly seen.

Peter and Velma soon realized that they needed assistance in looking for their son and contacted park officials. Inside of two hours, there were a hundred people looking for Kevin. The Reimers advised Royal Canadian Mounted Police (RCMP) officials that Kevin was wearing only a bathing suit and tennis shoes. He did not know how to swim and knew a little about being in the outdoors.

After four days of intensive searching, the RCMP was utilizing 350 searchers, aircraft, helicopters, and Bloodhounds. Rescue personnel were walking through the swamps with no more than two feet between each person in order not to miss anything. On July 3, Constable Donald Spitke made the following statement in the *Lethbridge Herald*: "It's most likely he drowned." Later in the article was the following description of the area that was being searched: "Some areas are so dense, searchers were required to register so they wouldn't get lost themselves."

RCMP put a series of divers in every pond and lake in the area. Survival experts told the press that the boy could live one week without food and that there was plenty of water in the area for survival purposes. Equestrians were also brought to the park and were roaming the land areas, trying to spot anything out of the normal from their higher perch. Infrared scanners were used in the helicopters, which were continually in the air above the search quadrants. They could not find a heat signature.

On July 10, low-risk federal prisoners were brought into the search to assist weary RCMP members. One hundred and forty-four Canadian Air Force soldiers from Lord Strathcona Field in Calgary were also brought to the park to assist in the ground grid search process. The July 10 *Lethbridge Herald* had the following statement about the search commander's feelings about the incident: "The RCMP constable coordinating the search said the disappearance appeared to be more than just 'a boy lost in the woods.'" Commanders on scene at the park admitted that they had been investigating the possibility of foul play from the very onset of the disappearance but did not supply any clearer information.

After eleven nonstop days of searching for Kevin Reimer, the effort to find the nine-year-old boy was terminated. Searchers did not find one shred of evidence: not clothing, shoes, or even tracks.

Seven years after Kevin vanished, RCMP commanders working Kevin's disappearance made a public statement that they did not have any new clues as to what had happened.

The effort to find Kevin included fifteen thousand search hours, eleven initial days of searching, countless days of follow-up investigation, and an unknown amount of volunteer hours, which included continued searching days after the disappearance.

Summary
I reviewed a weather chart for this region of Alberta and found that for the weeks I checked, it rained six of the seven days. This specific area in and around the park has hundreds of small lakes and ponds inside of a ten-mile radius.

Searchers did not have an overwhelmingly large area to search. Elk Island National Park is approximately four miles wide and ten miles long. The Reimer family was camped at the north end of the park near Asotin Lake, and Kevin was last seen in the northern end.

For readers that have followed the missing-persons cases I have highlighted in past books, you will recognize several factors in this case. Many Bloodhounds were used to locate Kevin; none found his scent. Helicopters with FLIR were used; no heat signatures were found on the ground. Hundreds of soldiers, RCMP, prisoners, and volunteers combed the park for eleven days; they did not find one clue as to where Kevin was located. Finally, when search commanders get stressed and facts are few, they start to present the abduction scenario. Commanders believed that some type of foul play might have been afoot when Kevin vanished.

The area where Kevin disappeared is similar to many locations where kids have vanished in North America. It's mind-boggling. Nobody will ever convince me that any child Kevin's age or younger is going to voluntarily wade through smelly, dirty swamp water on the mere possibility his parents are somewhere where they cannot be seen. It doesn't seem reasonable that the child would leave the safety of the roadway or paved path to go cross-country through swamps into the unknown. In past incidents with topography similar to this park's, the child is found in an area where searchers did not believe they could possibly reach.

I did an extensive search of the archives, and I could not absolutely confirm that Kevin or his remains were ever found. I did find a website on missing people with a forum where discussions about Kevin's case were discussed. One of the contributors on the forum advised that Kevin's remains were found by a lone hiker in an extremely remote area of the park in June 1989. There supposedly was an article in the June 1989 edition of *The Record of Kitchener Ontario* that outlined the elements of Kevin's remains. I could not find or confirm this article's existence, but if he was found in an extremely remote area of the park, it matches the facts in past cases.

James Christopher Caraley
Missing: 07/18/79, Columbia Ice Fields, Jasper, Alberta
Age at disappearance: 22

James Caraley was a hiker and climber. He enjoyed the outdoors. He parked his vehicle in the Columbia Ice Fields parking lot and notified friends that he was going to attempt to climb Mount Andromeda, located directly in front of the parking lot.

Mount Andromeda and Mount Athabasca sit next to each other and are part of the same continuous mountain. Both of the summits are approximately 10,500 feet. Andromeda has a fairly easy route up the southeastern side, but it is not known which direction James went. There were extensive searches by law enforcement, but they were unable to find any evidence of James's whereabouts. His case is still listed on Canadian Web sites as an active missing person case.

Hiking in this area is extremely common. There are thousands of vacationers that visit this spot every month during the summer. This is the first of two cases I have uncovered at this attraction.

Steve Thomas Maclaren
Missing: 06/30/81, Capital Trail Crew Camp, Kananaskis, Alberta
Age at disappearance: 25
Cluster Zone• Point of Separation•

In June 1981 Steve Maclaren was working on a trail crew at the Capital Camp near Kananaskis, Alberta. This is the entry point for the Canadian Rockies off of Highway 1, directly west of Calgary. This is a very picturesque area with remote regions just beyond the highway.

Steve was working on the crew in the wild when he disappeared. Searchers scoured the region for over a week and never found a trace of Steve. I have documented other cases where trail crew members have disappeared and never found. There are few details on where he might be located. There are other cases of missing people in this region.

Shelly Anne Bacsu
Missing: 05/03/83, Hinton, Alberta
Age at disappearance: 16

Hinton hides several dark secrets, and the whereabouts of Shelly Bacsu is one. Shelly was last observed walking down Highway 16 toward Highway 40 in Hinton. There was a documentary made about the Bacsu case. There are supposed to be witnesses who saw Shelly abducted by up to three men in a van. The RCMP of Alberta and British Columbia are investigating up to fifteen women who have disappeared on a highway or adjacent roadway. Shelly's case is the furthest east and may not be related to the other fourteen cases, which have been named the Highway of Tears cases. Canada formed a special law enforcement task force to investigate the highway cases, and they are still working on leads. There are no named suspects.

Sharel Vance Haresym
Missing: 09/04/84, Bentley, Alberta
Age at disappearance: 35
Water•

Sharel Haresym was supposed to be en route to the Twin Lakes Campground five miles west of Red Deer near Gull and Sylvan lakes. The landscape in this area is filled with hundreds of small family farms. Sharel was traveling approximately forty miles from an area south of Breton to the campground. He never arrived and was never seen again. A massive search of the area could not locate anything related to the disappearance.

Jesse Rinker
Missing 5/04/87–4:30 p.m., Sunchild In-
dian Reserve, AB
Age at Disappearance: 2 years

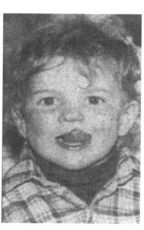

Jesse Rinker

The Sunchild Indian Reserve is locat-ed forty kilometers northwest of Rocky Mountain House, Alberta. The reserva-tion is fifty-two square kilometers in size and sits in an area just east of the Rocky Mountains and national parks. It is in a re-gion where several other people have also vanished and never been found. The area around the reservation starts on the east as plains and quickly escalates in the west to large mountains and rugged terrain.

Roger and Karen Rinker were Christian missionaries that came to the Sunchild Indian Reserve to educate and inform the local First Nation Cree Indians of the Christian word. The Rinker's had one son, Jesse, who was just over two years old.

The Rinker's lived in a home on the reservation that was situat-ed adjacent to a very wild area. On May 4, 1987, at approximately 4:30 p.m., Karen left Jesse in the front yard playing on his swing for just a few minutes as she went to attend to family chores. When Karen returned, Jesse was gone. Karen hollered for Jesse, walked the circumference of the yard, and then started to get extremely nervous. Karen couldn't find her boy, and she soon contacted the local tribal police and Royal Canadian Mounted Police (RCMP) along with Jesse's father.

RCMP from Rocky Mountain House immediately took charge of the scene and assigned several canine tracking teams to search. There was also a call for multiple helicopters with forward-looking infrared radar (FLIR) to assist in the search. There were initially several hundred ground searchers that made their way to the reservation to assist in the search effort. After a week of searching, the numbers dwindled down to thirty to forty people.

The canine search teams and the helicopters could not find one clue as to where Jesse went. A May 8, 1987, article in the *Lethbridge Herald* outlined some of the difficulties searchers were confronting: "Searchers were being hampered by difficult terrain, including muskeg and bogs." The area was very thick with vegetation, and there were many swamps and bogs in the vicinity.

The search for Jesse was taking place on the Sunchild Reservation and on the nearby O'Chiese Indian Reserve; both are close to each other.

Throughout the search for Jesse, the RCMP continually made a plea to the community for additional searchers. This plea is an unusual gesture, and it shows that there were few leads and that the RCMP did believe that the boy was somewhere in the countryside.

Three full-time RCMP detectives were initially assigned to the Jesse Rinker case, and they interviewed dozens of members of the community. On June 15, 1987, almost five weeks after Jesse disappeared, Roger Rinker made a statement to the press that he was unhappy with the RCMP and its response to his son's disappearance. He stated that he didn't feel that the RCMP was doing enough searching, and they were not following up on some leads. The police force did respond and stated that it was their fault for not keeping the father more informed of what they had done, but they felt that they had been doing plenty.

Near the end of June 1987, the RCMP made a statement that they were concentrating their investigation on the Sunchild Reservation, as that was the place they felt they should be looking.

Summary

The manner that parents are informed and kept updated about the disappearance of their child has changed significantly since 1987. Today, parents are briefed daily and sometimes more as details emerge. Police have agreements with family members that the information they are told must be held confidentially, and they aren't allowed to discuss much of what they know with the press. This is a two-way trust relationship between police and family.

In the many pages of documents I reviewed for this piece, I never found anything that indicated RCMP had a suspect in the case. Every article tended to indicate that volunteers and RCMP were still searching the swamps, bogs, and rugged terrain around the reservation for Jesse.

This is one of the rare disappearances where the news articles mention that family members were affiliated with any religion. I know that many readers of my past books have been interested to understand if there ever was a religious affiliation connected with the disappearance of a child.

Jesse Rinker was never found. His photo and personal information were placed on many milk cartons, bulletin boards, and public poles throughout North America. His disappearance will be added to the cluster of missing people in the Alberta Rocky Mountain area.

Brian Adrian
Missing: 02/04/91, Ware Creek Provincial Recreation Area, AB
Age at disappearance: 37 years
Canines• Cluster Zone

When a SAR team enters a case, they are faced with a multitude of questions that need answering. The personality of the individual and their interests are essential. If they disappeared in a wilderness setting, was the person an outdoorsman, did they know survival techniques? Had they been to the area before? Did they usually travel with

Jesse Rinker

others, or did they like to hike alone? What was their physical conditioning level? How far would they regularly hike? All of these questions come into play when SAR teams set grids and parameters that they will search.

Brian Adrian lived in Calgary, and that is where his family and friends resided. Numerous articles described him as a loner, but what does that mean? I think some would describe me the same way, just because I spend hours alone doing research and writing. I also like the solitude of being in the outdoors and enjoying nature on my terms.

The center point of this event was the Ware Creek Provincial Recreation area located approximately twenty-five miles southwest of Calgary. It was an area that Brian knew very well and had hunted many times. His companion in life was a seven-year-old Brittany Spaniel, Kin, that he loved to be with on the trails.

When Brian went out to hunt or hike, he never spent the time to notify others where he was going or when he was coming back, a huge mistake. This is one point I pound home in every conference presentation I make. A thorough search of many articles stated that Brian was last seen on February 4, 1991. His silver and gray Ford Bronco was seen by a cougar research team on February 5 in the Ware Creek area at the far eastern end of Kananaskis country. The vehicle was unlocked, and his keys were in the ashtray. It was not until a local rancher checking on his livestock saw the car encased in frost that suspicion started to grow. The rancher called the RCMP, and they ran the license plate, determining that it belonged to Brian. This started the process of contacting friends and relatives and determining if Brian was a missing person, which he was.

The search for Mr. Adrian started several days after he was last seen. This February 16, 1991 article in the *Calgary Herald* had details of the event, "A preliminary air search last week when Adrian failed to show, and on Wednesday a full-scale search began involving a helicopter, tracker dogs and more than 20 people. A pair of Adrian's boots, found in the vehicle was used to provide a scent for the dogs, Norberg said. Also missing is Adrian's dog, a six or seven-year-old Brittany Spaniel described as having a white to light brown coat with orange patches and an orange nose."

To understand how thorough and comprehensive searches can be is to know how diligent SAR team members take their work. The thoroughness of this search is described in the same article noted above later in the article, "Ironically, the search did turn up a hunting arrow that belonged to him," Morberg said. "It was broken and badly weathered, and Mounties concluded it was from a past expedition to the area." The RCMP were able to identify the arrow because all arrows used by Alberta hunters are required to have the hunters identification number on the shaft.

As SAR teams were scouring the mountains, someone in southern Calgary made an exciting find and is described in the October 7, 1991 edition of the *Calgary Herald*, "His Brittany Spaniel dog was found wandering around southern Calgary shortly after Adrian disappeared." There was never any mention if searchers took Kin back to the search site and tried to see what they'd do.

Friends and family of Adrian went to the search location dozens of times and searched on their own after the formal six days SAR terminated. A February 24, 1991 article in the *Calgary Herald* had this statement, "Rick Walker, a Calgary store manager, and Adrian's best friend said he's sure his buddy will turn up. "I think he just went camping for a while," he said. "Something might have happened to him." In the same article was this, "Meanwhile, Adrian's parents, Doug and Alice, are waiting anxiously for word on their only son. "I don't know what's happened," Doug Adrian told the Herald. "I have a thousand thoughts."

The area that Adrian disappeared is a series of rolling hills that lead to much larger mountains. The official parks page describe bears, coyotes, and cougars that roam the area. If Adrian had been attacked and killed by a predator, I do believe that SAR members would've found his remains. He was a very experienced hunter and outdoorsman and had been in this specific area many times in the past. The thought that he might have gone lost and died in the wild seems a very remote possibility. The fact that Kin was found on the southern edge of Calgary is an indicator that something devastating happened. I have documented several stories where a hiker dies in the wild, and their canine is found lying next to them, waiting for assistance. I tend to think that if Kin left the Ware Creek area, something unusual occurred to Brian.

I applaud the SAR teams, RCMP and the parks department in Alberta for placing significant resources into finding Brian. As I stated earlier, the finding of the arrow is proof of the thoroughness of the SAR.

One of the last statements made by SAR commanders on this event was their hope that hunters working in this area would stumble across evidence of what happened to Mr. Adrian. I searched hundreds of pages of articles surrounding this area and event. I could not locate anything noting that additional evidence had been discovered related to Brian's disappearance.

I have deep compassion for Mr. and Mrs. Douglas Adrian. The loss of their son without knowing what happened will eat at their heart for a lifetime.

Lillian Owens
Missing: 06/28/91, Hinton, Alberta
Age at disappearance: 46
Lillian Owens was last seen by her husband when she left her house to pay bills at a local bank. Sometime during her trip to the bank, she disappeared. After an extensive search, law enforcement found her vehicle on a rural road near the Athabasca River. Once her vehicle was found, police conducted an extensive search of the river and surrounding fields without finding any trace of Lillian.

According to the 2009 Canadian census, Hinton had a population of 9,825 and a land area of ten square miles. Hinton is known as the gateway to Jasper National Park. It sits in the Athabasca River Valley 176 miles west of Edmonton. The elevation of the city is 3,291 feet and it gets significant snowfall.

Donald Jean Belliveau
Missing: 01/27/95, Columbia Ice Fields, Jasper, Alberta
Age at disappearance: 28
Donald Belliveau left Calgary in his vehicle en route to the mountains for hiking. His path took him across the plains to the

mountains and onto the Columbia Ice Fields. The ice fields are a major tourist attraction with a visitor center and special transport buses that can take visitors out onto the ice. Visitors pay a small fee and are driven in huge buggies onto the glacier. They are given a presentation and allowed to ask questions about the geological features of the region.

This is also a jump-off point for many hikers and climbers, who head into the backcountry.

Donald's vehicle was located in the parking lot of the glacier, and it is presumed he hiked into the mountains and never returned. Searchers spent a week looking in the backcountry, and pilots searched from the sky. No trace of Donald was ever found.

Rhonda Laureen Runningbird
Missing: 03/26/95, Swan Lake Recreation Area, Rocky Mountain House, Alberta
Age at disappearance: 25
Hunter• Missing Clothing

Rhonda Runningbird, her husband, their eighteen-month-old baby, and her husband's aunt drove into the Swan Lake Recreation Area for hunting. The truck supposedly got stuck in the mud and the husband hiked into the bush to get help. The closest residence or business was approximately thirty miles away.

Darkness hit the area, and the aunt states that it was at this point that Rhonda also left to get help. Rhonda was supposedly in bad health. Relatives state that Rhonda wore a kidney colostomy bag and was scheduled for surgery five days after she was reported missing. Relatives do not believe that Rhonda could have walked far because of her condition. Early the following morning, Rhonda's husband returned to the truck. The aunt and the husband were stranded an additional night with the baby and still had not seen Rhonda. Another truck eventually came by, and the husband used the driver's cell phone to call a relative to obtain assistance.

The husband and the aunt eventually got home and reported Rhonda missing. After an exhaustive search, law enforcement stated that they found an unused colostomy bag, a set of Rhonda's clothing that she may have been wearing, and eyeglasses. Law enforcement officials did not believe that Rhonda could have survived the elements. They called off the search several days later.

It is presumed that Rhonda died in the wild, but she is still listed as missing. How did Rhonda's clothing become removed from her body?

Knut Thielemann
Missing: 08/04/95, Athabasca Falls, Jasper, Alberta
Age at disappearance: 22
Water•

Knut Thielemann was vacationing in the area of Athabasca Falls on the Athabasca River near Jasper, Alberta. On August 4, 1995, he was walking somewhere near the falls when he disappeared.

The Athabasca River starts in the Rockies and flows east through Hinton toward Edson. The falls are approximately eighty feet high and have a beautiful backdrop against the huge mountains of the Rockies. The falls are not known for their height, as it's the sheer volume of water that flows through the pass that makes it gorgeous to view. The waterfall itself is considered a class five because of its height and associated danger.

Knut is still listed in Canada as a missing person. This is the second person that vanished near this river.

Melvin Paul Hoel
Missing: 03/12/97, Cataract Creek, west of Longview, Alberta
Age at disappearance: 64
Water•

In March of 1997, Melvin Hoel was somewhere in the Cataract Creek area west of Longview along Highway 40. His exact whereabouts during this time are not known, and he could not be located. This region is at the base of the eastern side of the Canadian Rocky Mountains and has significant wildlife. It is very desolate in this area.

Approximately one year after Melvin went missing, his father died in a nursing home in Lethbridge. There are no other relatives.

Tom Howell
Missing: 09/12/05, Limestone Mountain, Caroline, Alberta
Age at disappearance: 46
Hunter• Water

Tom Howell was an avid outdoorsman and bowhunter. In September 2005 he went sheep and moose hunting near Limestone Mountain outside of Caroline, Alberta. The mountain is approximately thirty miles southwest of Rocky Mountain House. The summit of the mountain is 6,200 feet and is part of an extended ridgeline running north to south.

Tom's boss filed the missing person report, and several days later RCMP found Tom's truck near the mountain on Forestry Trunk Road. Tom had parked his vehicle and apparently taken his ATV, loaded with equipment, to drive closer to his hunting location.

SAR personnel found Tom's covered ATV at the base of Limestone Mountain. They dropped a ground crew at the location, who performed an extensive search of the mountain but found nothing. At his truck, they did find receipts for one hundred dollars' worth of groceries he had purchased prior to his hunt.

Bowhunters are quite different from hunters who use firearms. Bowhunters must use stealth, quiet, and surprise to get their trophy. The hunter must sneak within a very close shooting range to get a quality shot. Part of that stealthy behavior also means that they may surprise predatory animals, which is sometimes dangerous. In Tom's instance it is very surprising they did not find his pack, bow, clothes, campsite—nothing. He completely disappeared. Tom's family was told by SAR that the area is so rough and dangerous that they made a decision not to participate in the search.

In my book, Missing 411: Hunters, I explained how bow hunters disappear at a higher rate from hunters using forearms.

Wai Fan
Missing: 09/28/05, Mount Temple, Lake Louise, Alberta
Age at disappearance: 43

Investigators believe that Wai Fan was attempting to climb to the summit of 10,500-foot Mount Temple, located just two miles south of Lake Louise. This is in a gorgeous area of the Canadian

Rockies. There are numerous large mammals that roam the country-side, but hiking in the area is very common.

Extensive ground and air searches for Wai failed to find any evidence of his location.

Robert Barrington Leigh
Missing: 08/13/2006-11:30 p.m., Edmonton, Alberta
Age at disappearance: 20 years
Intellect• Water• Canines• Previously Searched

In past books I have written about a group of intellectuals who have disappeared under unusual circumstances throughout the world. Robert Barrington Leigh qualifies as a genius-level student who vanished without an easy explanation.

From the day that Robert was born, he was destined for great-ness. He was the son of a physicist and thus was given genius-lev-el genes. At a very young age, he was doing math equations that caused people around him to scratch their heads. When he was in high school, he was one of six students that beat 20,000 others across Canada to be on the national math team. He traveled at a young age to compete in Newfoundland and later went to Scotland to compete in the International Mathematical Olympiad.

Robert decided to attend the University of Toronto at the Saint George campus. He majored in mathematics and physics. In his sec-ond year of studies, he was already taking graduate-level courses and was challenging professors with his brilliant mind and polite demeanor. This young man wasn't one-dimensional. He was an ac-complished pianist, an outdoorsman, and an experienced sound and lighting technician.

At this point you should have a profile of this student, son, and boyfriend. Lucy Zhang and Robert had been seeing each other for several months. Lucy was taking classes during the summer, and Robert took a break to visit family at their home at 9820 Eighty-Fifth Avenue in Edmonton.

On August 13, 2006, at 10:30 p.m., Robert said good-bye to his mother, got on his blue Raleigh mountain bike, and rode to meet friends at the Folk Fest Music Festival being held at Gallagher Park. This would've been a ride of no more than two miles. His home was on the south side of the North Saskatchewan River, as was the festival. The ride would've taken him over Mill Creek and through a neighborhood he knew very well.

At 11:30 p.m., Robert sent Lucy a message saying that he was at Queen Elizabeth Park. He wished her well with her exams. Lucy later stated that there was absolutely nothing abnormal with the communication or the message. This was the last time anyone heard from Robert.

Queen Elizabeth Park is no more than twelve short blocks from Robert's home and on the same side of the river. He hadn't traveled far from his home in that hour and he never contacted his friends. The search started quickly.

The Edmonton police department headed the SAR for the twenty-year-old student. I could not find an article that mentioned finding his Raleigh bicycle. The five-day search included helicopters flying over Mill Creek and the North Saskatchewan River; this was followed by Bloodhounds searching the area from his home to the water. They found nothing. The police had Robert's cell provider ping his phone. They got nothing of value. They also reviewed his phone calls and text messages and found nothing relevant. Police had canoes work the river areas. They found nothing.

During the search, John Barrington (Robert's father) made a statement that Robert was one of those straight, honest, good kids that wouldn't get into trouble. He was worried that Robert may have run into trouble and foul play may be involved.

On August 18, 2006, the Edmonton police called off the search for Robert.

On August 22, 2006, the owner of River Tours West, Alan Flynn, decided to walk the area to see if he could find the body, and he did. Alan called the police, and they subsequently responded to the area on the north side of the Saskatchewan River near Ninety-Second Street and Ninety-Ninth Avenue. This was on the opposite side of the river and the creek from where Robert sent his last text message.

Reports indicated that there were no marks on the body and it was fully clothed; he was wearing a wristwatch and his wallet was in his pocket. Different jurisdictions have different rules about what they will release about the cause of death, condition of the body, blood alcohol level, etc. The only statement from the Edmonton coroner was: "Death was non-criminal."

Many individuals have voiced concern about this case. There are no explanations that make sense.

As with many, many cases we've reviewed and investigated, the key to these disappearances is within the coroner's report. Did they test for GHB? How long was the body in the water? Was there lividity within the body? What was the stage of rigor mortis? Were there abrasions, scratches, or other injuries to Robert? What was his blood alcohol level? What did the toxicology screen indicate? All of these are questions that need to be answered. The basic profile of Robert's disappearance fits within the confines of the profiles in Missing 411: A Sobering Coincidence.

Stephanie Stewart
Missing: 08/26/06, Athabasca Fire Lookout, Hinton, Alberta
Age at disappearance: 70
Canines• Point of Separation

Of the thousands of missing person reports I have researched, the case of Stephanie Stewart is one of the most puzzling. The facts surrounding her disappearance defy common sense and will cause great concern for any fire lookout attendant anywhere in the world.

Stephanie was an eighteen-year veteran of the Alberta Natural Resources Group that maintains a vigil at 128 lookouts across the province. For thirteen years Stephanie called the Athabasca Lookout her seasonal home. Twenty-five miles east of Hinton, the lookout is perched on a ridge with a commanding view of the surrounding valleys. There is a remote and desolate road that leads from the valley floor to the cabin and adjacent lookout where Stephanie worked and lived.

The lookout residence is a beautiful one-story log cabin that anyone would be proud to call home. Directly adjacent to the cabin is a forty-foot-tall lookout that is no easy climb. The lookout has something similar to a modified ladder inside a cage that makes its way to the top. The description of this climb should help explain that Stephanie was no normal seventy-year-old lady—she was fit! Stephanie had recently completed a climb and summiting of Mount

MISSING PERSON

RCMP are seeking your help in the disappearance of Stephanie STEWART, age 70, missing from the Athabasca Fire Lookout, between Friday the 25th of August and Saturday the 26th of August.

STEWART is described as 5' 2", 105 lbs., with grey/auburn shoulder length hair.

If you have any information regarding her whereabouts or disappearance, please contact
HINTON RCMP ph: **(780) 865-5544**

or if you wish to remain anonymous, please contact
CRIME STOPPERS 1-800-222-TIPS

Royal Canadian Gendarmerie royale
Mounted Police du Canada

Canada

Stephanie Stewart

Kilimanjaro in Tanzania. She may have been a small woman, but Stephanie Stewart would not have been an easy target for abduction.

Attendants at lookout towers are required to call their command center three times per day to report their status. Stephanie was diligent on her calls, and when she missed three in one day, a supervisor was sent to check on her.

On August 26, 2006, a supervisor drove to Stephanie's cabin and found a very unusual scene. There was a pot of water on the stove, with the stove burning. The supervisor noticed that her two pillows, blanket, and sheet were missing. The supervisor found her truck parked where it usually was, but Stephanie was nowhere on the grounds. Within hours, twelve law enforcement officials were on the scene; within twenty-four hours, hundreds were at the tower. What followed was one of the largest searches ever undertaken in the Alberta forests. Almost every resource available to search was utilized—canines, helicopters, planes, vehicles, and ground teams. Everyone wanted to find Ms. Stewart.

Stephanie has one daughter, Lorie. Lorie gave an interview to the press and stated that her mom was "an old pro at tower work." According to Lorie, Stephanie was "well known in the community of Hinton."

Police have stated that they are handling Stephanie's case as a homicide in an effort to keep resources working the abduction. One of the investigators assigned to comment on the case, Sergeant Taniguchi, stated, "We have been led to believe that Stephanie was likely attacked by a human being." The union that represents the lookout attendants issued a $20,000 reward for Stephanie or clues about her disappearance.

On August 27, 2009, RCMP stated that they had no clues in Stephanie's disappearance.

Subsequent to Stephanie disappearing, the resource department that manages the lookouts removed all directional signs that indicated how to drive to the lookouts. They have also placed locking gates at the roadway entrances to all lookouts throughout the province.

There are several elements to Stephanie's disappearance that don't make sense when dealing with a predator abducting a victim. When criminals plan a major crime, one of their main concerns is having multiple routes to leave the area. They do not want to be seen, heard, or later recognized with their vehicle in the area. In the Stewart case, there is one long and lonely road to the lookout. There is no way for a predator to know if someone is going to drive up the road and interrupt the crime, or observe the suspect as they are leaving the scene with the victim. Anyone with any sense could see that this is a very, very risky abduction location and subsequent escape. This is a dirt road without significant traffic. Anyone driving to the lookout would leave tire marks, especially the last vehicle in. The RCMP should know the type and size of tire that was last visiting Stephanie, and that would be a major clue as to the type of vehicle that visited, but the RCMP has not commented on this.

If the RCMP had a significant clue that a vehicle had participated in the abduction, it is doubtful they would expend thousands of dollars in flight time for helicopters and airplanes to search the vast openness that surrounds the lookout. I also don't think they would have placed hundreds of people on the ground in this area.

Stephanie was in great shape for a seventy-year-old woman, but with the advent of FLIR on helicopters, they can fly over any area and see radiant heat coming from a body. If Stephanie had been abducted and was being forced to hike out, she would have been seen. She also would have been seen by satellites that the government could utilize in a search. Yes, the Canadian and United States governments do have the ability to direct a satellite camera into a specific area and monitor the region to a degree so finite they can read a license plate from space.

Did the Alberta Sustainable Resource Department really believe that Stephanie walked out of that area? Sergeant Taniguchi stated that the RCMP believed she was attacked by a human being. That's an odd choice of words. Why would the sergeant state she was attacked and not abducted? Were there clues at the scene that Stephanie may have been assaulted or worse? I can guarantee that the RCMP has interviewed the family members of Stephanie at length. The RCMP would want to know if she was concerned for her safety, if she had problems with someone in the recent past, or if there were something about the lookout tower and that surrounding area that had caused her concern. Maybe she had witnessed illegal drug activity, another type of crime, or maybe this was a completely random act (doubtful).

Two other women—Shelly Bacsu, 16, 1983; and Lillian Owens, 46, 1991—disappeared from the Hinton area. It may be pure coincidence, but notice the ages of the victims. The victims ages increase with time: 16 in 1983; 46 in 1991; 70 in 2009. Is this a coincidence or is their rationale to the increasing ages? It is very odd for a small community such as Hinton to have three women disappear in a twenty-three-year period—all in remote and rural areas.

Lastly, the items that are missing from Stephanie's room, two pillows, blanket and sheet are a clue. Many burglars take pillow cases and stuff them with items to carry from a residence. Could Stephanie have been wrapped in her sheets and blanket and carried away?

Robert Samuel Neale
Missing: 05/02/07, Peers, Alberta
Age at disappearance: 77

Robert Neale was the owner of a ranch/farm near Peers, Alberta. His residence sat close to the Macleod River at the foothills on the eastern side of the Canadian Rockies. The topography in this area is fairly flat, with some slight elevation increase as you travel west.

It is believed that Neale was working on his ranch and either walked off or somehow disappeared in the immediate vicinity. This case sounds very similar to other ranchers and farmers you will read about in their respective chapters of *Missing 411: Eastern United States*.

Kevin Kennedy
Missing 8/21/11, Peter Lougheed Provincial Park, AB
Age at Disappearance: 59 years
Canines• Point of Separation• Cluster Zone• Weather

Kevin and his wife made the trip from their home in Australia to visit his wife's mother in Alberta. The trip was an annual summer affair and one that Kevin always enjoyed. He was in very good condition, enjoyed hiking, and liked the big mountains of the Kananaskis region. This area can be very rugged with many large mammals. The terrain is gorgeous, steep, and can be treacherous but is an area where someone who is lost should be found. The elevation where Kevin vanished was near 7,800 feet with dozens of small lakes in the vicinity.

On August 21, 2011, Kevin was dropped at the trailhead for Tyrwhitt Loop in the Highwood Pass area for his four-hour hike over Grizzly Col. Kevin's wife arrived back in four hours, but Kevin never arrived.

On that August 21 when Kevin was hiking the loop, there were a number of other hikers on the trail enjoying a beautiful day. The RCMP put sixty searchers into the mountains looking for Kevin; they found nothing. Search dogs were brought to the scene and could not locate Kevin's scent. The effort to find the Aussie went on and off until winter storms hit the region. In 2012, searchers went back into the area where Kevin had vanished and still never found the man. A September 27, 2011, article in the *Calgary Herald* had the following response from Royal Canadian Mounted Police: "'In virtually every search we are doing there is some sign of something, but in this one we've got nothing,' said RCMP spokesman Patrick Webb. 'We've got no sign of him at all. We've got no indication of a bear attack, no indication of him falling off the mountain.'" Something very unusual happened to Kevin Kennedy.

Rhonda Cardinal
Missing 07/31/12, Calling Lake, AB
Age at Disappearance: 42 years
Canines• Point of Separation• Illness/Disability• Berries• Hunter• Lack of Memory

The disappearance of Rhonda Cardinal is not only highly unusual, but she survived to explain in slight detail what might have happened. The incident occurred at Calling Lake, approximately one hundred miles north of Edmonton, Alberta, Canada.

Rhonda's case is one of the few where an adult goes missing and then can explain why she got lost. Rhonda was at a remote hunting cabin near Calling Lake when she disappeared. In a July 16 article in the *Globe and Mail*, Rhonda explains how she initially got lost: "Ms. Cardinal can't explain why she left the first cabin, she 'blacked out,' woke up lost and started wandering through the bush." A relative reported Rhonda missing, and the RCMP took the case and started to search. The eight-day effort to find Rhonda included ATVs, helicopters, and ground searchers. The effort to find Rhonda was terminated without finding any evidence of where she might be.

I'd like readers to recount in their minds all of the strange disappearances I have documented. Think about how many of the disappearances make no sense at all. Rhonda now comes forward and states that she somehow blacked out, got into the woods, and was lost. What caused Rhonda to black out? What prompted or forced her into the woods?

Later in the same story, it explains how Rhonda acted: "After a few days, she ditched her wet and torn shoes and ripped up her t-shirt to wrap around her blistering feet." Does this make sense to any of you? Later in the article, it says: "One day, a black bear startled her, she said. It aggressively stood up on its back legs." The bear supposedly walked away. Rhonda stated that she ate berries and drank water for the almost two weeks she was missing.

At one point in Rhonda's disappearance, she came across an abandoned cabin and forcibly entered and got supplies to stay alive. She eventually got enough strength to find a roadway, where she found someone driving on a rural road that stopped to assist her. The Royal Canadian Mounted Police made an estimate about how far Rhonda had traveled from the point where she vanished—it is explained in the same article: "RCMP estimate the location (where she was found) was about 22 kilometers from where Ms. Cardinal was reported missing." Rhonda was transported by helicopter to a hospital for observation and was subsequently released.

Summary

This case is disturbing, because it brings into the light that people may be "blacking out" in the woods when they are alone. They lose their memory and they somehow slip into a state where they do not remember what happened, why they were lost, or where they are. This "blacking out" may be one of the causes as to why people disappear in the mountains and woods. The real question is what is causing the "blackouts"? How do the people make their way from the location they are last seen to the place where they are eventually found? During the time people are missing, what are they doing?

British Columbia

Population: 4,700,000
Capital City: Victoria
Largest City: Vancouver

British Columbia (BC) is the third-largest province in Canada with 367,699 square miles. It has 29 regional districts that govern the specific area, very similar to counties in the United States.

BC has four hundred provincial parks, one hundred and thirty ecological sites, six national parks, and 3 UNESCO designated parks. The province is continually adding more locations for open space.

If you like to drink wine, you'll love the 850 vineyards that occupy the inland regions.

The most prominent industries in BC are forestry, tourism, mining, and fishing. There are five species of salmon, multiple species of trout and thousands of miles of creeks and remote rivers where you could drop a line and not see another person.

One up and coming industry that does not get much public attention is filming. The first five years of the X-Files was filmed in Vancouver, a fact that many do not know. If you watch the series and you know BC, you'll recognize many local landmarks throughout the episodes. There have also been many films shot in different areas of the province, 50 Shades of Grey, Tomorrowland, Apollo 18, Fantastic Four, I Robot, and many more.

You need to hike with caution throughout British Columbia. They have a lot of large mammals that include deer, elk, bighorn sheep, mountain goats, cougars, and bear. They have a vast population of black bear, and they even have Grizzlies. You will need to carry bear spray while hiking in certain areas, check with locals to understand the dangers presented and take the appropriate safety items.

You need to bring many layers of clothing when you visit this most western province. The coastal zone can have high humidity, extreme winds, and cold temperatures. The coast can also get warm and have the perfect beach vibe.

One of the areas that I have spent considerable time in is Whistler, north of Vancouver. It is a ski resort in the winter with a great open mall area that leads to the lifts. In the summer it's a big mountain biking area. I was there several times for hockey tournaments and always enjoyed the scenic drive up the coast and the mountain community of the city. The weather in this high altitude area can change quickly, dress accordingly.

British Columbia is one of many provinces in Canada that I do not doubt that there are areas where nobody has ever walked. I could spend weeks traveling throughout the northern regions and never be in a big city, and stop at a gorgeous location every night. If you like water, mountains, wildlife, and magnificent scenery, you'd love British Columbia.

British Columbia- List of missing people by date.

Name	Date/ Time Missing • Age • Sex • Location
Danny Schlicter	10/17/35-AM• 3• M
Eric Catchpole	10/22/41- noon• 2 1/2• M
Kenneth Duncan	11/27/43-3:00 p.m.• 21• M
Leslie Heal	11/05/44-1:30 p.m.• 26•M
Frank Johnson	09/06/45• 65•M
Louis Majers	11/03/45•39•M
Alma Hall	06/09/51• 28• F
Raymond Hall	06/09/51• 6• M
Leo Gaspard	07/31/51-Unk • 60 •M
David Anderson	05/20/53-10:00 A.M.• 3 1/2• M
Arthur Tibbett	11/09/53•29•M
Helena Jackson	04/11/54•46•F
John Last	09/26/54•24•M
Herman Jungerhuis	11/10/57• 55• M
Cindy Lou Maclane	09/09/58-9:00 A.M.• 2• F
Tony Beauchamp	09/16/58-3:00 P.M.• 2• M
Betty Jean Masters	07/03/60- 8:00 P.M.• 20 MOS• F
Gezo Peczeli	09/18/60• 21• M
Wallace Marr	11/19/62• 30•M

Leslie Evans	06/11/66•39•M
John Evans	06/11/66•14•M
Clancy O'Brien	08/20/66 P.M.• 9• M
Roger Olds	08/25/66•19•M
Myron Shutty	07/09/67-2:30 P.M.• 5• M
Kenneth Vanderleest	07/14/67–PM • 3 • M
Alphonse Boudreault	11/09/70•22•M
Michael Bryant	11/14/70-5:00 p.m.•32•M
Richard Wenegast	10/27/73-1:30 p.m.• 31• M
Margaret Andersen	07/06/74- 7:00 p.m.•59•F
Yehudi Prior	09/23/74•2•M
Henry Hansen	09/22/75• Unk• M
Wendy Riley	02/11/83-PM• 29• F
Nicholas Vanderbilt	08/22/84• 25• M
Francis Glenhill	08/22/84• 29• M
Janice Pedlar	02/08/86- P.M., 37• F
Lynn Hillier	07/24/86• 2• F
Charlie Musso	09/07/87-5:00 p.m.•61•M
Emerson Dobroskay	10/28/88-p.m.•21•M
Wally Finnegan	11/04/89• 51•M
Raymond Krieger	08/28/92-9:00 p.m.• 48•M
Steven Eby	11/14/93-3:00 p.m.•29•M
Richard Grey	04/14/94•22•M
Samuel Wright	06/03/95- 6:00 P.M.•66• M
Ian Ralph Sutherland	08/15/96•30•M
Karl Walter	06/28/97-5:00 p.m.•65•M
Brian Faughnan	07/12/02–Unk • 35 • M
Richard Milner	09/29/03•43•M
Juaqueline Bob	07/06/04• 41•F
Jared Stanley	01/10/05•25•M
David Koch	05/25/05 at 8:00 p.m. • 36
Tom Leonard	10/02/05• 40•M
John Kahler	11/04/07-4:00 A.M.• 29• M
William Pilkenton	02/15/08• 7• M
Michael Raster	08/08/08• 43• M
Tyler Wright	08/10/10–Unk • 35 • M
Rachael Bagnall	09/08/10-Unk • 25•F

Jonathan Jette	09/08/10-Unk • 34•M
Darcy Brian Turner	06/20/11–Unk • 55 • M
Matthew Huszar	12/16/11-p.m.•25• M
David Christian	03/27/12-11:30 p.m.•27• M
Raymond Salmen	05/28/13• 65•M
Sylvia Apps	07/13/14 at 4:00 p.m. • 69 • F
Sukhjeet Saggu	06/05/15 at 4:00 p.m. • 20 • M
Neville Jewell	09/12/15-6:00 p.m.•52•M
Deanna Wertz	07/19/16 • 46 • F
Gordon Sagoo	08/14/16 at 2:00 p.m. • 50 • M
Debbie Blair	09/29/16 at noon • 65 • F
Alison Raspa	11/23/17- 1:15 A.M.• 25• F
Travis Thomas	08/07/18•40•M

Danny Schlicter
Missing: 10/17/35-AM, Bear Creek Valley, Kelowna, BC
Age at disappearance: 3 years
Water• Weather

Kelowna is considered part of the wine belt of British Columbia. This area has a very mild climate compared to much of
the province and has several successful wineries. The city sits
on Okanagan Lake east of Vancouver and approximately twenty
miles north of the United States border. The lake is narrow and
stretches north to south over eighty miles and varies in width from
2-3 miles. One of the creeks that feed the lake is Bear Creek on
the western shore just northwest of Kelowna, that's where this
story starts.

The archives in this incident spell the victim's name two different ways, Schlicter and Schlecter. The majority of the reports used
Schlicter, which is what I will use.

The Schlicter family lived in a home up Bear Creek Valley from
Lake Okanagan. This was a rural existence on the side of the lake
with few businesses and residences.

On Thursday, October 17, 1935 in the morning hours, three-year-
old Danny Schlicter was playing in the front yard. Mrs. Schlicter went
to check on the boy and could not locate him. She called for the boy,
searched the region around her home, and started to panic. It wasn't

long before the family had friends and neighbors, helping them scour the mountains. This October 22, 1935 article in the Vancouver Sun described the extent of the SAR, "More than 150 searchers, who have been combing the district since the boy was reported missing four days ago returned Monday without having found a trace of the youngster, and were unable to continue the search in the face of a sharp change in weather." The change in weather was extreme cold and snow.

Different teams over a dozen times searched bear, Creek. The flow was described as very low and slow. Nobody found anything in the water or creek bed. It was at the end of the full second day of searching that people started to talk openly about the possibilities of what may have happened. The creek had been excluded. This statement in the October 22, 1935, The Province discussed another option, "Suggestions that cougars, coyotes, other animals, eagles, and rattlesnakes caused the lad's death have been discarded, as at present there is no predatory wildlife in this area. The belief is that he wandered away as he has often done and went too far and lost his bearings." I've read similar statements by the press on dozens of disappearances. The implication is that the boy wandered so far and that he'd never be found. This search had over 150 people on the scene that covered thousands of acres up to a two-mile radius from the Schlicter residence. Searchers did not find any tracks, any dropped clothing, etc. One passage in an article described how the group walked shoulder to shoulder across the mountains. I do not believe that a three-year-old boy could walk farther than 150 searchers.

Danny Schlicter was never found. There are no easy answers on these disappearances, and I'm sure that the Schlicters never looked at their homestead the same way.

Eric Catchpole
Missing 10/22/41- noon, Kitsilano, West Vancouver, BC
Age at disappearance: 2 1/2 years
Weather• Canines• Previously Searched• Water

The disappearance of a young male in conjunction with their inability to speak is something that I have written about many times.

If a child cannot explain what happened to them, how are we to ever understand the facts surrounding a disappearance?

Kitsilano is a small sector in West Vancouver that sits on a small peninsula with Vancouver International Airport to its south and the Burrard Inlet to the north. The Strait of Georgia would be the largest body of water to the west of the community.

On October 22, 1941, at approximately noon, two and a half-year-old Eric Catchpole was playing in the alley behind his home at 3276 West 11th Avenue, Kitsilano. The boy was playing on his bicycle while his mom was in their residence. Mrs. Catchpole had not heard her son in several minutes and went out to check on him. She found his abandoned bike sitting outside the garage at 3226 West 11th Street. Eric Catchpole was nowhere in sight. Mrs. Catchpole yelled and screamed for her son; there was no answer. After several minutes searching the alley, the garage where the bike was near and calling his name, she called the Vancouver Police.

The police responded and initially searched the neighborhood without finding anything. They called for more reinforcements, and the uniforms responded in mass. Hundreds of police officers responded into the well-knit community. Mr. Catchpole came home and started to canvass the neighborhoods looking for his boy. There was a concern that the boy walked toward the Burrard inlet, just 3000 feet north of the home. The police roamed the streets, speaking to neighbors, and learning that a boy matching the description had been seen several streets away walking in traffic. There was a growing fear that Eric may have been abducted.

The October 23 edition of the *Vancouver Sun* had these details of the search, "Fears for the safety of a 2 1/2-year-old Eric Catchpole, 3276 West Eleventh Avenue was openly expressed by police as they search for the baby passed the 24-hour mark at noon today." The article went on to describe the possibilities that police described as what may have happened to the toddler. The first theory was that he was hit by a car and disposed of in some remote area. Another option was that he fell into the water somewhere and is not being seen. Lastly, police thought he might be tangled in foliage somewhere. The same article quoted above had this, "A Doberman-Pinscher dog, brother of the late "Ruffy" of Vancouver Police was put to work on the case this morning. On three occasions the dog worked his way west in the lane behind the Catchpole home to a park at Twelfth

Avenue and Alma Road and there appeared to lose the trail." The path the dog took following the scent is confusing. The canine was tracking in the opposite direction from the Catchpole home as to where the tricycle was located. The bike was east, and the park was west of the residence.

As patrolman were searching the streets, homes, and garages, detectives were doing a follow-up on the possibility that Eric had been kidnapped. There was a local call for all homeowners to search their years and garages.

Several articles mentioned heavy fog at the time Eric disappeared and while police were on scene. There were many statements that the boy may have been confused and lost while wandering in the fog and walked in the wrong direction from his home. The police and Eric's family were perplexed that Eric was not being located.

There was nothing new on the case until just after midnight on October 24. This October 24, 1941 article in the *Victoria Daily Times* has the details, "The little fellow was found by a neighbor, Gordon Marshall, in an automobile in a garage a few doors from the home of Mr. and Mrs. George Catchpole from which he had disappeared Wednesday afternoon. Marshall heard a police broadcast appealing for automobile owners to look into their garages as it was known that Eric like to play around parked cars and it was thought he might have fallen asleep in one. "I came down the lane and noticed a car in a garage with 1938 license plates sitting in a garage," Marshall said. There was a load of wood in front of the doors. I climbed over the wood into the garage and found the little fellow lying awake on the front seat of the car. All he said was "Mummy." Mr. Marshall took the boy home and called the police.

Eric Catchpole was in excellent condition. He was taken to his parents and had a visit with the local emergency room physician. The boy was hungry but in otherwise good condition.

The owner of the residence with the garage where Eric was located was Mrs. Wright. An October 24, 1941 article in *The Province* had these details, "Mrs. Wright said the car had been stored in the garage for four years. A woodpile blocked the large doors, and the small doors were closed. She had been out to the woodpile half a dozen times but heard nothing coming from the car." In the same article, his mom made this statement, "And if Eric wanted to make a noise, he could," she said. "He could really holler." Later the article had this, "How long the child had been in the car will probably remain a mystery. It is apparent, however, that he returned to the car after dark following a visit to the corner of fourteenth and Collingwood, where a child answering his description was nearly struck by an automobile at 5 p.m. Wednesday. The child was pulled from the roadway by an unidentified motorist."

Over one hundred Vancouver Police were scouring the neighborhoods near the Catchpole residence at 5 p.m. the day he disappeared. The idea that Eric made his way back to the garage without being seen by the police seems a bit unreal.

Articles about this incident differ on the actual amount of time Eric had been missing. Some say 36 and others state 34 hours. The amount of time he was gone is of little value in understanding where he was and how he got into the car. If there was a large woodpile blocking the car doors, how did the toddler get in? I am not the only one having a difficult time understanding this disappearance and believing the surrounding facts. The November 1, 1941 article in *The Province* had these headlines, "Parents Suspect Mystery in Case of Missing Child." The same article had this, "The fact that he was found so near home may appear queer, and while we don't doubt that we shall never learn the actual facts, as our youngster cannot talk, we don't for one minute think he was in the car where he was finally found all of the 34 hours he was missing," read the letter from the Catchpole's. "As to how he got there is mere theory. We think that if he been there the first day he would have been found. The district was well searched, and Mrs. Wright was in her garage several times for wood." Mrs. Catchpole's letter was sent to the editor of the newspaper and later published.

In reviewing the facts of this disappearance, readers need to remember a few key facts. The canine tracked in the opposite direction that Eric and his tricycle were found. Did Eric go towards the park at some point? The intersection of 14th and Collingwood is relatively close to the location where the canine tracked and is also the point where a motorist removed a boy from the roadway matching Eric's description. All of this sounds plausible until you realize the number of police that were combing the region. You'd think that the police or neighbors on the street searching for the boy would've seen him.

Kenneth Duncan
Missing: 11/27/43- 3:00 p.m., Shawnigan Lake, BC
Age at disappearance: 21 years
Weather• Point of Separation• Area Previously Searched• Cluster Zone

Kenneth Duncan

When I see a headline that reads, "Mysterious Death Baffles Police," I'm hooked. When the story involves a missing hunter in a location that is a geographical cluster zone, I'm investigating it.

In November of 1943, Kenneth Duncan was a shipyard worker at the Victoria Machinery Depot on Vancouver Island in British Columbia. Kenneth worked the night shift and did work the evening of November 26. He slept for an hour and then joined his friend, Claude Collington for a drive to the area of Shawnigan Lake for deer hunting.

Just before dawn on November 27, Gordon and Claude arrived at a location called the Silver Mine Trail Cabin near Shawnigan Lake. Kenneth was a novice hunter, Claude was a very experienced outdoorsman, 60-years old and knew the island quite well. The pair met with other hunters, Albert Lamb, and two Gillespie brothers. The group left that morning and together hunter the area around the cabin, shot one deer and returned to rest that afternoon. This December 1, 1943 article in the *Times Colonist* explains what happened next, "Duncan, according to other hunters did not want to go out into the woods again, and the four left him while they went on a second hunt. On returning to the cabin, Duncan was missing." The hunters called for the young hunter and then shot off several rounds just before dark. Later in the evening, three of the hunters walked to a high plateau a half mile from the cabin and fired off a series of 12 shots; there was no response. It was at this point that the group decided to contact authorities. Several articles made a special note that the hunters had stated that the woods were very foggy the day they hunted, and it could've been easy to get lost

Hundreds of searchers converged on Shawnigan Lake. Groups from logging camps, Militia Rangers, game wardens, local law enforcement and family all scoured the mountainsides looking for Kenneth. The Militia Rangers called in 80 men who searched shoulder to shoulder out to a distance of three miles from the cabin; they found nothing. Family members and friends could not believe that nobody had seen anything related to Kenneth. The searches continued for weeks. Here was a standard description of the search efforts as was found in the December 2, 1943 edition of the *Vancouver Sun*, "More than 50 rain-soaked searchers returned from combing the thickly-wooded area between Shawnigan Lakeland Kokailah Ridge Wednesday night without finding a trace of Kenneth Duncan, 21 Victoria hunter missing since 3:00 p.m. Saturday."

This case took an odd twist months after the disappearance. There was a rumor that Kenneth had been murdered and his body dumped in the lake. Police dragged the water looking for a body, interviewed witnesses and essentially came up with nothing to support the allegations. It was an odd twist to a hunter lost in the woods.

The case went stale for almost three years until a group of hunters was back in the same area where Kenneth vanished and made a surprising discovery. This October 17, 1946 article in the *Windsor Star* explains what was found, "Last Sunday three Victoria hunters, J.F. Wratten, T. Magnall, and Bob Redgrave found an army-type boot with human foot bones encased in a gray sock. Provincial police were notified and with Wratten, and Magnall found the boot. Within 30 yards of the skeleton was found with a 35 caliber Winchester automatic rifle close by an Indian sweater among the bones. The skeleton was left where it lay until a coroner and doctor reach the spot." The location of the remains was only a mile and a half from the cabin where Kenneth was staying. The Duncan family was notified, and Kenneth's dad identified the sweater and rifle as belonging to his son.

After the discovery of the remains, there was this statement in an October 17, 1946 article in the *Times Colonist*, "The area where the remains were found had been thoroughly searched by the Pacific Coast Militia two days after Duncan had been reported missing."

The coroner's office on the island did an inquest into Kenneth's death. A determination was made that he died of natural causes. There were no gunshot wounds to the body, and a live round was found in his rifle, meaning he had not accidentally shot himself. Readers need to understand that the coroners were guessing on the reason the young hunter died. They had a skeleton to deal with, nothing else. They could not determine if he died from exposure, natural causes or some other cause. They did make a note that the remains were scattered, indicating there had been post-death predation to the remains.

This case contains facts I have written about hundreds of times.

Kenneth Duncan was located close to his cabin. Hundreds of people crisscrossed the area where his body was eventually found, and they discovered nothing. Three years later his remains are located in a region that had been previously searched, probably many times. When Kenneth entered the woods, it was foggy, when SAR members went out to search, they encountered rain. Weather played a significant role in the disappearance and search. When the hunting group was together in the morning hours after they first arrived, everything was fine. It was only after three hunters left the cabin and Kenneth remained behind did something happen. Why did Kenneth leave the cabin alone when he told the others he didn't want to go out? We do know that he had only one-hour sleep and was probably exhausted and needed rest. This is one of many cases that have similarities associated with missing people on Vancouver Island.

Leslie Heal
Missing: 11/05/44- 1:30 p.m., Cowichan Lake, BC
Age at disappearance: 26 years
Weather• Point of Separation• Cluster Zone

You just read the story about the disappearance of Kenneth Duncan on November 27, 1943, from Shawnigan Lake. Twenty miles southeast from Shawnigan Lake and 343 days after Duncan vanished, another hunter disappeared under very similar circumstance, this time the location was Cowichan Lake.

In November of 1944, Leslie Heal was a member of the Royal Canadian Air Force (RCAF) and assigned to Patricia Bay. He was married to his wife, Yvette and they had two children and lived near Sidney. He was known as a very experienced outdoorsman and hunter.

Leslie was off on weekends and on November 4, he and friend J. Macbeth joined another buddy, and they went to Camp 10 near Lake Cowichan deer hunting.

On November 5, the three friends got separated while hunting. At 1:00 p.m. J. Macbeth heard one shot fired and a loud shout. He didn't think much about it and

Leslie Heal

thought he'd hear from Leslie at the end of the day. The hunters went back to camp and Heal never arrived. They fired shots that night and heard nothing in return. They waited at camp till early Monday morning and then drove back to the city to report Leslie as missing. Macbeth knew something serious had happened because both were supposed to return to their duty station, Patricia Bay, that morning.

The search for the RCAF member got started in earnest Tuesday morning. Seventy soldiers from Colwood camp, 55 airmen from Patricia Bay, 50 area woodsmen and guides and countless local citizens all responded to search for Leslie. It was a three-hour hike from where vehicles could be parked to the location Macbeth last saw Heal. It was explained to searchers that Heal would hunt at the mountain top, and the others would be downslope. Searchers were told that their target was last heard from at 1:00 p.m. when they heard a shot and thought they heard him shout. Tuesday's efforts produced no results.

On Wednesday, 75 additional soldiers arrived for more search support. People were walking areas just feet apart and were not seeing anything of value.

In Missing 411- LAW I wrote about the disappearances of aircraft and their association with missing people. This November 7,

1944 article in the *Vancouver Sun* had these shocking details, "Heal is lost not far from where a bomber crashed last April 25. The crew of the bomber, killed in the crash were buried on the mountain." This was not the only aircraft that had an odd association with the disappearance of Heal.

Seventy miles east of Cowichan Lake is Abbotsford, British Columbia, three miles from the United States border. Just as the search for Heal was heating up, this November 10 article in *The Province* had these facts, "All available aircraft in Western Air command are still searching for a Liberator bomber and its eleven-man crew missing since early today after leaving it RCAF Abbotsford Base on a routine flight." Then there was this article in *The Province* on November 15, 1944,"Ten men are aboard an RCAF Canso flying boat which disappeared during a routine flying patrol from its West Coast base late Tuesday (11/14). It is the third mishap to RCAF planes in lower Mainland and Vancouver Island areas since Friday, and brought to 22 the number of RCAF personnel missing in this area." One last disappearance is explained in this December 4, 1944 article in the *Times Colonist*, "Fog and rain today prevented an aerial search for an RCAF Canso flying boat with a crew of nine which has been missing since Saturday (12/2) night in the vicinity of Victoria from Patricia Air Base," yes, the same base that Leslie Heal was assigned.

The search for Leslie was compromised because of heavy rain and wet condition. Searchers had gone from the mountains and had searched all the way towards the western coast of the island. This November 16 article in the *Lethbridge Herald* had this statement from searchers, "Belief that LAC Leslie Heal, 26-year old airman stationed at Patricia Bay perished in a little-known canyon on Lens Creek, said to be 1700 feet deep was put forward Wednesday. Bill Palliser said on his return to Victoria that searchers had followed footprints (footprints or boot tracks?) and broken twigs which they were satisfied were those of Heal to the edge of the canyon." There were other articles that stated that these men had to climb cliffs hundreds of feet high to remove themselves from the canyon. They were under the belief that Heal died climbing out and that he'd probably never be found. It was not long after this that the search was terminated.

There were many searches for Leslie over the following years and nothing was ever found.

It's hard to believe that identifiable remains would be found after 25 years, but it happened. The police were called to a hillside near Dymple Lake by a logging companies tree planting crew. They found a watch, whistle, gumboots, service rifle and a signet ring with the initials "LH" were located. The area had been logged years earlier, and the slash had been burned the previous year. The fire charred the butt of the rifle. Leslie's brother, Victor of Saanich made a positive identification from the property that was recovered. This April 12, 1969 article in the Times Colonist had these interesting details about the location and initial search, "Saanich Police Sergeant William Stephenson was in the air force with Heal and recalled being one of the searchers climbing arm's length apart up that unnamed forested hill where the hunters separated. The weather was cold, wet, miserable he remembers, but three-quarters of the squadron was out there." As it turned out, Leslie was located far from Lens Creek, as was noted in an earlier article. The question remains, what tracks had searchers found at that location?

When you start to string together the coincidences in this case with Kenneth Duncan, missing air force planes, missing RCAF member, both hunters not located for years and each located in an area previously searched, proximity to each other, weather problems, etc., it starts to be overwhelming. The number of people missing in southwest British Columbia and northwest Washington are some of the most significant clusters I've documented.

Frank Johnson
Missing: 09/06/45, Manson Creek, BC
Age at disappearance: 65
Weather• Canines• Hunter

This is far and away the most unusual story about someone that would not be considered a traditional hunter. This man had an affinity for bears, specifically Grizzlies. He either loved or hated the predators, I'm not sure which. The story starts in one of the most remote parts of North America, the headwaters of a creek with the same name as a notorious killer.

In the early 1940s, Frank Johnson was a loner, prospector, miner, trapper, and hunter. He had come to Canada from Sweden 59 years ago and had been living in northern British Columbia for the last 18 years. The prospector had three relatives that all lived in one home at 1542 West Sixty-Third Street in Vancouver, Norma Johnson and Rose Baillie were nieces, and E.A. Johnson, his sister in law. The women said he was reasonably wealthy, didn't spend money and he had securities and cash in several British Columbia banks.

Frank Johnson

Johnson traveled with his Doberman Pinscher, a dog that was given to him by Norma Johnson. After thinking through this man's travails, it might have been that dog that kept him alive. He was known to spend many months in the woods alone with the canine prospecting, mining or trapping, all with the intent of making money.

Frank was supposed to be out of the woods on September 6, 1945, when he didn't come out, a group of friends went to one of his cabins to check on him. Searchers found that nobody had been there for weeks, his buddies got concerned and contacted the local RCMP. It wasn't until October 3 that notification got out of the mountains and made it into a city to report the disappearance. At this point, nobody knew where Johnson was, what may have happened or if he was even alive. Friends reaching out to law enforcement started one of the most extensive searches I've ever documented.

Constable B.E. Munkley and Game Warden Philip Brown left Fort St. John and first went to the cabin his friends knew Johnson had utilized, they found nothing, and it appeared Johnson had not been there in weeks. By the time searchers got into the woods, the prospector had been out for the majority of the summer, and they had no idea where he might be, but they did have a list and map of cabins that he owned and used. The constables stated they had been deluged with constant rain and cold temperatures for their majority of time in the mountains and usually crawled into their sleeping bags wet. They knew the hunter had owned over a dozen cabins along Manson and Germansen Creeks, an area heavily infested with Grizzlies, per the constables.

This October 18, 1945, edition of *The Province* had these details on the search, "In a 150-mile search through mountains "swarming with Grizzlies" Constable B.E. Munkley and Game Warden Phil Brown failed to find any trace of Johnson, who has been missing since September 6." In the same article was this, "Frank Johnson, 65, the veteran hunter who had bagged more than 37 Grizzlies, may have himself been killed by bears. Discovery of an ax and the body of a starved pack dog have led police to believe that bears had killed the elderly man." I liked the wording in that article and how Johnson was described as "elderly," he was quite a ways from slow and old. The same article stated they found his dog and equipment near timberline at the headwaters of Manson Creek. Law enforcement said that they believed that he left to go hunting, but never returned. There was no evidence to show a bear killed him, it was mere conjecture.

Johnson's dog was found starving in the cabin with porcupine quills in its nose. The RCMP shot the dog to put it out of its misery. This may seem like a cruel act, but considering the remote location, it's understandable.

There was another article describing Johnson's hunting prowess in the October 19, 1945 edition of *The Province*, "The trapper had 36 Grizzlies to his credit and would "rather hunt bear than eat." It was his habit to kill animals and leave their carcasses near his cabin to attract a bear."

I have a good friend that owns a fishing lodge in the Yukon Territory and many times when I've been there the conversation will turn to Grizzlies. He has told me that they are not an animal to play games with, they are dangerous, fast and you can't predict what they will do. He has told me that any time they arrive onto his property and are lingering near guests or cabins, he has to shoot them to protect his customers.

It's hard to tell from these articles if Frank Johnson loved or hated bears. When you are prospecting, many times your head is down in the dirt and your backside is open and susceptible to attack. He might have learned at an early age that he couldn't allow Grizzlies to loiter near his work for fear of attack.

Johnson's relatives in Vancouver stated that they never believed he would leave his dog to starve, they thought something fatal must've taken his life.

If there was one photo that would encompass the life of Frank Johnson, it's the one I included in this article. The two-week search of 150 miles and the checking on a dozen cabins failed to produce Frank's body, and he was never found.

Louis Majers
Missing: 11/03/45, Elk Valley, British Columbia
Age at disappearance: 39 years
Hunter • Weather

British Columbia has steep, unforgiving mountains that have many mysteries, several described in the *Missing 411* books. The Canadian Rockies are very similar to their cousins to the south as they also hold many missing people.

Louis Majers was a Czechoslovakian citizen when he decided in the mid-1930s he needed a better life for his family and moved to Michel, British Columbia. He left his wife at their home country and found employment at the mines in this area. He loved the outdoors and Elk Valley; Michel and Natal were very wild regions in the 1940s. Every day off, Louis would hike into the mountains and scout the hunting grounds preparing for the season to start, he knew these areas very well.

On Saturday, November 3, 1945, the Czech citizen had a rare day off. He decided to grab his rifle and hunt the ground in Elk Valley. When he didn't turn up for work on Monday, his friends got a group of miners and hunters together to look for their friend. This November 8, 1945, article in the *Lethbridge Herald* had some related information, "The prevailing cold weather is making it difficult for the search parties to locate him due to the heavy snowfall up in the Elk Valley mountains where he was last seen. Under the direction of the local police, the first clue was found by the searching party when his bicycle was found Wednesday, some two miles west of Natal."

The area where the search was being conducted was a very rugged region. Just to the west of the area Majers was hunting is the Top of the World Provincial Park and to the west of that is the city of Skookumchuck. When people go missing in small communities, it is usually a challenging task to find able-bodied searchers in large numbers, especially when the weather is challenging.

Snow continued to fall in Louis' hunting area, and temperatures were frigid. After being missing for 1 week, searchers gave up. When the weather got slightly better and warmer in December, there was another push to locate the hunter, nothing was found. I cannot remember a much more difficult area to search than what was presented in this incident. Cold temperatures, snow, steep mountains, small community, and a lack of relatives pushing the search agenda meant the effort to locate Louis would not be extended. When they found his bicycle, that presented a real opportunity to track him. This is another incident where we will never know what happened as his body was never found.

Alma Hall, 28 years old
Raymond Hall, 6 years old
Missing: 06/09/51, Woss Logging, Englewood, Vancouver Island, Water•

Alma Hall and her son, Raymond, left their Saskatoon residence to visit Thomas Glen Hall, the boy's father and Alma's husband. Glen worked for Woss Logging at "W" Camp in Englewood, outside of Alert Bay. This is a rural camp near the Nimpkish River.

On June 9, 1951, Alma took Raymond for a hike in the woods to a waterfall on the Nimpkish River. Loggers saw the boy and the woman near the falls, but this was the last time anyone ever saw the pair.

Glen was quickly made aware of the disappearance. He notified the RCMP and gathered a group of the best loggers and woodsmen in the area to search for his family. The RCMP dragged the river while the others focused on the land. A search of over a week failed to find the two people, and neither body ever floated up in the river. It was as if the mother and son had vanished.

Leo Gaspard
Missing: 7/31/51-Unk • 60 • Pitt Lake, BC
Age at disappearance: 60 years
Cluster Zone• Lights in the Sky• Weather•

This story centers on an old gold mine near the headwaters of the Pitt River, forty-five miles northeast of Vancouver, British Columbia.

The stories about this incident vary slightly, but they all begin in 1890. An Indian named Slumach or Slummack was prospecting in the headwaters when he supposedly found a very wealthy vein of gold. Slummack was a very private person, but it was noted that he had returned to civilization with bags of fine gold. Sometimes he would realize he needed more gold, and then he would disappear for forty-eight hours and return with another bag, some nuggets as big as walnuts.

Slummack wasn't a model citizen. One story stated that he murdered a person and was hanged on January 16, 1891. Another story, more complex than the first, indicated that he brought a Native American woman with him on each trip to cook for him. Each time he returned alone and said that the woman either died of a variety of reasons or disappeared. On one return trip, other miners found his female companion in a river with Slummack's knife in her back. He later confessed and was supposedly convicted of eight murders. He was offered life in prison if he told the court where his mine was located. He refused. Between 1891 and 1951, twenty miners reportedly entered the headwaters of the Pitt River looking for the Lost Creek Mine and disappeared, never to be found.

There are strange stories associated with this area of the Pitt as were described in the February 21, 1943, *Milwaukee Sentinel*: "Strange lights recently have been flickering in the skies above the Pitt Lake Mountains in the icy wilderness of British Columbia. The aged Indians of the district say the weird illumination is caused by the spirits of the 11 murdered squaws of Slummack, a strange Indian killer who disposed of women to protect the secret of his fabulously rich Lost Creek mine."

In July 1951, Alfred Gaspard entered the offices of Okanagan Air Services and asked to be helicoptered into the headwaters of the Pitt River. He stated that he wanted to contract for four hundred pounds of food to be dropped four months after he originally left. Carl Agar was the manager of the air service and the man who Gaspard spoke with. He stated that Gaspard was one of the few legitimate and well-prepared prospectors he had ever met. He said that ten to twelve people a year ask him to drop them at the Pitt, and he normally refuses. He said that Gaspard was one of only two he has agreed to allow his pilots to fly in. Agar stated that the area is too dangerous for anyone who isn't extremely experienced in mountain life and well prepared for all types of weather.

After Gaspard was originally dropped on the Pitt, two other prospectors remembered seeing him hiking north into the woods. After this initial observation, the prospector was never seen again.

In October 1951, two RCMP officers went into the headwaters to search for evidence of what had happened to Gaspard. The area had incurred snow, and it rained on the officers during their search. They spent two weeks in the rugged wilderness and did not find any information about where the man had set up camp or any evidence of his death. Every news article that I reviewed indicated that Gaspard was the twenty-first victim who had gone into this area in an attempt to work the Lost Creek Mine. He was never found.

Summary

I've always been interested in this area of British Columbia. The region is considered some of the roughest mountain landscape in all of North America. Many segments of these mountains have probably never been walked by humans. There have been several First Nations stories about this area being a place just for Indians and not for white people.

In another odd twist to the Gaspard story, he left a letter for relatives to read should he disappear. In the letter he stated, "By the time you are reading this note, I have passed on." Yes, he had a premonition about his own death on this last trip of his life.

David Anderson
Missing: 05/20/53-10:00 a.m., Metchosin, BC
Age at disappearance: 3 1/2 years
Water• Missing Shoes• Weather• Canines• Cluster Zone

Even if a story doesn't seem exciting, researchers need to be true to their work. If the incident matches the profile points that have been established after years of refining, the disappearance is included.

Metchosin is a small city on the southern end of Vancouver Island. The south end of the town is across the Strait of Juan De Fuca and across from Port Angeles, Washington. There are a series of small boys that have disappeared from Port Angeles to Neah Bay and across the Strait to Tofino and then south to Metchosin. All of these cases happened very close to the coast. This disappearance happened off Wishart Road near Turners Shingle Mill, approximately 4000 feet from the ocean.

Little David Anderson was playing at his home at 10:00 a.m. on May 20, 1953. Somehow David got out of sight from his mother and vanished. Mrs. Anderson searched the yard and then the neighborhood and called the local RCMP. The RCMP did a cursory search of the region, realized the boy wasn't anywhere nearby and immediately called for additional resources. A May 21, 1953, edition of the *Nanaimo Daily News* had these details, "Almost 1000 police and civilians searched for David Anderson, the son of Mr. and Mrs. Peter G.L. Anderson, who disappeared from his home at 10:00 a.m. The search started late on Wednesday by 10 RCMP constables and assisted by a search dog. By nightfall, 40 persons, including members of the South Vancouver Island Rangers and members of the Langford Volunteer Fire Department, had joined the hunt.

SAR teams worked until 2:00 a.m. searching and calling for David. They didn't hear anything, and they did not have any witnesses that had seen him. The parents stated that David never wandered far from home and was surprised he wasn't quickly located.

The search on May 20 was fully functional with hundreds of volunteers and professionals. Near 11: 00 a.m., there was a development in the case as is mentioned in the May 21, 1953 edition of the *Times Colonist*, "Sir Roderick's (Canine) handler, Ron Mason, stated he could detect tiny footprints where the dog was tracking, but they, too, disappeared." Searchers were now formed into a shoulder to shoulder search to walk through the forest. Later in the same article was this, "Through the darkness of the night, hampered by intermittent rain, and the heavily wooded region, uneven terrain, the men carried on the search. The Navy and the Army committed hundreds of personnel members. A May 21 article in the *Times Colonist* had this, "The mass sweep through the hinterland surrounding the boys home was an all-man venture. Three dogs sent to trace the boy failed to find a sign of him."

On May 21, the Canadian Army, Navy, RCMP, local volunteers and SAR officials were still walking shoulder to shoulder calling the boy's name and not getting a response. The May 21 paper of the *Nanaimo Daily News* had this, "RCMP stated the boy was found asleep under a tree near one of his shoes that were found. He was located about one mile from his home in a shoulder to shoulder sweep of the country which started at noon. He was transported to a hospital for a thorough exam. There were no details on his condition.

As a side note, the *Times Colonist* article quoted in the previous section had this interesting note, "The RCMP Bloodhound Rip, and the islands Ranger's hunting dogs Sir Roderick and Joe, picked up a faint scent at the point the shoe was found, but it petered out. A Searcher found the shoe. The exact location wasn't explained but that it was somewhere near where the boy was located. What I find interesting is that if the boy was located near the shoe, the dogs should've been able to pick up the scent and track straight to the owner, they didn't. Why the dogs didn't follow the scent is puzzling.

I have documented dozens of stories where searchers state that when the small child was located, they were sleeping. If they weren't sleeping, they were described as tired. David was found at 1:00 p.m., maybe it was nap time. The press never tried to interview the parents or obtain a statement from David.

How did David avoid the Canadian Armed forces, 1000 searchers who were all beating the bush for him? He was located approximately one mile from his home, sleeping under a tree.

Arthur Tibbett
Missing: 11/09/53, Mount Seymour, British Columbia
Age at disappearance: 29 years
Canines• Disability• Weather• Cluster Zone

When missing people are around others, just before the disappearance they often report feeling ill, tired, something that takes them away from the people they are with; this specific profile point becomes an integral part of this story.

In November of 1953, twenty-six-year-old Arthur Tibbett was a world war II RCAF (Royal Canadian Armed Forces) veteran who was living with his wife and seven-month-old son in Deep Cove, British Columbia. Arthur had gained skills in the military as a radio technician and transferred those to civilian life into a job in Vancouver.

On November 9, 1953, Arthur was working with technicians from CBC television on a new transmission tower on Mount Seymour, approximately 15 miles from his home. While he was working on the project, he started to feel ill as is reported in this November 10, 1953 article in *The Province*, "He (Arthur Tibbett) was reported to have gone into the lodge with technicians from CBC (Canadian Broadcasting Corporation) television transmitter, now being built lower down the mountain, and asked for aspirin for a headache. Then he disappeared." There were no other details about the facts surrounding Arthur going missing.

Arthur failed to come home from his assignment and his wife called RCMP (Royal Canadian Mounted Police). She knew he was working on Mount Seymour and the police sent a car to search the area. They located his vehicle in the Mount Seymour Lodge parking lot, and this is where the search started. A November 12, 1953 article in *The Province* had this, "The search got underway immediately and was intensified Wednesday when volunteers worked at 15 to 30-foot intervals through deep brush on each side of the mountain highway. Heavy rain impeded the search." There was one interesting notation on the canine search as is described in the November 12, 1953 edition of the *Vancouver Sun*, "The dog was given Tibbett's scent at 7:00 a.m. Wednesday from the car he left in the parking lot on the side of the mountain Monday afternoon. Searchers followed the dog to a small creek high up the mountain, but there Tibbett's trail was lost."

Several articles stated that Arthur had described his pain as a "a splitting headache," something we know that can be debilitating. Fellow workers stated that Arthur felt fine when he left the business and left for Mount Seymour, it was only after he started to work did he begin to feel ill.

The effort to locate the missing technician included canines, forty-four members of the Mountain Emergency Squad, skiers and dozens of volunteers from Arthur's business, Regal radio and Television of Vancouver.

A four-day search failed to find Arthur or any of his clothing or shoes.

Imagine when you have had a "a splitting headache," the last thing you want to do is exude enormous power and climb uphill on a trail. The exertion of energy usually would cause the headache to get worse. If the scent trail was correct, why would Arthur voluntarily make this journey when he knew he was working with CBC down the hill? Many times victims are found near bodies of water, which can be creeks, rivers, ponds, marshes bogs, etc. I have been reminded many times by readers that creeks are an excellent location for something or someone to walk in and leave no tracks. Why would the canine lose the scent high up the mountain?

Why wasn't Arthur ever located?

This is case number one on Mt Seymour.

Helena Jackson
Missing: 04/11/54, North Vancouver, British Columbia
Age at disappearance: 46 years
Canines• Missing Shoes• Cluster Zone

The City limit of North Vancouver travels north from the water and ends on the edge of thick wilderness. The city sits on a peninsula surrounded by water on three sides and mountains to the north. From west to east the mountains just north of the town are Mount Cypress, Grouse Mountain, Mount Fromme, and Mount Seymour. Each of these locations is within miles of large population centers.

One of the furthest north streets in North Vancouver that is on the edge of the wilderness is Borthwick Street, the victim in this story lived at 1365.

In April of 1954, Mrs. Helena Jackson lived on Borthwick street, a gorgeous neighborhood of thin roads, expensive homes that enjoy the picturesque nature of North Vancouver.

On April 11, 1954, in the morning hours, Mrs. Jackson's daughter (Sharon) helped her mom put a dressing gown over her nightgown so she could go outside. Sharon looked for her mom throughout the day but could not locate her. At 7:00 p.m., the RCMP was called. After the first officer arrived and collected details, more police responded and started a search of the area. On April 12, 1954, there were these details about the search in *The Province*, "Forty volunteers searched all day Monday helped by RCMP tracking dog Bobby, but didn't find a single clue."

The location of this incident is between Mount Seymour and Mount Fromme. The distance from the Jackson residence to Mount Seymour Provincial Park is approximately four miles.

The investigation by police indicated that Mrs. Jackson was possibly seen at the Sunshine Nudist Club higher up the mountain where it was claimed she left her shoes behind. The four-day search included ninety volunteer searchers, tracking dogs, forty soldiers from Jericho and the Grouse Mountain Emergency Squad.

Barry Jackson was the son of the victim and was irritated that searchers gave up after four days. He was able to rally friends and work employees to spend several additional days scouring the area for his mom. There were random reports that Helena was seen walking around the city and at various shopping centers, none of these sightings were corroborated.

One of the reports about Mrs. Jackson's demeanor stated that just before the vanished, she was "nervously upset," but nobody knew why.

There was never an inkling that the 46-year-old housewife had issues of dementia, etc.

Three months after Helena vanished, the Vancouver court placed a curator on the family's estate to take care of the children and the assets. This move by the courts is an acknowledgment that Helena Jackson was deceased, even though she was never found.

John Last
Missing: 09/26/54, Gunn Lake, Lillooet, British Columbia, Canada
Age at disappearance: 24 years
Point of Separation• Canines• Weather

British Columbia had notoriety in the 1950's-1960's for gold mining. This disappearance deals with the Pioneer Gold Mine located forty miles west of Lillooet, British Columbia near Gunn Lake. The area has very steep mountains, several that rise above timberline. It also has many lakes, rivers, and creeks that have ground covered by thick brush and trees.

Every mine has an assayer, a professional that examines the ore coming from the ground and determines the quantity of gold or silver in the rock. In this incident, the person missing was the Pioneer mines assayer.

In September of 1954, twenty-four-year-old John Last was a resident of Sussex, United Kingdom. He was working for the last several months as an assayer for the Pioneer gold mine. John was a Korean War veteran and described as in excellent shape.

On Sunday, September 26, 1954, the mine had a day off. Mr. Last and two co-workers decided to take a day hike of the area and John didn't make it back. They were not carrying food or heavy clothing because it was a gorgeous morning and they'd be back for dinner. Something happened during the hike and is explained in the September 29, 1954, *The Province*, "A Pioneer Mines spokesman said, "He must be hurt. He's been with the mine about a year now and knows the country around there fairly well. He'd have walked out if he'd been ok." There were more details about the missing man in the September 30, 1954 edition of *The Province*, "John Last vanished Sunday because he was impatient. He was one of a party of three hiking above timberline near Gunn Lake, in the Bridge River Area. But he became impatient with the slow speed of his companions and forged ahead. That was the last they saw of him." Once Last's companions reached the mine and realized he didn't make it back, supervisors organized a search, found nothing and then called the RCMP.

The Mounties sent a float plane that landed on Gunn Lake. They also requested a canine officer from Coquitlam. Corporal

R.P. Stone and his dog "Bobby" was flown into the area and met with mining officials. The best conditioned miners that worked for Pioneer were chosen to help with the search. The group included Austrians, Swiss, and Norwegians that spent six days climbing high altitudes looking for their work companion. The Mounties new the area was vast; they sent a second canine to search after the third day of the SAR.

Corporal Stone's dog searched for five days and was severely injured walking over sharp rocks high in the mountains. Stone made the following comment in the October 5 edition of *The Province*, "There was no chance of a track, because of rain, the dog had to rely on scent." The article went on to say, "The group searched a 10-mile radius without finding a trace of the missing man."

At the end of the six-day effort to locate John, there were a total of seventy searchers, two canines and two RCMP airplanes. John Last was never found.

This case is unusual for a few reasons. Mr. last was seen hiking away from two friends above timberline, meaning, there was no ground cover, no trees, just rocks, and boulders. RCMP pilots should have been able to see a body in the boulder fields if it was there. This incident is an excellent example of something happening after the point of separation. When the group was together there were no issues, once the assayer separated from his friends, something deadly occurred. Hikers should always stay with a group when in the mountains.

There were comments in the newspapers about the feelings of RCMP and mining officials on what may have happened. Some people felt that John may have encountered a Grizzly bear and was consumed. Bear experts warn against hiking in grizzly territory alone and recommend hiking in groups of three or more. I doubt that a bear devoured John, canines would've found torn clothing containing scent and small body parts and blood on the trail. It would also seem doubtful that he was injured and died. According to mining officials, the Brit knew the path to the mine. If he became injured it would be close to that trail and canines and ground teams would've found him.

John Last was never found.

Herman Jungerhuis
Missing: 11/10/57, Monte Lake, BC
Age at disappearance: 55 years
Point of Separation• Weather• Water• Canines

The victim's name in this story has been spelled two ways, Jungerhuis and Jongerhuis. I will utilize the first rendition.

Herman Jungerhuis was a native of Austria and had moved to Canada in 1951 and took up residence near Kamloops.

On November 9, 1957, Herman and friends decided to go hunting in the area of Monte Lake, 25 miles southeast of Kamloops. The trio decided to split up and meet back at their car at a designated time. When the agreed-upon time arrived, and the hunters started to meet together, Herman did not show up, and his friends began to search. They combed the area where they last saw Herman, and they continually called his name and did not receive a response. After exhausting all options they knew about, the RCMP was called.

The search for Jungerhuis was comprehensive and explained in this November 15, 1957 article in the *Edmonton Journal*, "Meanwhile, the search is continuing for a 55-year old immigrant- Herman Jungerhuis-missing near Kamloops since Sunday. More than 50 searchers, supported by a helicopter, a tracking dog and walkie talkies, are searching an area 25 miles southeast of Kamloops." The actual area of the SAR is Monte Lake, which has highway 97 traveling to it. The area west of the search area is rolling hills with thick vegetations. There was another description of the conditions searchers faced that appeared in the November 16, 1957 edition of the *Nanaimo Daily News*, "They said mud conditions had made travel in the area almost impossible. Every inch of the ground in the area where Jungerhuis is presumed to have disappeared had been covered several times without revealing a trace of him."

The last article in 1957 about this incident appeared in the November 18, 1957 edition of the *Vancouver Sun*, "Bad weather Friday forced police to abandon a six-day search 25 miles southwest of Kamloops for a Dutch immigrant in Canada for six years." The three-week search for Herman found nothing.

There were no additional details about Herman's disappearance until September of 1960 and those facts are found in the September

20, 1960 edition of *The Province*, "The remains of a North Kamloops man missing since he went on a hunting trip November 11, 1957, were discovered by two hunters on the shore of Ernest Lake, 12 miles south of Kamloops." The article stated that a skeleton was found along with a rifle and some clothing. The wording in the report implies Herman was found on the beach, strange place for a body to be found, especially when he was last hunting in the area just west of Monte Lake. If he died on the beach, he should've been able to be seen by the air search that the RCMP had completed. The puzzling part of this information causes the reader almost to think he was washed up onto the shore. If you go that direction with your thinking, it doesn't make sense because they found his rifle with him. Why didn't he fire three shots and notify his partners where he was located, and he needed assistance? Three shots in rapid succession are the accepted method for a hunter to say they need help.

One of the last reports I reviewed stated that Herman was located 5 1/2 miles from where he was last seen. Ernest Lake is in the Roche Lake Provincial Park and is an area with dozens of small lakes and ponds.

Why didn't canines pick up a scent? Why didn't the airplanes in the sky see the hunter? This is another disappearance of a hunter that revolves around water, weather, canines, and separating yourself from others.

Cindy Lou Maclane
Missing 09/09/58–9 a.m., Willow River, BC
Age at Disappearance: 2 years
Water• Canines

Willow River, British Columbia, is located eight miles northeast of Prince George. It sits between a main tributary to the Fraser River and Eaglet Lake. The town had only eighteen roads in 2012, so you can imagine it wasn't a very big city in 1958. It sits in a region with hundreds of small bodies of water, and even today, it still has significant overgrown and wild areas at the city's perimeter. In 1958, Willow River was supported by one small sawmill where most of the men were employed.

On September 9, 1958, Cindy Lou Maclane was at her home with her mother, twenty-two-year-old Gladys, while her father, Gerald, was working at the local sawmill. At 9 a.m., Cindy vanished from playing in the yard of the family home. Mrs. Maclane searched for the girl and couldn't locate her. The local RCMP was called, and Mr. Maclane came home from work to assist in the search. In an oddity to this event, the MacLane's were only in this home for two days as they had moved from their previous residence just one mile away.

The Maclane home was located on the perimeter of the town, where there was little to no vehicular traffic. It was the general feeling that Cindy must've wandered into the forest. Almost immediately, several hundred volunteers flocked to the Maclane home and started to cover the area, looking for the two-year-old.

When Cindy wasn't found after the first day, the RCMP sponsored radio broadcasts asking for volunteers to respond to the Maclane residence to assist in the search. Eventually, every sawmill in the area closed, and hundreds of able-bodied men committed to searching. The RCMP had sentries stationed deep in the woods at the end of every night of searching. They were listening for the sounds of an injured or crying girl.

There was some strangeness in this search as several men had heard odd noises in the forest in the middle of the night and is described in the September 11, 1958 edition of the *Vancouver Sun*, "The man who heard the strange cry in the bush Wednesday evening is another neighbor, F.D. Glynn. Five other men with Glynn heard the sound which they said was "exactly like a child whimpering." In conjunction with the strange sounds, a tracking dogs behavior could not be readily explained and is discussed in the same article just quoted, "But Mrs. Peters (canine handler) claims there's something strange about his (Tracking dog) and is far from certain the child actually went in the water. He's never lied to me yet. I don't know what to make of it, she said. Chamounte (canine) has been running around in a tight circle at a spot near the river bank." The river was approximately one mile from the residence and nobody had a feeling that the child entered. The RCMP did put several divers into the water and pulled grappling hooks for many hours, finding nothing.

A body never did come up downstream from this location. The oddity of the canines behavior was the location, a spot near the bank, not near the water.

As searchers completed their sixth day of searching, they were coming to the realization that they had found nothing of the girl. They had come across several black bears in the region and had killed each one they had seen. The bears were gutted in an attempt to see if they had eaten Cindy; they had not. There was still the feeling that a bear had taken her, even though they hadn't found the suspect.

Just as the exhausted community was beginning to terminate the search and get back to their jobs, another child went missing.

Tony Richard Beauchamp
Missing 09/16/58–3 p.m., Bonnet Hill, BC
Age at Disappearance: 2 years
Water•

Bonnet Hill sits approximately twelve miles southwest of Willow River, and oddly enough, each city is an equal distance from the Fraser River. Bonnet Hill sits three miles east of Prince George and in a location between the Fraser River and Tabor Lake. The landscape that surrounds Bonnet Hill and Willow River is very similar. Both cities are very small in size and would be considered suburbs of Prince George.

Exactly one week after Cindy Lou disappeared and while the search for her was still ongoing, Tony Beauchamp vanished. Tony was in the front yard of his home with his brothers and sisters. They were waiting for their dad, Gilbert, to get off work at his sawmill at 3 p.m. It appears that Tony walked partially down his rural road, looking for his dad, and vanished. Tony was last seen wearing rubber boots, blue jeans, and a light blue sweater.

The Beauchamp family immediately started to look for the boy and then notified the local RCMP. Searchers were now split between the Beauchamp and Maclane search.

On the first night searchers were looking for Tony, it was reported that searchers found a boot, but the paper couldn't absolutely confirm it was his.

On Wednesday, the United States Air Force joined the search for Tony. I realize that this seems like an odd addition for a Canadian search, but Captain George Knight was flying his Beaver aircraft looking for the boy.

Between the Beauchamp residence and Prince George, there was a pipeline that crossed the territory in a north-to-south direction. The pipeline would look a lot like large electrical lines, in that the area around the pipe was mowed and there was little vegetation in close proximity to the pipes. This was the area that Captain Knight was flying. At 2 p.m., he made a remarkable discovery. A September 18, 1958, article in the *Lethbridge Herald* had the following statement: "A 2½ year old boy, missing 23 hours from his home near here was found asleep near a pipeline right of way Wednesday about two miles from his home." Tony was taken back to his residence and found to be in good condition. There was never a statement about what Tony was or wasn't wearing or his physical condition.

Summary

In the thousands of missing-persons cases I have investigated, it is highly unusual to have two missing in such close proximity of the Canadian bush, as is the case with Cindy and Tony. Imagine that both kids were two years old, missing less than fifteen miles apart, and disappeared exactly one week apart. One child is never found, and another is found in the same condition as a vast majority of all missing children—unconscious or semiconscious. Was it pure coincidence that two children exactly the same age disappeared miles from each other in an extremely rural area of British Columbia? There was never a clear reason listed in any article why a United States Air Force captain was participating in the search.

The fact that both fathers of the missing children worked in a sawmill isn't unusual. Employment in a sawmill would've been one of the few types of work available in this part of Canada in the 1950s. It does seem opportunistic that both children vanished when their fathers weren't at home.

I spent a significant amount of time trying to find any articles that indicated that Cindy was located. I found that the search for

Cindy continued briefly after Tony was found, and then there was no additional information available.

Where is Cindy Lou Maclane?

Betty Jean Masters
Missing: 07/03/60- 8:00 P.M., Red Lake, BC
Age at disappearance: 20 Months
Water• Canines

When I speak at conferences, I routinely ask the parents in the audience how far their two-year-old child would wander if alone on a trail. I get answers from three miles to nowhere; they'd lay down and sleep. I ask the question because I place a table up showing the unreal distances small children have been found from where they were last seen. Every parent knows that a small child couldn't manage those distances on their own, the question, how did they get there?

Red Lake British Columbia is approximately 35 miles northeast from Kamloops. This is a very remote location with a few residence, a post office, and two small businesses and a sawmill down the road, and this was in 1960. The mountains around this tiny city are rugged and very wild.

On July 3, 1960, the Master's family took a day trip from their residence in Copper Creek and drove to visit friends in Red Lake. Betty Jean was playing outside with other children when something happened and is described in the July 11, 1960 article of *The Province*, "The girl disappeared while playing with other youngsters outside the home of friends her parents were visiting. Red Lake is a logging community in mountainous country in which the going is tough even for woodsmen."

The other children that were with Betty never saw anything unusual and could not explain how she vanished at around 8:00 P.M. This area of Canada has daylight in the summer until very late.

The parents for both families called Betty's name, searched the region around the home, and did not get a response. The owner of the house called other friends at the sawmill and asked to help with the search.

Betty disappeared on a Sunday, they closed every sawmill in this area of Canada, and the men responded to search. The area around this town was so rugged; only the fittest men went into the hillsides to look. This July 5, 1960 article in the *Vancouver Sun* had details on the SAR, "A day-long search for the child by Red Lake residents Monday failed to find her. The tracking dog couldn't pick up a scent."

The RCMP questioned Robert, Betty's dad, about what he thought happened to his daughter? Mr. Masters never had his daughter disappear and had no idea where she was located. The police questioned every resident within five miles. Nobody saw anyone unusual; nobody heard anything odd; there was nothing unusual. On the third day of the search, the RCMP brought in a famous game hunter to see if his dogs could find any bears or cougars in the area. After a several-day search, the hunter came up with both, a bear and cougar; unfortunately, they were not the culprits.

After seven stressful days and nights searching for Betty, nobody had found anything. Canines never picked up a scent; nobody found any of her tracks in the woods. The investigation into local residents by the RCMP had not turned up anything odd. There were several statements made by the police about what they thought may have happened to the girl. The comments ranged from a cougar or bear got her, even though there was zero evidence of this, to she was possibly kidnapped. The RCMP downplayed the kidnapping theory because the location was so remote and isolated, it made no sense.

I have written several stories about young children that had vanished while visiting a relative or friend's home. In almost every instance, there were no witnesses, no leads, and no explanation of how they got away so quickly.

One police officer was asked in the July 7, 1960 edition of the Times Colonist to explain the incident the best he can, he said one word, "queer."

Mr. and Mrs. Masters lived a lifetime with the horror of not knowing what happened to their daughter; I cannot imagine their grief.

Gezo Peczeli
Missing: 09/18/60, Mount Baldy, 50 miles northeast of Kamloops, BC
Age at Disappearance: 24 years
Water• Canines• Weather

It took a bit of an effort to locate the exact location of this incident. The Baldy Mountain, in this case, is located approximately fifty miles northeast of Kamloops and sits above Shuswap Lake on its southern shore just west of Sorrento. This is not a huge mountain, but it sits in a gorgeous location above the water.

In June of 1960, David Anderson owned a sheep ranch that had his herd grazing on land northeast of Kamloops. He met twenty-four-year-old Hungarian immigrant Gezo Peczeli and offered him a job as a sheepherder for two hundred of his sheep on Mount Baldy. On June 26, Gezo went up to the mountain with Mr. Anderson and was shown his quarters in an old cabin. He was given a rifle for protection and supplies. He was told that he'd be visited monthly and re-supplied with what he needed.

Everything was going smoothly for Mr. Anderson's operation until he arrived for a regular check on Gezo and the flock on September 20, 1960. This September 26, 1960 article in the Nanaimo Daily News explains what was found, "The shepherd was not at his lonely camp, and four inches of snow had fallen. His rifle and other belongings were at the camp, but there were no signs of footprints in the snow." Mr. Anderson now started to search the mountains for Gezo and the sheep. The sheep were located 2000 feet further up the mountain huddling together where there had been eight new inches of snow. Gezo could not be located anywhere in the area. Mr. Anderson went back to town and called the RCMP and forestry officials.

The RCMP got to the camp on September 23 and continued on-site through the weekend with the assistance of a forestry crew. The September 26 edition of the Vancouver Sun had these details, "A 10-man party made up of RCMP and forestry men familiar with mountain woods, and a searching dog set out early today. The team located Peczeli's rifle and supplies in the cabin, but no indications he had been there recently. The RCMP told the press that they faced blizzard conditions up the mountain that compromised their search efforts.

There was a four-day search that did not find any indicators showing what happened to Gezo.

In 1961, Mr. Anderson went back into the mountains after the snow had cleared, still looking for his sheepherder. Gezo Peczeli was never found.

In Missing 411: Eastern United States, I wrote an entire chapter about missing sheepherders. I realized early in my research that this was a dangerous occupation where many disappeared without a trace. Montana had the most missing sheepherders with three. Some of the stories behind those cases are fascinating. When you realize that these men spent weeks in the wild alone with no human contact and no assistance for miles, it's easy to understand how they could become prey. The unusual part of that chapter was I could never find a case of predation; the vast majority just vanished.

Wallace Marr
Missing: 11/19/62, Yale, BC
Age at disappearance: 30 years
Weather• Point of Separation

There are dozens of people missing in the Cascade Range of mountains in the United States. If you continued that range north into Canada thirty-five miles, that's where this disappearance happened, five miles north of Yale, British Columbia.

Wallace Marr was an avid outdoorsman and hunter that lived in Calgary, Alberta Canada. In November of 1962, he made the 450-mile drive from Calgary, Alberta to Yale, British Columbia. He then drove five miles northwest to his hunting camp where he met his friend Fred Bascoe. The pair would be hunting very thick forests and steep land.

On November 19, 1962, Fred and Wallace had hunted and were getting cold. They started a small fire on a logging road and rested until Fred saw deer tracks entering the woods. He told Wallace he'd follow the path to see if he could find the animal. Wallace said he'd stay by the fire.

Fred eventually made his way down the mountain to the main road and then back up to the hunting camp. He waited for several hours, checked the logging road, didn't find his friend and then went back to camp, Wallace never arrived. It was at this point that the RCMP was notified.

The SAR commanders contacted all hunters in the area and advised them of the situation and requested assistance. Seven hunters joined police and SAR officials in combing the mountain for the thirty-year-old hunter. This November 23, 1962 article in the *Nanaimo Daily News* had these details, "They said Thursday the lightly clad Marr is missing in an area 120 road miles from Vancouver, where snow, rain, and fog and low temperatures have been prevalent since the weekend."

The RCMP put forth two theories over five days about what may have happened to Wallace. The number one theory was that he fell into a river and drowned. Theory number two was that he fell off a cliff and died. They never answered the question about why they couldn't locate tracks in the forest or why they never found a body or equipment. They never stated that he possibly died of hypothermia even though temperatures were below freezing.

It's amazing how many times hikers and hunters separate, and something happens, and the individual vanishes. I have had several readers tell me that it appears that someone or something is watching these people, waits for the appropriate time, moves in when nobody is watching and takes these victims, leaving behind nothing.

The six-day SAR for Wallace located nothing. He was never found.

Leslie Evans
Age at disappearance: 39 years
John Evans
Missing: 06/11/66, Golden Ears Park, BC
Age at disappearance: 14 years
Boulders• Cluster Zone• Inclement Weather• Water

I am notified of missing cases from a variety of sources in a multitude of ways. This incident was told to me by my good friend, Randy Brisson from British Columbia. Randy lived in the same neighborhood of the victims and clearly remembered vital details that led me to an understanding of this disappearance, thank you, Randy.

Leslie Evans lived in a suburb of Vancouver, British Columbia with his wife and thirteen-year-old son, John. He was a correctional officer at the Haney Correctional Institute. Leslie enjoyed living in British Columbia and the proximity it offered to the remote outdoors. It was his love for nature that led to his trip in June 1966.

On June 10, 1966, Leslie had a rare weekend off work from the prison and decided to head into the woods with his son, John and try to climb a local mountain, Edge Peak in Golden Ears Park. The park was just north of the Evans residence and would be a short drive to the trailhead.

John and Leslie Evans

On Saturday morning, June 11, 1966, Leslie and John Evans packed their sleeping bags, two sand-wiches, a few eggs, a couple of canteens and made the drive to the Gold Creek Camp trailhead, parked their car and started to hike. Other hikers reported seeing the pair on the trail and had a brief con-versation about where they were headed, Edge Peak.

Late on Sunday night, June 12, Mrs. Evans became very con-cerned when her son and husband failed to return from their week-end getaway. Leslie was always punctual and stated he would be home that night, he never arrived. She called the RCMP.

It wasn't long after Leslie and John were reported missing that the Haney Correctional Institute was notified. The prison told the correctional staff, and several guards went to the mountains to aid in the search effort.

The RCMP initially thought the pair was hiking to a different location in Golden Ears Park. Searchers quickly found a witness that had spoken with Leslie and determined they were headed for Edge Peak. The search effort had its complications, as is described in the

June 16, 1966, edition of *The Province*, "The helicopter completed a rescue mission in the area Wednesday after Don Quoron, 40, a member of the 12-man team from Mountain Rescue Group from Vancouver, broke his right leg when a rock hit him. Green was flown to Maple Ridge Hospital in Haney then taken by ambulance to Vancouver General Hospital."

The area that searchers had focused was a region just north of Alouette Lake towards Edge Peak. They knew that Leslie was in outstanding physical condition and that John had the energy of a fourteen-year-old. The forest in the area was very thick with foliage and was challenging to see through with a helicopter, yet the RCMP had committed air time to the search. At the height of the SAR, one hundred searchers from the RCMP, Rover Scouts, Mountain Rescue, and even the Canadian Army joined the effort and put 50 soldiers on the ground to look.

Leslie had several very close friends that refused to give up looking. Many of their efforts lasted for weeks and found nothing. The September 26, 1966 edition of *The Province* had these details of SAR efforts, "Hume said he had counted on having 60 persons take part in the hunt but inclement weather kept most of them away." There were some theories that Leslie and John were caught in an avalanche and died, yet months after the event when the snow cleared, and no bodies were located. One focus of the SAR was a boulder ridden chute that led to the top of Edge Peak. The peak stands high and mighty, seen from miles with a summit of 5,512 feet. It is a massive granite monolith that can be seen for miles. The chute was repeatedly searched and nothing was found.

Months of repeated SAR efforts failed to find John or Leslie or one item that belonged to the pair. It's a real mystery of what happened to the Evans.

Clancy O'Brien
Missing: 08/20/66- P.M., Green Lake, Clinton, BC
Age at disappearance: 9 years
Berries• Point of Separation• Water• Canines

Mr. and Mrs. Patrick O'Brien lived with their nine-year-old son, Clancy at 362 East Keith Road in Vancouver, BC. Patrick was an active member of the Teamsters Union of Vancouver and had a summer vacation planned for his son, Clancy and his wife. The family drove to Green Lake thirty miles north of Clinton, and approximately 200 miles north of their residence.

On Saturday, August 20, 1966, the family went to visit a rancher that was a friend of the family just outside of the Green Lake Provincial Park. It was in the afternoon hours that something happened and is described in the August 26, 1966 edition of The Province, "The boy disappeared after he left a picnic lunch to get some wieners for himself and three friends. He did not turn up at a ranch his parents were visiting near Green Lake." The parents and friends

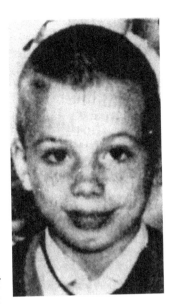

Clancy O'Brien

frantically searched through the muskeg and could not find the boy. It wasn't long before the local RCMP was called. When the family questioned the boys, it was believed that Clancy was returning to their cabin to get more hot dogs.

The first day of the search was a wake-up call for local police. They were not finding any indication where Clancy maybe and this caused them to ask for more assistance. It wasn't long before the search had 150 volunteers from local ranches and summer visitors. Within five days the Teamsters union in Vancouver had contracted for five buses to transport members to the search area. At one point there were 250 searchers, 25 equestrians, three helicopters, tracking dogs. Five mills in the area closed and sent their employees to the region to search.

The weather during the search was mild during the day and cold at night. Questions about the boy starving were addressed in this August 27 article in the Vancouver Sun, "Much of the area is covered with berry bushes," said a police spokesperson. The boy could stay alive and well for a long time eating nothing but these." In my first few Missing 411 books, I specifically wrote about cases of missing people where they were picking or eating berries, and it was an odd association. Because so many cases involved berries, I made it a profile point to track. Refer to Missing 411: Eastern United States for a chapter on missing berry pickers.

Green Lake sits in the central portion of British Columbia surrounded by hundreds of small bodies of water. The location is remote, which makes the response by hundreds of searchers remarkable.

The search for Clancy lasted until September 2. During the thirteen-day effort, search commanders thought they had located small tracks deep in the woods. When the SAR officials put their canines on the tracks, they showed no interest. Because the dogs showed no interest, the tracks were discounted. I've read about canines exhibiting this behavior hundreds of times only to learn later the tracks may have been essential.

The effort to locate Clancy produced nothing that could positively be related to the boy. SAR manuals state that a nine-year-old boy should be found 95% of the time in a mountain environment in a radius of 4.5 miles or less. I do not doubt that RCMP covered this area multiple times.

I lay in bed at night, thinking about these cases. I cannot imagine being Patrick O'Brien and driving the family car back to North Vancouver without my boy; it would ruin me as a person.

Clancy O'Brien was never found.

Roger Olds
Missing: 08/25/66, Sentinel Glacier, Squamish, BC, Canada
Age at disappearance: 19 years
Weather • Canines• Cluster Zone

The area of British Columbia's coast, north of Vancouver is genuinely gorgeous. On the east side of the road are thick woods that are very wild. To the west, you have the Pacific Ocean, islands and views to behold. Approximately half-way to Whistler from Vancouver you will come to Squamish. Eighteen miles north of Squamish is Mount Garibaldi, a remote tall, rugged and glacier covered peak. One of the glaciers that sits on the northeast side of the mountain is Sentinel Glacier.

Dan Harris was a surveyor for the British Columbian government and working on the Sentinel Glacier with a team of other scientists. Harris had a friend in North Vancouver, 19-year-old Roger Olds. Dan knew that Roger wanted to travel up to the glacier and spend a few nights visiting. The plan was that the North Vancouver resident would be hiking from Squamish on August 24 and arrive on scene after a 2-day journey.

This is a description of Garibaldi Park from the provincial governments website:

"In 1860, while carrying out a survey of Howe Sound on board the Royal Navy survey ship H.M.S. Plumper, Captain George Henry was impressed by a towering mountain dominating the view to the northeast. Captain Richards chose to name the 2,678 metre mountain Mount Garibaldi, after the great 19th century Italian patriot and soldier, Giuseppe Garibaldi, a guerrilla general whose exploits and valour were held in high esteem. In 1907, a party of six Vancouver climbers reached the summit of Mount Garibaldi. The views from the peak inspired the establishment of summer climbing camps at Garibaldi Lake. This early interest led to the creation in 1920 of a park reserve. Garibaldi Provincial Park was legislated as a Class A park in 1927, a 195,000 hectare mountain wilderness just 64 kilometres north of Vancouver."

August 26 came and went, and Roger never arrived. Dan was under the belief that something came up and he didn't make the trip and continued working. On September 5th, Dan left the glacier and arrived into Vancouver September 7 to inquire about his friend. The surveyor was told that he departed on August 24th to make the hike into the mountain. Almost immediately SAR was called, and the motion was put into place to locate the 19-year-old. The monumental task in front of searchers was that they were 13 days behind their victim. The September 9, 1966, article in the *Nanaimo Daily News* had details of the event, "A rescue helicopter was scheduled to airlift 20 loggers into Garibaldi Park, 30 miles north of here today to search for missing hiker Roger Olds, 19, of North Vancouver. The loggers were to join ten RCMP and civilians combing the area with the aid of police dogs."

Searchers were told that Roger had a sleeping bag and at least a week's supply of food when he embarked on his journey. September

15 came and found the search had not slowed. More searchers continued to arrive. Nobody understood why they weren't locating anything associated with Roger. The headlines in the September 15, 1966, *Squamish Times*, "Clouds Hamper Search for Hiker." Rescuers weren't getting many breaks, and they couldn't locate any witnesses.

The majority of the SAR effort was focused between 4,500–5,000 feet elevation. SAR helicopters were trying to fly daily and were only held back because of bad weather. The mission had as many as fifty people in the field scouring the mountain in a precise grid pattern; they weren't finding anything.

The path to the glacier is pretty easy to follow. There are distinct valleys, a big mountain, rivers, huge glacier, and the sun to guide you on your journey. It was completely baffling to local RCMP about where Roger could've gone. There was little snow on the ground, temperatures at night got down into the mid-twenties, but everyone knew he had a warm sleeping bag and backpack.

The Olds' family rented a helicopter for several days to supplement the search effort. September 23, 1966, edition of the *Nanaimo Daily News* highlighted the last attempt to locate Roger, "The father, brother and four friends of Roger Olds, 19, of North Vancouver, missing in Garibaldi Park north of here since August 26, Thursday started a final search for the youth. They chartered a plane to fly over sections of the park they think Roger may have hiked through." The 19-year-old hiker just trying to meet his friend was never located. Nothing of what Roger was carrying was ever turned in or determined to be his.

I've written about many stories in British Columbia very similar to this. One of the more baffling parts of this event is SARs failure to locate anything related to the victim. I'll say this for the hundredth time; this is not an indictment of anyone in SAR, I don't believe anything was there.

This story emphasizes the need for every hiker to tell someone you trust where you are going and when you are coming out. This person is your lifeline and only trust this responsibility to someone who won't forget. Not knowing the specifics of what happened to Roger, I can't comment on the equipment that may have saved his life.

Myron Shutty
Missing: 07/09/67-2:30 P.M., Seneca Creek Provincial Park, Nelson, BC
Age at disappearance: 5 years
Water• Canines• Point of Separation

I've documented some very unusual stories over the years; this is one of the strangest. When a young boy disappears in the wilderness, the vast majority of the time they are located quickly. If the child is not swiftly found, search teams bring in trained canines that can usually track down them down. When the missing person walks into the campsite that they disappeared from and surprises everyone, that's an unusual story.

On July 9, 1967, a very unusual event started to unfold at the Seneca Creek Provincial campgrounds on the east shore of Kootenay Lake thirty-five miles north of Nelson, BC. The story involves Mr. and Mrs. Joseph Shutty and their two boys from Nelson, BC. This July 12, 1967 article in the *Vancouver Sun* had details, "Shutty said he, Myron and his other son, Johnny, 8, had walked down to the creek for a wash after eating lunch. "Myron washed up first and then headed back to his mother. We followed him a minute later, but when we got back to our campsite he wasn't there," Shutty said. "He went missing in the 300 feet between the creek and the car. It just seemed like he disappeared into thin air." One article stated that the family was washing their dishes in Lockhart Creek. Since there is not a location called Seneca Creek Provincial Park, it appears the family was camping in Lockhart Beach Provincial Park.

I have documented dozens of missing children cases where the parents say the child was right next to them, they turned their back, and they were gone. Joseph Shutty's statement about Myron, "disappeared into thin air," reflects a similar statement of many other parents who have lost their kids in the wilderness.

The Shutty's searched the area around their campsite, the path from the creek, the region around the water and continually called Myron's name. They never got a response and soon called for law enforcement.

The mountains and region around Kootenay Lake are rugged, steep, and remote with very few people. A search of the British

Columbia Provincial Park website says that the activities at this park include, cycling, fishing, hiking, canoeing, and swimming.

Once law enforcement was called, they responded with a large contingent of searchers, as is described in the July 11, 1967 edition of the *Vancouver Sun*, "More than 100 people, including eight members of the Kimberley militia, assisted by a police dog, are taking part today." The Shutty campsite was 60-70 yards from the lakeshore. Rescuers were focusing on the forest area and the region near the creek without finding a clue. A helicopter arrived late in the first day of the search and flew the skies looking for the boy.

The SAR group established their headquarters near the Shutty campsite. Two days after Myron vanished and 100 yards away from the campsite, Myron walked out of the woods and into the arms of a volunteer searcher. The July 13, 1967 edition of *The Province* supplied these essential details, "How he got out of the woods is a real mystery," said his father, Joseph Shutty. "Myron tells us he was carried out of the woods by a person he calls a teenager. Nobody has seen this teenager or person, but we have to believe Myron's story. "Myron says the teenager found him way back in the woods, picked him up, carried him down the mountain, across the creek near where he disappeared and then showed him all the cars and people and told him if he walked to the people he would find his parents. It's weird. When I asked him where the teenager went, he said, "back into the woods."

The teenager that Myron described also claims they asked him if he had any money? When Myron said he didn't have any coins, the teenager gave him twenty-five cents and stated that all boys should have money when lost. Joseph said he is positive that his son didn't have any money when he vanished, but did now.

The SAR team went back into the woods from where Myron exited and did find an abandoned cabin five miles away. Myron stated he had walked past it with the teenager but had not stopped. Myron was located by a searcher on the opposite side of the creek from where he was last seen. Joseph said that his son was afraid of water and had no idea how he got across.

Rescuers knew that Myron had traveled at least five miles into the woods because he recognized the cabin. This location was up a mountainside, a big trek for a small boy. SAR manuals state that a 4-6-year-old child will be located 95% of the time in a mountain setting 2.3 miles or less from the location they were last seen. Myron was at least double the distance quoted in SAR books. How did Myron get on the opposite side of the creek? The location of this park is nowhere near a mid-sized city; it is remote. Canines brought into the search never picked up Myron's scent. How was the boy able to get from the area without leaving a scent trail?

Myron described his rescuer as a teenager that was wearing an orange baseball cap. There was no other description supplied. He never gave a name, said where the person came from, never stated a sex, what the person was wearing. The conversation about money is very odd. Why would anyone give a five-year-old twenty-five cents and say that anyone lost should carry cash? There was never any indication that the rescuer had abducted Myron or had molested him in any way. I probably wouldn't have given this story as much press if the incident hadn't happened in such a remote area. The facts that Myron disappeared in almost Joseph's presence and then was returned by a stranger that also vanished, that is odd!

SAR team members searched for Myron's rescuer and could never locate them.

Kenneth Vanderleest
Missing 7/14/67–PM, 14 miles northeast of Hudson Hope, BC
Age at Disappearance: 3 years
Water• Weather• Previously Searched• Missing Shoes

The location of this incident is near the center of British Columbia, slightly on the eastern end. The site is just east of the large Williston Lake and sits in an area known as Drayton Valley. The region is now known for farming, and much of it is settled. The part of the province that isn't farmed is predominantly swampland. Hudson Hope is approximately fifty miles from the Alberta border.

Leo Vanderleest was a construction supervisor for Kiss Construction in Edmonton and was in the Peace River Basin conducting a land survey. On July 14, 1967, Leo was traveling in a Jeep with another Kiss employee, Ray Penay, and Leo's three-year-old son Kenneth. The men were driving on a very muddy rural road when they got the Jeep stuck. Both men told Kenneth to wait in the Jeep, and they would walk down the road a short distance to ensure it was clear so they could pass.

Leo and Ray walked a few hundred yards down the muddy and rutted road and returned after ten minutes. The men found that Kenneth was not in the Jeep. In a very strange discovery, they found one of Kenneth's boots in the Jeep. The boot was a very unusual find, because the road and surrounding area was extremely muddy and swampy. Nobody could understand why Kenneth would remove his boot and walk off. Leo and Ray yelled for Kenneth, ran up and down the road, and tried to find tracks in the mud. After several minutes, one man left to get assistance.

The Peace River Project was under development several miles from where Kenneth was lost. The entire project was shut down, and all the employees started to search for the three-year-old boy. The region had temperatures that went into the low thirties and rain continued to inundate the search area. There were several helicopters put into the air looking for the boy; they found nothing. Bloodhounds were brought into the marshy area; they couldn't pick up a scent.

Searchers were covering a three-mile radius. Law enforcement felt they had the area saturated very well and had already searched many areas two times. Three days after Kenneth disappeared, searchers were walking through a cut-line area that had been searched two times en route to a new area, when they found the boy lying on the ground.

Kenneth survived his three days in the swamplands. A July 19, 1967, article in the *Brandon Sun* had the following: "The boy had said nothing about his experience alone in the bush near Hudson's Hope in British Columbia's Peace River District." The same article explained how the boy was found: "He was sighted in a relatively open area 100 yards from a cut-line trail through the bush for seismic crews, in the same area where two previous parties had searched the previous day without success."

I looked extensively for any articles that described Kenneth's condition when he was found or explained what he may have been wearing. The only description given was that he was found with scratches and bruises, and obviously without at least one boot.

Summary

The story of Kenneth Vanderleest's disappearance defies conventional common sense. It's hard to believe that Kenneth removed his boot before stepping into the cold and wet mud. Kenneth obviously watched his dad and friend walk down the road—why wouldn't have Kenneth walked down that same road toward his father? His father and friend returned in just ten minutes and started to call for the small boy; he didn't answer. How far can a three-year-old travel on an isolated muddy road in the British Columbia wilderness? Two different teams specifically searched the site where Kenneth was found—why hadn't they found him?

It's amazing in the stories that I present how many of the children refuse to talk about their ordeal. It would be interesting to gather a number of these people together in a large room, where they would be supported by others who have survived equally disturbing disappearances, and hear their recollections.

Alphonse Boudreault
Missing: 11/09/70, Great Beaver Lake, British Columbia
Age at disappearance: 22 years
Water• Point of Separation• Canines• Weather• Hunter

The area of this disappearance is an extremely boggy, wet region with hundreds of lakes in the central of British Columbia. The exact location was Great Beaver Lake, fifty miles northwest of Prince George and fifteen miles east of Fort Saint James.

It's very rare that I have written about the disappearance of an active member of the armed forces, but this incident involves a military man. Alphonse Boudreault was born in Spiritwood, Saskatchewan which is another area with dozens of small lakes and waterways. He joined the armed forces in 1967 and in November of 1970, he was assigned to the armed forces base at Comox on Vancouver Island, British Columbia.

On November 9, 1970, Alphonse was on a short leave from his base and traveled with friends to a hunting area near Great Beaver Lake. The November 17, 1970 edition of the *Vancouver Sun* had these details of what happened, "Private Alphonse Boudreau, 22, of Prince Albert, Saskatchewan separated from his hunting companions November 9. More than 40 men from the Canadian Armed Forces, RCMP and the B.C. Forest Service are scouring the remote area, about 45 miles northwest of here, in ground parties and two helicopters."

Canadian Armed Forces sent a Buffalo aircraft from Comox filled with supplies to keep the search for the soldier going. Several articles about this incident stated that it was snowing on searchers in the lake area.

A ten-day SAR for Private Boudreault failed to locate him. It was a massive, expensive and comprehensive effort to find the soldier. The region of the search was very thick with trees, water and lots of game. The RCMP used canines and two helicopters to cover the search area.

In the middle of the search to locate this soldier, another man was going missing on the western side of British Columbia. Is this a mere coincidence, or is something more complex at work?

Michael Bryant
Missing: 11/14/70- 5:00 p.m., Mount Seymour, British Columbia
Age at disappearance: 32 years
Canines• Weather• Cluster Zone

New residents of an area are sometimes eager to go out and experience their environment; this was the part of the circumstance in this incident.

Michael Bryant and his wife Janet had moved to North Vancouver in September of 1970. In October of 1970, Michael started an engineering job with a local firm that gave his wife and nine-week-old baby the security they relished.

Michael Bryant

On November 14, 1970, at noon, Michael told his wife he was going for an afternoon hike on Mount Seymour and that he'd be home for dinner. He took his company car and drove it to the parking lot on the mountain, strapped on his hiking boots and headed for the trail.

Michael's wife Janet, became concerned when it started to get dark and Michael wasn't home, she called the North Vancouver Police who contacted the RCMP near Mount Seymour. Mounties responded to the parking lot on the mountain and immediately located Michael's car and started a hasty search.

The formal search started on November 15 and included over four hundred searchers, two helicopters, multiple canine teams and dozens of volunteers. Search commanders interviewed Janet and found that Michael was going to hike to Mystery Lake, a location that will appear again in this chapter. SAR leaders focused their effort on the summit, lake and surrounding areas of the mountain looking for any clues to Michael's whereabouts.

A November 20, 1970 article in the *Vancouver Sun* had stated that a light snowfall hit the mountain yesterday and searchers had hoped that this may reveal tracks of the new father.

SAR commanders announced that a five-day effort to locate Michael was ending. A November 21, 1970 article in the *Vancouver Sun* had this, "By the time we finish today we will have had 100% coverage of the mountain (Search Commander Ed Nicholson)," he said. "This will be it today. There's just no use following it up because we don't know what else to do. The odds that he's still alive are slim, and if he's alive, he's not on the mountain, if he were, we would have found something." I have never heard any SAR commander state that any area was 100% covered, a pretty bold statement.

It always helps that a family keeps pushing government officials or knows someone that can push the envelope to get more assistance and this is explained herein the same article noted above, "The search was originally called off Friday, but a message from Solicitor General George McIlraith resulted in the extension today. The missing man's brother, Alan Bryant, 27 of Toronto, a special prosecutor for the Ontario Water Resources Commission, said some of his friends in government asked McIllraith to intercede and extend the search. Alan Bryant has been here since Wednesday to join the search for his brother, who he said was an experienced outdoorsman and avid skier."

The search for Michael continued for three additional days. Search coordinator Ed Nicholson was interviewed for the November

19 edition of *The Province* and made this statement, "This is a very dangerous mountain, and this was the most frustrating and puzzling search I have ever been involved."

Michael Bryant was never found, the heartache his young wife and new child experienced in a life of living without a husband and father are unimaginable.

Richard Wenegast
Missing: 10/27/73- 1:30 p.m., Cassiar, BC
Age at disappearance: 31 years
German• Canines• Weather

If the location of this incident were in the United States, it would be classified as an Environmental Protection Agency Superfund Toxic site. The area of the disappearance was Cassiar, British Columbia, a very remote region of the province forty miles south of the Yukon border and eighteen miles west of Good Hope Lake.

Starting in 1950, Cassiar began to exist as an open-pit asbestos mine. It was the opening of the mine that the town began to flourish. The mine was known as a location with a lot of dust with a nearby city that boomed for a portion of the time the pit was open. In 1970, the population of Cassiar was 1500 full-time residents that supported two churches, a small hospital, theater, and a small pool. Cassiar was also the home to two famous National Hockey League stars, Scott and Rob Niedermeyer.

In 1973, Cassiar had approximately 1400 residents that occupied the town during the summer months and up until the snow started to cover the ground. In late October 1973, Richard Wenegast was a German immigrant who had worked at the mine for the previous season and was then the janitor for the means bunkhouse.

On Saturday, October 27, 1973, the mine workers had a day off. Some of the guys drove off to a local town, and others relaxed in their bunks, and still, others were like Richard and enjoyed the outdoors. He was someone that liked to take hikes into the mountains that surround the mine. It was reported that Richard was last seen in the afternoon hours hiking up a small canyon and heading into the higher elevations. It was thought that he was going to return to the mine that night.

On Sunday, friends of Richard hadn't seen him in camp and realized he hadn't slept in his bed. The alarm was sounded on Monday when the janitor failed to report for work. The November 9, 1973 edition of the *Whitehorse Daily Star* had these details, "October 30 he was still missing so there was a searching party out on October 31, 1973. Some on snowmobiles, some on foot going up the southside of Cassiar townsite and the area up to 4-5 miles from town. From 25-50 men had been searching, some thought they had seen his track; only the snow got deep about 18 inches of snow. But it is pretty hard to find tracks because the snow was too deep." There were notes that searchers were fighting deep snow and harsh weather. There was also one line in the June 28, 1974, edition of the *Whitehorse Daily Star* that stated the RCMP brought a canine into the area to search. The police went back to the valley where they thought the missing man went to see if they could recover his remains. There were rumors that he might have been caught in an avalanche, but nothing was ever found.

There was a four-day search for Richard; he was never found. His parents were in Germany, and RCMP sent word that their son had disappeared in the mountains.

It's hard not to be numb to the number of disappearances that happened in BC. The numbers are unprecedented, and this is not normal.

Richard Wenegast was never found.

Margaret Andersen
Missing: 07/06/74- 7:00 p.m., Burke Mountain, Coquitlam, BC
Age at disappearance: 59 years
Water• Point of Separation• Weather• Canines• Boulders• Cluster Zone

Margaret (59 years old) and her husband, Edward (68 years old) lived in Maple Ridge British Columbia on the east side of the Pitt River.

On July 6, 1974, the couple left their home and drove to a parking lot on Quarry Road at the base of Burke Mountain in Coquitlam. They planned on making the day hike to Munro Lake.

The pair made it to the lake and had a difficult time finding the trail to Quarry Road and decided to follow Mcintyre Creek down the eastern side of the mountain and towards the Pitt River. It was near 7:00 p.m. when the following incident happened as is described in the July 8, 1974, edition of the *Vancouver Sun*, "She was ahead of me leading, and I was following behind," Andersen said today. "She just disappeared behind a rock, and that was it. Visibility was poor in the bush although it was still light and there was no mist."

Edward Andersen soon realized he couldn't locate his wife, he yelled and called for her but did not get a response. He knew he was now lost and decided to wait it out on the mountain until the following morning.

On the morning of July 7, Mr. Andersen made his way down the mountain, located Quarry Road and eventually located his vehicle. Once the car was found, he called the local RCMP.

In the same article quoted earlier was this statement from RCMP, "About 30 searchers and a helicopter team today (Monday) resumed the search for a Maple Ridge woman who became separated from her husband on Coquitlam's Burke Mountain on Saturday. Searchers aided by a helicopter and a tracking dog failed Sunday to find Margaret Andersen, 59 who became separated from her husband."

Late on Monday, searchers located Margaret Andersen's body, which is described in the July 8, 1974, edition of the *Vancouver Sun*, "A 59-year old Maple Ridge woman missing on Coquitlam's Burke Mountain since Saturday was found dead at the 2300 foot level by search teams today. It was not immediately determined whether Margaret Andersen died of exposure or a fall." When I read this article, it was apparent that if Mrs. Andersen fell, her visible injuries were slight because search teams couldn't determine that the injuries might have been fatal.

There was further clarity on Mrs. Andersen's death in the July 9, 1974, edition of the *Vancouver Sun*, "A Maple Ridge woman found dead on Coquitlam's Burke Mountain Monday after being missing for 40 hours, died after falling 150 feet, RCMP said today." The autopsy report indicated that she suffered fatal head injuries.

Mr. and Mrs. Andersen became separated when she disappeared behind a boulder. Boulders are part of the profile points that we have identified in missing people. The incident happened in very close proximity to the Pitt River and Mcintyre Creek. RCMP brought in a canine to search, which failed to locate the victim, why? Why wouldn't Mrs. Andersen have replied to her husband's call for her during the time she was missing? The words used by Mr. Andersen to describe his wife vanishing, "disappeared behind a rock," is revealing.

Yehudi Prior
Missing: 09/23/74, Wild Duck Lake, Vancouver Island
Age at disappearance: 2
Berry Picker• Distance Traveled• Point of Separation• Canines

William Prior took his son Yehudi berry picking at an old tribal area four miles north of Wild Duck Lake, which is located in the southern area of Vancouver Island. As the father was picking the berries, the boy suddenly disappeared. William immediately started to call out the boy's name, but there was no answer. He frantically searched the entire area but couldn't find the boy. It was at this time that William contacted authorities.

At the height of the search, multiple tracking dogs, helicopters, and over fifty trained searchers scoured the mountains looking for Yehudi. The searchers found no evidence of the boy anywhere in the area.

Six days later, there was one last big push to find Yehudi. Late on September 29, searchers found Yehudi in rugged brushland four miles north of Wild Duck Lake. The boy had died. A September 30 article in the *Edmonton Journal* had some very enlightening statements by the search leader, Hal Orrick: "The boy's body was found near Hope Creek in the next valley north of Wild Duck Valley where he had spent most of his life. It was a fantastic long distance … It seemed so impossible that he could go that far." It appeared the boy had died of exposure. There was no inquiry into the death of Yehudi, and the case was closed.

Henry Hansen
Missing: 09/22/75, Garibaldi Park, BC
Age at disappearance: Unknown
Cluster Zone• Water

It is imperative that when you go hiking or enter the woods for any reason, that you notify someone exactly where you are going and when you are coming out. It is your responsibility to notify that person and advise them you are safely out. If your contact does not hear from you, they need to call search and rescue immediately. There are dozens of examples in my books of people who never told someone where they were going or changed their destination without notifying anyone. Failure to tell the contact your destination could lead to your demise.

This incident is peculiar for 1975 because of its lack of specific details. In September of 1975, Henry Hansen (no age given) lived at the Cecil Hotel at 1336 Granville in Vancouver, BC. The man loved the outdoors and frequently traveled to the woods and explored the region in southern British Columbia.

On September 22, 1975, Henry left his hotel and traveled to Garibaldi Park, approximately fifteen miles northeast from Squamish, BC. Here is what the British Columbia Provincial Parks website states about this destination, "Garibaldi Provincial Park, named after its towering 2,678-metre peak, Mount Garibaldi, was designated as a provincial park in 1927. In honor of the 19th-century Italian patriot, Giuseppe Garibaldi, the park is known for its natural beauty and its endless hiking opportunities. Garibaldi Provincial Parks rich geological history, diverse vegetation, snow-capped mountain, iridescent waters, abundant wildlife, and scenic vistas all contribute to the immense beauty. The park is located in the heart of the Coast Mountains just 70 km north of Vancouver.

Offering over 90 km of established hiking trails, Garibaldi Provincial Park is a favorite year-round destination for outdoor enthusiasts."

The park is remote, isolated and filled with wildlife, including grizzly bears.

Henry didn't return from his trip when his friends thought he was supposed to and they called the RCMP. He was believed to be hiking in the Cypress Bowl area. Searchers focused on this area and could not locate anything. A helicopter was put in the air and discovered Henry's car in a parking lot in the Diamond Head area, and SAR switched their focus. This delay in finding the exact location where Henry was hiking could've contributed to the complications of the search.

The RCMP helicopter continued to fly the skies along with three private fixed-wing aircraft. They flew all of the hiking paths near Diamond Head that led to Atwell Peak, Opal Cone, Mamquam Lake, and Garibaldi Neve. This is one of the higher altitude roads in the region that leads to several rugged hiking paths. The last area of the searcher's focus was Black Tusk Mountain, one of the most spectacular mountains in the park. The description of the climb states it can be made in one day. The area around the summit does not have any foliage and is above timberline. Ground and air searches around this area did not locate anything pointing to where Mr. Hansen was located.

There was an intensive nine-day search for Henry that did not find anything but his car. The SAR was terminated on October 2, 1975.

Wendy Riley
Missing: 02/11/83-PM, Lynn Canyon Park, North Vancouver, BC
Age at disappearance: 29 years
Cluster Zone• Point of Separation•
Weather

Wendy Riley

In February of 1983, Wendy and David Riley had been married for several years. The pair were living in Santa Rosa, California, but had roots in the Toronto area. David was a photographer, and Wendy had been helping her husband in his photography shop and had also been working at another gallery.

Wendy Riley was born and raised in Toronto, Canada. Her father, Joe Sherkin, was a tire broker and was married to Wendy's mom, Ruth. Wendy was the youngest of the three kids in her family, and they lived in the Forest Hill area of the city. She lived in the home until she left for college. Ms. Riley ended up getting a psychology degree from Guelph University.

David and Wendy met when Wendy was in college. They lived in Toronto for the first few years and then moved to Vancouver. After approximately two years in British Columbia, the couple moved to Santa Rosa, where David's family had roots.

On February 11, 1983, David and Wendy were in the later stages of a four-week vacation. The couple had spent three weeks in Toronto visiting friends and family and were now scheduled to be in Vancouver until February 14. At 1:30 p.m. on the eleventh, Wendy was driving her green Honda Civic Hatchback and dropped David at West Hastings and Bute in downtown Vancouver as David was heading for the Bombay Bicycle Club. The couple made plans to meet that night at a party. Wendy had two open hours until she was meeting a friend and then later meeting David at the party. David said goodbye, and Wendy drove off.

At 6:00 p.m. on February 11, David started calling Wendy and did not get an answer. He called her every half hour until 9:00 p.m. Wendy had not met with her friend and didn't arrive to meet her husband at the party. David knew that something was desperately wrong and decided to call the RCMP.

At 7:30 a.m. on February 12, Wendy was officially listed in the RCMP computer as a missing person, and her car was flagged as being associated with the case. This February 26, 1983 edition of the *Vancouver Sun* had details of what happened next, "The last indication of her whereabouts was the next day when her car, a green 1978 Honda Civic was found in the parking lot at North Vancouver's Lynn Canyon Park." The RCMP had located Wendy's car and searched it. Inside the vehicle, they discovered her purse with money and credit cards inside. Everything associated with the car seemed to be normal. David was questioned about Wendy's association with the park. He confirmed that she had been there before when they both walked a friend's dog. He said his wife would not usually be considered a hiker, and he thought it was odd that she would stop at the park and hike the area on the eleventh because it had been raining.

The RCMP immediately put resources into searching the park, looking for Wendy. Teams searched the nature trails of the park and attempted to search the creek bed, but were thwarted because of high water levels. It wasn't until the park went without rain for three consecutive days did SAR go into the creek. The press grabbed this story and gave it extensive coverage. They had a missing 29-year old woman who had virtually vanished. This February 20, 1983 edition of the *Press Democrat* had these opinions from the police, "However, a police official said there was no sign of a struggle having taken place at the car. " This is an important point. The park wasn't a new place for Wendy. If there wasn't a struggle at the car, could there have been one in the woods? Ms. Riley was not a small target; she was 5'7" and 130 pounds, not a pushover in the world of crime.

A February 20, 1983, article in the *Press Democrat* summarized the feelings of the RCMP on Wendy's disappearance, "Investigators have combed rugged Lynn Canyon Park for the second time Saturday, but failed to turn up a clue into the disappearance of Wendy Riley of Santa Rosa. "It's just a complete mystery," said Sgt. Earl Stinson of the Royal Canadian Mounted Police. "We still don't know anything definite." Other articles stated that the disappearance of Wendy was entirely out of character.

In early March of 1983, the RCMP made a press release that they had put divers into Lynn Creek and found clothing of the size of Wendy's. A March 8, 1983 edition of *The Province* said that the RCMP had located Sheepskin coat and pair of jeans in the size Wendy would've worn. The article stated they had determined that the clothes had not been in the creek more than three months. The article never said that the clothing was Wendy's; it just implied they might be hers. I must admit, this was a bizarre article and press release. Why would the RCMP ever release such a report without confirming with David if the items belonged to his wife? Well, eventually the clothes were shown to David, he couldn't confirm that they belonged to Wendy. The clothing offered nothing. If Wendy owned a sheepskin coat, I think David would know.

Wendy Riley vanished in an area where there have been other disappearances. This is an area that is relatively close to a population zone, but gets remote and thick with foliage quickly. There is something extremely unique about the region where Wendy and others have dropped out of sight. There have been zero leads or evidence of where these people went. Look at a map of this region and then take a ruler and measure an eighty-mile radius from this case, the numbers of missing is staggering.

Some readers may believe that a serial killer stalks the trails of North Vancouver, I doubt it. A killer needs to do something with the bodies. Dragging, pulling or carrying one hundred and thirty pounds any significant distance is tiring, even for a strong man. They body won't be moved far until the person is completely exhausted. After carrying it, then the killer has to bury it, or, the odor from decomposition would encompass the park and easily be located. In reviewing dozens of cases for inclusion in this section, I never saw an instance where the police thought death was related to a human to human attack.

Nicholas Vanderbilt- 25 years
Francis Glenhill- 29 years
Missing: 08/22/84, Mt. Robson, BC
Weather• Point of Separation

Nicholas Vanderbilt

I've done significant research on hundreds of people in my career. It is a rare day that you read about a persons dedication to helping the underprivileged and their commitment to their religion. These personality and moral traits are even more unique when you are dealing with someone who was raised in a life of privilege and money. You are going to read about a person in this story that was born into one of the wealthiest families in North America. He made a life decision to help others and not align himself with his family's staggering wealth and make a name for himself without using his family's position to help him.

Mount Robson, British Columbia, is located in the far eastern area of the province. The mountain is just eight miles west of the Alberta border and is the tallest peak in the Canadian Rockies at 12,972 feet. The mountain is located approximately fifty miles northwest of Jasper, Alberta, and is part of UNESCO and has been dedicated as a world heritage site. It is regularly climbed in the summer months with an average of 10-50 climbers per year successfully reaching the peak with an overall average of 10% of the attempts being successful.

Nicholas Vanderbilt was the son of racehorse owner Alfred G. Vanderbilt of Austin, Texas. Nick was the great-grandson of Cornelius Vanderbilt, who was the founder of the New York Central Railroad. He attended Harvard University, where he became president of their Mountaineering Club. After graduation, the graduate moved back to a modest apartment in Austin. He volunteered two days per month at a local soup kitchen called Angels House and was committed to his Catholic faith where he attended weekly. His friends described Nicholas as someone that never wanted to talk about the wealth in his family. If he met someone who wanted to center the conversation on the Vanderbilt fortune, Nicholas would not see them again. He was a freelance writer with his latest work appearing in Vogue. Just before leaving for British Columbia, he had taken an advance from Sports Illustrated to write a piece about his favorite sport, mountain climbing.

In August of 1984, Francis Glenhill was a 29-year old from Berkeley, California. He met Nicholas when they were both attending Harvard. Francis and Nicholas immediately bonded over a love of the outdoors and explicitly climbing mountains. The pair had been exploring and climbing since the late 1970s and had made ascents together in the Sierra's, New England, Canadian Rockies, and French Alps. The pair were considered as cautious, experienced, and conservative climbers. They had each attempted to summit Mt. Robson two years earlier and had been turned back by weather.

In mid-August of 1984, Nicholas and Francis arrived into British Columbia and purchased some supplies for their ascent of Mount Robson. By every account I could locate, the two men were well equipped and experienced for their journey. A September 5, 1984 article in the *Vancouver Sun* described their attempt, "The park's supervisor said the two climbers set out August 17, in fairly good weather, and reached the climber's hut August 19. Like many other alpine huts, the hut contained a logbook where climbers could enter their names and describe their climbing plans. In this case, the log is the only record of Vanderbilt and Glenhill's plans, since they did not seek advice from the park office before setting off. According to the log, the climbers left the hut the morning of August 21 in good weather." It usually takes at least two days to reach the summit from the hut when you are taking the route that the pair used, the Wishbone Arete. The guys would have had to sleep one night on the side of the mountain before they reached the top. Later in the same article described above was this, "On August 22, in the afternoon, heavy clouds rolled in. It began snowing. Tierney said the climbers would have been near the peak. Vanderbilt and Glenhill were due back August 27. A search began the next morning at 6 a.m."

Mount Robson is located in the Mount Robson Provincial Park and is administered by British Columbia Parks. A decision was made early in the disappearance that the RCMP would take control of the SAR. Once a decision was made that Nicholas and Francis were missing, the RCMP made several attempts to fly under the clouds in a helicopter to an area where some believed the pair might be staying. The helicopter was turned back multiple times because of weather issues. SAR administrators decided to send climbers to the hut to hold in that position until the weather improved. An August 31, 1984 article in the *Edmonton Journal* had these details about what was located, "The climbers left their wallets, food and a note at the hut at the 2600-meter level. They indicated they would try to ascend the Wishbone area of Mount Robson, near the summit. Menzis said the note indicated the pair would be back by last Monday." It was approximately another 1200 meters to reach the summit from the hut.

Once Francis and Nicholas were declared to be officially missing, many friends and relatives responded to the search headquarters and volunteered their assistance. The group of volunteers was briefed about what the SAR knew and were given the following information that appeared in the September 6, 1984 edition of the *Vancouver Sun*," Pfisterer (alpine specialist for parks Canada) said he speculates the two climbers ran into difficulty just above the most difficult part of the climb, called the Crux. It is at the 3400 meter level of the 3954-meter mountain. If they fell, he said, there would be no hope of surviving. If they did fall, off....they could fall almost a mile. They would go down an ice shoot, and it would be very difficult to find them," he said. Vanderbilt and Glenhill did not make the summit, Pfisterer said. A climbing party spotted them on August 23, within a day's climb of the summit. The party, taking a different route, lost sight of them at The Crux, but found no sign of them at the summit."

One of the friends that immediately responded when he heard that Nick and Francis had vanished was Brinton Young, a longtime friend. Young was a very experienced climber and volunteered to lead a team into the weather to locate his friends. Brinton and his group made their way into the region where the pair was last seen. They found no evidence that Francis and Nicholas were alive and turned back.

Nicholas' mother, Jean Vanderbilt, responded to the search center and was flown by the parks department to the area where they believed the men were last seen. She later stated that she appreciated the explanation by the parks department and does not see any chance that her son could still be alive.

A park's administrator made the following clarifying statement in the September 4, 1984, edition of the *Edmonton Journal*, "But Roger Tierney, Robson Park Warden, said conditions on the mountain were believed to have been stable during the dates the men gave for their climb." This statement implies that there were no avalanches recorded during the time that Francis and Nicholas were climbing. Avalanches are recorded on seismographs stationed in the mountain range.

There were many articles I reviewed for this piece. There were several statements from SAR and park administrators that Francis and Nicholas were regarded as expert climbers. The climb they were attempting was described as challenging but not outside their skill or experience level. There were other climbers on the mountain at the time that Nicolas and Francis were climbing. Nobody saw or heard anything that can be attributed to their demise.

I did a lengthy search for more personal information about Francis; sadly, I could not locate much. I do know that Mr. Glenhill must've been a high quality and intelligent person to be a friend of Nicholas. Nicolas Vanderbilt didn't leverage his wealth; he made his own way in our world. He never wanted to discuss his background or family business. Nick wanted to explore the world on his terms, at his own rate with his own money that he earned through writing. He understood the importance of volunteering and helping the underprivileged, something I greatly admire, especially in a young person.

There were a few articles written in the years after this SAR, many explaining the disappearance and the fact that neither Nicolas or Francis were ever found.

Janice Pedlar
Missing: 02/08/86-P.M., Chetwynd, BC
Age at disappearance: 37 years
Canines• Weather• Mechanical Issues

The location of this incident centers at the far eastern section of British Columbia, just two miles from the Alberta border, Dawson Creek. The small city sits in the northeastern part of the province and is quite remote.

In early February of 1986, Janice Pedlar was a single mother of three children (ages 4, 7, and 15). She was living in Dawson Creek and was actively looking for a job. She landed employment and was scheduled to start her new work on February 10.

On February 8, 1986, Janice had a busy day dropping and picking up her kids in her 1969 Dodge Dart. She was scheduled to attend a friend's party in Taylor, approximately thirty miles northwest from Dawson Creek. She left her home at 6:00 p.m., with many believing she was headed for Taylor.

The Pedlar kids were staying with a friend when Janice was out for the night. When the mother didn't arrive home after the party, the alarms started to go off. When she didn't come home the following morning, the RCMP was notified. The police put her name into the computers as a missing person and logged her car into the provincial wide system flagged as related to Ms. Pedlar. The police made a few initial calls and quickly realized she never went to the party.

Janice's car was found, and the SAR was explained in this February 14, 1986 edition of the *Vancouver Sun*," Mounties using tracking dogs and volunteers are searching dense bush east of here for 38-year old woman, whose car was found on an isolated logging road. Janice Pedlar, a mother of three children who lived in Dawson Creek, was last seen by her family when she drove off from her home. Her car was found 53 kilometers east of here on a logging landing, an area where fallen trees are gathered for loading onto trucks., "but there was nothing obviously suspicious about the condition of the vehicle," an RCMP spokesman said." Another article was written on March 22, 1986, in the *Vancouver Sun* that explained more details of the SAR, "Chetwynd RCMP Sgt. Bill Phillips said police conducted several searches of the area with dogs and aircraft, and are "reasonably certain" they did not miss Pedlar. Phillips said that had Pedlar left her vehicle and walked away into the woods, the dogs would have had a "good chance" of picking up her scent."

Janice's car was known to have many mechanical issues. The RCMP stated that it appeared to them as though the Dodge stalled in its location, and Janice had to walk away. They made this statement based on the spot the car was found. Her car was located in the opposite direction of the party and towards the home of her boyfriend. To get to her friend's house, she missed the turnoff and went the wrong direction at a "Y" in the road. The RCMP interviewed and cleared the boyfriend of any involvement. Temperatures at the time Janice would have walked away from her car were frigid. It was the belief that Pedlar walked away from her vehicle and froze to death in the woods.

There were a few articles that reported some people had seen a young man in Janice's car the night she disappeared. The RCMP discounted those sighting and put no credence in the reports.

The RCMP says on one day that if Janice had walked from the car, their canines would've tracked her. On another day, they made the statement that it appears to them that she walked from her car and died in the elements, sort of conflicting statements.

Janice vanished four days before her 38th birthday, and two days before starting a new job, it was an important time in this mother's life.

This February 18, 1986 edition of the *Vancouver Sun* has a comment from the police on Pedlar's car location, "Police cannot explain why the car she appears to have abandoned because it had stalled, started when Police turned the key. "It's definitely strange," Sgt. Barry Shaw of the Dawson Creek RCMP said Monday." I have written several stories about missing people who had left their cars in odd areas under very unusual circumstances. One evolving profile point is mechanical issues associated with the missing people. Maybe Janice saw something and drove to get a better look, and her car stalled, and she couldn't get it going again. It was freezing outside, she might have been forced to walk, and something happened.

After several extensive searches over a several month time frame, Janice was never found.

Lynn Marie Hillier
Missing: 07/24/86, Horne Lake, Parksville, BC
Age at disappearance: 2
Point of Separation• Water

Colleen Hillier and her parents took Colleen's daughter, Lynn Marie, for a short vacation to the Hilliers' cabin at Horne Lake on Vancouver Island. The lake sits approximately four miles from the eastern shore of the island, just west of Spider Lake Provincial Park and Horne Lake Caves Provincial Park. Horne Lake has a ridgeline coming down to it that terminates to the north and sits in a bowl with a large opening on the eastern side of the lake. A steep, rocky road runs in front of the cabin, which sits in an isolated location downhill from the main road.

On July 24, 1986, Lynn Marie went outside the cabin and vanished. The grandparents and parents searched and found no evidence of her. They contacted the RCMP and a massive search was immediately started. People were yelling her name and driving the roads, all looking for the young girl. Four hundred people volunteered to search for Lynn Marie; they found nothing. The RCMP brought in canines to pick up a scent; they could not locate a scent, or refused to track. The RCMP brought in airplanes with infrared scanning equipment to look for body heat, but they didn't find anything on their air-to-ground search.

After a week of searching for the girl, Lynn Marie's great-grandfather, Ernie Miner, posted a $25,000 reward for her return. Ernie was interviewed by the *Toronto Star* and stated, "I don't think she is here." He later stated, "She doesn't like water, and she doesn't wander." I believe the implication of Ernie's statements was that Lynn Marie was nowhere near the family cabin.

The formal search for Lynn Marie was terminated after almost ten days.

On August 19, 1986, almost four weeks later, two men were scouting for hunting locations on a steep hillside 3½ miles from the Hillier cabin. They thought they saw something under a fallen log. They looked closer and found the body of Lynn Marie Hillier. The RCMP was notified and recovered the body. Formal notifications were made to the Hilliers. An RCMP officer had stated that they felt it might be possible that the girl walked to the location where she was found.

On August 21, 1986, Colleen Hillier responded to the RCMP statements about their daughter being found. The *Windsor Star* ran the following article on the same day: "Colleen Hillier, 25, mother of the little girl, refused to believe her daughter walked up a mountain to her death. 'There's no way,' she stated in an interview Wednesday night. 'It just doesn't seem possible. It's so hard to imagine her making it there on her own.' ... Relatives couldn't explain how the little girl climbed up the rocky road behind their cabin. Les Hiller stated, 'I don't believe she could have walked there herself.'"

The coroner stated that Lynn Marie Hillier died of exposure on her second or third day away from her home.

Case Summary

Readers need to remember that Lynn Marie Hillier was two years old. Children who go missing almost always walk downhill, not uphill, as Lynn Marie had done for 3½ miles. Parents are generally a good judge of their children's stamina and abilities. If parents state that a child would not walk into the woods or couldn't climb a hill at two years old, I tend to believe them. It's hard to imagine a two-year-old girl leaving a cabin, not her home, and immediately walking up a steep, rocky road. Considering searchers were looking for the girl within three hours, all yelling for Lynne Marie, why wouldn't or couldn't she respond?

I think it's an amazing coincidence (if you believe in coincidences) that the RCMP put up aircraft equipped with FLIR (forward-looking infrared radar) to look for heat signatures on the ground, did not find her, and then Lynn Marie was found by hunters underneath an old log. In all of the searches I have ever read about, this is one of the rare times that FLIR was used, and one of the only times a child was found under something as penetrable by FLIR as a log.

Charlie Musso
Missing: 09/07/87- 5:00 p.m.,
Mount Seymour, British Columbia
Age at disappearance: 61 years
Cluster Zone• Canines• Disability

Charlie Musso

In Italy, Charlie was called Carlo, but in Burnaby, he was Charlie or dad. In September of 1987, Charlie Musso was a sixty-one-year-old insurance salesman living with his family in Burnaby, British Columbia. He had immigrated from Italy where climbing in the Appenine Mountains was a normal part of his life. In 1956 Charlie came to British Columbia where he met his wife of twenty-two years, and they had a family. He still loved to exercise and regularly rode his bike up Mount Seymour and then did calisthenics every morning. He knew he had to exercise because he had high blood pressure and was taking medication for it. He knew that rigorous exercise would help control his condition.

September 7, 1987, was a national holiday in Canada, Labor Day. Charlie woke up, went through his daily regime and knew he had to drive his seventeen-year-old son, Carlo to at the Pacific National Exhibition at 7:00 a.m. Carlo was dropped off, and Charlie drove off knowing he had to pick up his son at 1:30 p.m. that afternoon, he never came back. Carlo eventually contacted his mom and explained that his dad hadn't arrived and was picked up and taken home. Charlie had told friends that he knew he had about six hours from dropping his son off and when he had to pick him up and wanted to get to hike to an old trappers cabin on Mount Seymour, but he hadn't told his family. Not long after 5:00 p.m., police received a report of the following as is described in the September 9, 1987, *Vancouver Sun*, "About the time a father and son were to meet (1:30 p.m.), two separate groups of hikers on Seymour heard cries for help from a man. The calls were about an hour apart and reported to have come from the same vicinity. That combined with the fact that Musso's car was the only one left in the parking lot Monday at dusk, prompted police to do a computer check in the license plate, they then notified the family." This phone call started a massive search for Charlie Musso. Police later reported that the calls for help were heard approximately five kilometers from the parking lot. The first two searches focused on the Dinkey Peak and three kilometers past Mystery Lake.

Later in the *Vancouver Sun* article quoted above was this description of the search, "RCMP dogs, two helicopters and eight Bloodhounds supplied by the West Coast Bloodhound Search and Rescue were also used. Family members and searchers are baffled. Musso, according to family and friends was an experienced hiker who knew the trails on Seymour well."

Charlie was a dedicated parishioner at St. Helens Parish in Burnaby. He helped sell advertising space in their newsletter and regularly volunteered for odd jobs. Father Ponti had a made a public statement, "Pray for this missing man and his family."

Hundreds of searchers scoured Mount Seymour for five days looking for the missing insurance salesman. They placed particular emphasis on the area where other hikers heard someone asking for help. SAR commanders stated they located one partial shoe print, but could not determine if it was Charlie's.

It's troubling when SAR commanders say they are baffled, not a good indicator that things are running smoothly. Several people stated that Charlie knew the trails of Mount Seymour very well, he should not have been lost. When two groups of people report hearing a man calling for help, the triangulation of the cries is a good marker of where the person was at the time. There have been several other cases I have documented where a person was heard calling for help, the witness was quite close to the voice and searched and couldn't locate anyone.

In 2019 I did a two-hour special for the History Channel called, Vanished. It chronicled an incident where a hiker vanished on a trail. What the segment editors refused to put in the show, two different sets of people on two different days heard a man calling for help in the same spot on different days. One of those witnesses was a reporter that heard the cry for help and actually told the park superintendent. Search parties were sent into the area and thoroughly covered the ground for several hours finding nothing. I posed this situation to theoretical Physicist John Brandenburg. He stated that portals are possible, it is also possible for an intelligent source to direct a portal. I asked him if it was possible for someone to be in a portal, see outside of it and for others not to see them, he stated it was probably possible. The purpose of the conversation was to develop a possible answer for searchers being unable to locate someone that two other groups had heard. I have no idea if this was a possible answer in Charlie's case, but if we never look outside the box for solutions, we may forever hit a dead end in understanding these cases.

Charlie Musso has never been found.

Case number 3 Mount Seymour.

Emerson Dobroskay
Missing: 10/28/1988-p.m., University of British Columbia
Age at disappearance: 21 years
Water• Intellect

I have continuously written about the disappearances of people with high intellect, ranging from physicians to physicists and a variety of very smart college students. The missing have been from various backgrounds and majoring in a multitude of degrees. This case highlights intellect and intrigue.

Emerson Dobroskay demonstrated the highest of intellect from an early age. He had a variety of interests, which

Emerson Dobroskay

included astronomy, meteorology, and even physics. While still in high school in Saskatoon, Emerson studied astronomy at the University of Saskatoon and reached a level of proficiency in his studies that when he turned nineteen, he was allowed to teach classes at the university. He finished his undergraduate degree in physics in less than three years. He was granted an honors status in his degree and looked into attending graduate school.

The astronomy program at the University of British Columbia (UBC) intrigued Emerson, and he applied and was granted acceptance. Articles state that he was studying meteorology even though his degree was in physics.

On October 29, 1988, students at UBC had just completed taking final exams. Emerson completed three tests in three days and was feeling relieved and happy that finals were behind him. He left his dormitory room and went to The Pit brew pub with friends. The group drank beer, hung out, and had fun. They left together and headed in different directions. This was the last time anyone had contact with Emerson Dobroskay.

The police searched Emerson's dorm room and found all of his clothing and personal items. They found approximately $2,000 in cash and checks that had not been cashed. Everything appeared just as it should for a college student. Vancouver and UBC police searched the entire region around the dormitory and the pub. They placed helicopters in the air and canines on the ground. Searchers found nothing. It should be explained that UBC sits in an area bordered by a wealthy Vancouver neighborhood, the city of Vancouver, the Salish Sea, and the Pacific Ocean. It's an idyllic setting that juts out to the water.

This case received significant publicity in the Canadian press. As is normal with missing person cases, the police got many reports of sightings of Emerson from throughout the coastal zone and on Vancouver Island. Each of the sightings was investigated, and none were substantiated.

This is another case in a long line of brilliant college students who went out drinking and vanished. The vast majority of cases occurred near bodies of water, and in many cases the victims were never found.

Wally Finnigan
Missing 11/04/89, Creston, BC
Age at disappearance: 51 years
Point of Separation• Disability/ Illness• Canines• Missing Clothing
The location of this incident is unique, and it could almost be considered in the United States. Creston, British Columbia is locat-

ed just five miles north of the Idaho border and 300 miles east of Vancouver. This is a very rural area with significant wildlife.

Wally Finnigan was a longshoreman living in Surrey, a suburb of Vancouver, BC. In November of 1989, he was a family man with children who enjoyed the outdoors. In the early days of November, Wally had not been feeling well. He had complained to his wife about chest pains but had minimized it knowing he had a hunting trip planned. The longshoreman had taken a few days off of work and drove his vehicle with his friend, Andy Wolfan three hundred miles east to Creston,

Wally Finnigan

BC. The pair was going elk and deer hunting in the mountains high above the city.

On November 4, 1989, Wally and Andy were hunting an area nine miles north of Creston, east of Duck Lake and south of Kianuko Provincial Park. The pair talked about their plans, they split up at Wally's truck and agreed to meet back in the afternoon, Wally was never seen again.

When Andy returned to the truck, he waited for Wally, called for his friend and hiked the trails looking for signs he might be injured. There were no indications that Wally was in the area. Andy drove into Creston and got the assistance of local police.

The local Royal Canadian Mounted Police (RCMP) mounted a search that included forty people to look for the Surrey resident. The formal search lasted six days and located nothing. The family did get a note from a psychic that was addressed in the November 10, 1989 edition of the *Vancouver Sun*, "Finnigan said the family was contacted by a psychic, who believes he fell down a mine shaft but is still alive." RCMP officials searched all possible mines in the area and found nothing. Wally's wife and five children did participate in the search in addition to locals and police. One longshoreman took his camper to the scene and fed searchers.

There was a strange report from Creston Police. After posters were put up in the community of Wynndel, a resident came to the police and stated that they had seen Wally walking down the road dragging his feet as though he was intoxicated. Nobody knew if the sighting could've been the hunter, but it was a sighting that had to be followed up by police. They never could locate that man.

The RCMP stated that they had brought their canines to the scene in an attempt to pick up Wally's scent. A December 11, 1989 article in the *Vancouver Sun* had these details, "Finnigan (wife) said tracking dogs followed her husband's scent along the road where he was last seen by the witness all the way to the main highway."

In late June of 1990, the RCMP and family members of Wally's made one last push to find his remains. As they were searching the mountainside where he was hunting, they found something of note, as is described in the July 7, 1990 edition of the *Vancouver Sun*, "Two weeks ago during a final search by RCMP of the area, police found Finnigan's clothes, hunting rifle and wallet containing his identification." A few bones were found in the area, but it was never confirmed who they may belong to, or even if they were human. Later in the same article was this, "Although she believes her husband may have fallen down a cliff and died, legally her husband still hasn't been declared dead." The coroner did state that the clothes appeared to be chewed on by animals, they never stated if this was post-death or the cause of Wally's demise.

This is another case where searchers don't find a victim at the time they disappear. It's only after the family pushes the issue is there any resolution. It's also an interesting note that the RCMP canines were not even close to finding the victim; he was nowhere near the road where they supposedly picked up his scent. The sighting of someone looking like Wally in Creston was also incorrect. Lastly, the psychic who stated Wally was in a mine, they were also incorrect.

Raymond Krieger
Missing: 08/28/92- 9:00 p.m., Fort Nelson, BC
Age at disappearance: 48 years
Canines• Disability/ Illness• Point of Separation• German

Several years ago, I started to track locations where people lived or were raised versus where they disappeared. The first time I was made aware of this issue involved the disappearance of two physical therapists from Alaska. Through a series of odd coincidences, I determined that they were raised in a different state close to one another (See Missing 411- Off the Grid). Since that first connection, I have been trying to determine where others lived and where they vanished. In this case, there are a few parallels that related to other missing hunters.

Earlier in this chapter, I documented two cases of hunters that disappeared on Vancouver Island, now you can add another. In August of 1992, Raymond Krieger was a 48-year-old man living in Parkville on Vancouver Island, just thirty miles from Cowichan Lake. In earlier years, Raymond had owned a logging company in Fort Nelson, BC in far northeastern British Columbia and later moved to Vancouver Island.

Raymond loved the outdoors and hunting. In mid-August of 1992, he joined friends by flying to Fort Nelson, visiting friends for a few days and then traveling to Tuchodi Lakes southwest of Fort Nelson. The group then rode by horseback seven hours into their remote hunting camp. This area has been described in travel journals as some of the most remote regions anywhere in British Columbia. I encourage you to go online and look at photos of the lakes; they are gorgeous.

On August 28, 1992, everyone in Raymond's camp went to bed at approximately 9:00 p.m. They woke at 6:00 a.m. and Raymond was gone. His friends searched the area and determined that no horses were missing and the following details were released in the September 11, 1992 edition of the *Nanaimo Daily Free Press*, "Although they scoured the area where Mr. Krieger disappeared, there were no clothes or tracks that would point to his whereabouts." Remember, this was a group of very experienced hunters and woodsmen, how could there be no tracks?

One of Raymond's friends made the long ride out of the wilderness to notify authorities of the disappearance. RCMP had people on site within two days as is described in this September 1, 1992 article in the *Nanaimo Daily News*, "The search for him began over the weekend, Monday, a search and rescue team was accompanied by two police dogs, their handlers and a regular RCMP officer."

Once the RCMP arrived at the hunting camp, they started to question other hunters to attempt to understand what happened. Lorne Scott was one of the authorities on the scene and made this statement in the September 4, 1992 edition of the *Vancouver Sun*, "Scott said that Krieger's companions reported that he appeared to become disoriented and delirious the day before he disappeared." Raymond's condition was further described in the September 11, 1992 edition of the *Nanaimo Daily Free Press*, "We know he was in a confused state of mind," said Scott. "Something happened that reduced his capacity to think normally." He did not know the cause of the man's condition."

RCMP canine units, other hunters in the region and friends of Raymond went into the forest looking for the man. They fired off round to attract his attention, and they called out his name, they never got a response. They never found any tracks and the dogs never keyed on a scent. The search lasted one week, and nothing was located to indicate where the hunter may have gone.

The symptom of being disoriented would cause readers to think that Raymond may have had a stroke or some other debilitating medical condition, if this were the case, the reality of him traveling far would not be reasonable and he should've been found. I have written dozens of examples of people in the wilderness where they suddenly feel ill; they become separated from their group somehow, it's at that point that they disappear. In this instance, Raymond went to his tent, and nobody saw him again.

There are always high risks associated with going deep into the wilderness. Tuchodi Lakes is a very remote area with extreme difficulty in getting to hunting locations. This difficulty can be a significant factor in obtaining medical care and searchers to the scene; thus the reason the RCMP were only able to send three officers and two canines into camp.

Raymond Krieger was of German heritage, he was never found.

Steven Eby
Missing: 11/14/93- 3:00 p.m., Mount
Seymour, British Columbia
Age at disappearance: 29 years
Weather• Cluster Zone• Unknown
Cause of Death

In my years of researching people
missing in the wilds of North America, few locations hold the mystery
of the missing like the area of North
Vancouver, British Columbia. There
have been many men and women that
vanished in this area. If the bodies are
located, they don't reveal what happened, and if they are never found, the
mystery deepens. It does not appear to
matter what season it is; people vanish

Steven Eby

in all months of the year. This region of the world is lush with thick
foliage, abundant predators and steep, treacherous mountains where
you can hike tens of miles without seeing a soul.

In November of 1993, Steven Eby was a student at the University of British Columbia attending their film school. He had
moved to British Columbia in the summer of 1993 from Montana
where he had lived in Bozeman. The student was in outstanding physical condition, worked out, knew the outdoors quite well
from taking wilderness classes in Montana and spending countless hours hiking and backpacking. His time spent in the Montana
outdoors should've prepared Steven for the mountains of North
Vancouver.

On November 14, 1993, Steven drove his car from his apartment near the university to the parking lot of the Mount Seymour
Resort and ski area. The weather was good as he exited and took
to the trails. One witness reported seeing Steven on the Mystery
Lake Trail at approximately 3:00 p.m. The path leaves the resort and
travels one-half mile north to Mystery Lake. The area of the lake is
surrounded by massive rock outcroppings, big trees, and a lush landscape. In the summertime, this area is known as a great swimming

hole after a good hike. In November, the lake would be frozen with several feet of snow on the ground.

On Tuesday, November 16 at 10:00 p.m., a close friend of Steven realized he hadn't been seen and saw his car was still gone. The friend notified Vancouver Police who had officers in the Mount Seymour area check the parking lot for the overdue hiker. Law enforcement located the vehicle on November 17 and the search was on.

The North Vancouver Search and Rescue Team led the effort to locate the former Montana resident. Friends notified Steven's family of the disappearance, and they responded from throughout North America. Steven's mother made this statement to the *Vancouver Sun* Newspaper on November 19, 1993, "Julie Medland said Thursday, her son, Steven Eby is a skilled outdoorsman and knows what to do if he is lost or hurt in the wilderness. "He is very experienced," said Medland, who flew in from Toronto after hearing her son had not returned from a solo hike on Sunday. I think he's either lost or had an injury, and I think he's probably found a shelter for himself. He knows how to build a shelter."

The SAR commander rallied assistance from Kamloops, Hope, Chilliwack, Comox, Lions Bay, Coquitlam, Maple Ridge, Squamish, Salmon Arm and Bellingham, Washington. In total, there were over 150 searchers that responded to the call for assistance. A November 22, 1993, edition of the *Vancouver Sun* had these details on the search, "Fog and near blizzard-like conditions hampered the search on Friday and Sunday, searchers had to battle more snow and freezing rain."

North Shore Search and Rescue had contracted two helicopters to scour the Mount Seymour area; the commander had stated that it was costing them $20,000 a day for air support. On November 18, 1993, there was this search update in the *Vancouver Sun*, "We haven't found any sign of him. We've spotted no tracks at all," said search manager George Zilahi, a member of North Shore Search and Rescue."

The SAR for Steven Eby lasted five days. Searchers were battered by severe weather conditions for two of those search days. This is a relatively short period for a search in the 1990s, but I can read the frustration in the search commanders statement, they were not finding any tracks in the snow. How is that possible?

As I stated earlier, this area of North America has some bizarre and unusual disappearances and body recoveries. A January 7, 1994 article in the *Missoulian* had this information about Steven, "Authorities in North Vancouver, British Columbia, have identified a headless body found near Mount Seymour Provincial Park as that of Steven Eby, a former resident of the Bozeman area. Cpl. Howard Curry of the Royal Canadian Mounted Police said the body was washed down Swift Creek and was badly battered. Curry said the cause of death has not been positively determined, but foul play is not suspected." I'm always amazed what some law enforcement will say and what reporters will print. A headless body is found, and they immediately assume there is no foul play, what? What happened to the head? In thousands of missing person cases I've read, this is the first time I've ever heard of a headless body found, and it's not suspicious to the RCMP? How do they know that Steven didn't have his head crushed in an attack? There were no other details about the find other than what I noted. I'd like to know what clothes, boots were found on the body if any.

It's essential that hikers tell friends exactly where they are going and when they will be out. If the friend doesn't hear from you when you're hike is completed, they need to immediately notify search and rescue and have them commence looking for you. The delay in the search starting for Steven could've played a role in him not being found alive.

Case number four Mount Seymour.

Richard Grey
Missing: 04/14/94, Strathcona Park, British Columbia
Age at disappearance: 22
Cluster Zone• Water

I have consistently preached hiker safety throughout every conference I have ever presented. Each hiker needs to tell one good friend where they are going (specific location) and when you'll be out. If that friend doesn't hear from you on that day, they must call SAR. It may seem like a burden to some to notify others, have them become engaged and follow your activities. An individual that understands the dangers that exist on the trail, this notification process is mandatory for safe hiking. If there was a clear understanding of where the hiker in this story was going, his life may have been saved.

In April of 1994, Richard Grey was a twenty-two-year-old resident of Quadra Island, just offshore from Campbell River British Columbia and Vancouver Island. On April 13, Richard left a note with his landlord that he'd be hiking Strathcona Park April 14 and would be back April 19. RCMP investigators determined that Richard hitchhiked to the park, left another handwritten note at the Elk River Trailhead. It was believed that he'd be on the north end of Strathcona and would be out on the 19th.

Richard's landlady called the RCMP when the renter didn't arrive home on the 19th. The RCMP went to the trailhead and found his handwritten note and then contacted his mom.

Beverly Pick was a professional artist living in Quebec and Richard's mother. She received a call from RCMP that her son had vanished. She immediately got on a plane and flew to the island. The RCMP probably didn't know Beverly's background when she arrived. The artist had once lived on Vancouver Island and had volunteered for many years as a search and rescue volunteer. She asked to be a partner of the SAR and soon after joined in for all meetings and strategy sessions.

A June first search deep into the park, with Beverly participating located items that she identified as belonging to Richard. The SAR found sweatpants, tuque and a towel lying on the bank of a park river. One opinion was that these items were left on the bank when the river was high, it lowered and left these items in place. Much of the later searches concentrated on Puzzle Mountain and the northern section of the park. No other things were located that were identified as belonging to Richard.

The search for Beverly's son went on for over a month until it was canceled. It has now been over 25 years without Richard being located.

Samuel Wright
Missing: 06/03/95- 6:00 P.M., Houston, BC
Age at disappearance: 66 years
Canine• Water• Point of Separation

Samuel and Verna Wright were a longtime married couple who lived in the small city of Houston, British Columbia near the center of the province interior. The town with 5,500 residents sits on the bank of the Bulkley River with Buck Creek bisecting the city and flowing into the river.

On June 2, 1995, after dinner, Samuel took the families Black Labrador, Chaz, for a walk in the nearby wilderness. For some reason, Chaz suddenly took off chasing something and was quickly out of sight. Samuel looked for him for over an hour, calling the dog's name and walking the trails south of town. As it got dark, Samuel gave up the search for the night and returned home to Verna.

On Saturday morning, June 3 at 8:00 A.M., Samuel loaded a small

Samuel Wright

knapsack with a few chocolate bars and a water bottle and told Verna he was going to look for Chaz and that he'd see her at dinner. The dog was last seen near Buck Creek near the southern area of Houston. The woods where Samuel was searching had thick wilderness with a small creek. At 9:00 A.M., Samuel met a jogger on the trail and had a discussion with them about Chaz. The conversation wasn't lengthy, but the jogger later confirmed they were speaking with Samuel. The meeting took place at a location south of Vanderploeg Road approximately two miles south of Houston. At 10:00 P.M., Samuel had not returned home, and Verna called the local RCMP.

Once the RCMP arrived at the Wright residence, Verna described to them the specifics of why her husband was in the woods and the fact that Sam was an outdoorsman, knew the woods intimately and would do well if he was alone in the elements.

A June 7, 1995 article in the Houston Today had these details, "RCMP immediately called the Houston First Responders, and Tim Smith, Wright's neighbor was put in charge of the operation. Smith says they physically scoured the banks of Bucks Creek, through a steep canyon and log jams, down to the Bulkley River. No trace of Wright was found in initial searches Smith says there was no sign he was in the water."

The first four days of searching had this development that was noted in the June 14, 1995 edition of the Houston Today, "7:30 A.M., RCMP dog master Lothar Bretfeld arrives from Terrace Detachment. Cannot pick up Wright's scent." A helicopter later that same day flew the creek area with FLIR finding nothing. In those first four days, hundreds of people from the community volunteered and set themselves in grid patterns and continually searched the area of the disappearance.

On June 5 a specialty tracking team entered the search to find any tracks of Samuel. They stayed on site for two days and found nothing.

On June 14, a local newspaper had the following headlines on an article about this SAR, "Over 430 volunteers take part in the ground, air search." To get a response of this magnitude in a small community is not that unexpected in Canada. Locals pull together and watch out for each other and relish the sense of community.

Six days after Samuel vanished, the RCMP made the following statement in the June 14, 1995, edition of the Houston Today, "Formal search operations suspended. Smith says all high probability areas have been covered. No further clues or leads to Wright's whereabouts." Those are the last words that any family wants to hear that is missing a loved one.

I could find only one other article near the time of this event, and it was an advertisement in the newspaper about missing people. This add highlighted the facts of Samuel's case. This appeared in the June 21, 1995 edition of the Houston Today, "Circumstances, Mr. Wright was last seen in Houston BC at approximately 9:00 A.M. Saturday, June 3, 1995. Mr. Wright was walking the undeveloped trail network in District Lot 2094 and 2090 just south of Four Seasons Park and between Buck Flats Road and Buck Creek. Mr. Wright was out looking for his lost dog, a black Lab named "Chaz." (Who is still missing).

On January 3, 1996, there was another page of highlights from the previous year in the Houston Newspaper. The article mentioned Mr. Wright's disappearance and how he had not been located.

I think it is relevant to review the facts in the case. This incident surrounds the disappearance of a man and a dog. The RCMP brought their trained tracking dog onto the trail, and it could not pick up a scent. The police also brought in a team of professional trackers who could not locate any tracks belonging to Samuel. Something happened to Samuel after he met the jogger on the trail, point of separation. These elements are essential.

Is it plausible to conclude that the reason Chaz was never found is the same reason Samuel wasn't located? How could Samuel vanish without leaving any tracks or a scent trail? All of this happened near the banks of Buck Creek.

After hundreds of searchers searched the area, planes in the sky and scent tracking canines, nothing is found, no backpack, no dog, no Samuel. If a cougar or bear attacked either Samuel or Chaz, there would be a massive scene of blood, torn clothing, etc., it would be very evident. In the years after Samuel vanished, hundreds of others have volunteered their time to comb the woods above Houston; nothing has ever been found.

I do not know what happened to Samuel or Chaz, but whatever it was is profoundly strange.

Ian Ralph Sutherland
Missing: 08/15/96, Green Mountain, Kersley, BC
Age at disappearance: 30 years
Point of Separation• Disability• Hunter

Kersley, British Columbia is approximately 65 miles south of Prince George on Highway 97. The region is known for harvesting lumber and its remoteness.

On August 15, 1996, Ian Sutherland was hunting on Green Mountain east of Kersley with a close friend. Sometime in the afternoon, something happened as is described in the August 21, 1996 edition of the *Quesnel Cariboo Observer*, "Ian Ralph Sutherland, 30, from Quesnel went missing last Thursday in the Green Mountain area, near Kersley. The RCMP said Sutherland was hiking with a friend when he slipped and hurt his knee. Sutherland's friend went for help, and when he returned, the injured hiker was missing. A thorough search of the area by police and Quesnel and Prince George Search and Rescue units turned up nothing over the weekend." SAR members numbered over 30 at the height of the rescue effort. There was a four-day effort to locate Ian; nothing was found.

Articles stated that Ian was hunting and a few others said the pair was hiking. I have written about several hikers and hunted that were injured in the woods, became injured, and their partner left to get assistance. When rescuers returned, the injured party was not located.

There were few details on this event.

Karl Walter
Missing: 06/28/97- 5:00 p.m., Mount Seymour, British Columbia
Age at disappearance: 65 years
Weather• Point of Separation• Cluster Zone• Disability• Canines• German

There are only a few cases that hit on almost every possible profile point for the area they disappeared, this is one. The disability profile point also includes ailments the individual may have where they are taking medication for a condition, something that may not be obvious by looking at the person.

On June 28, 1987, in the early morning hours, Mr. and Mrs. Karl Walter left their home in North Delta, British Columbia and drove twenty-five miles north crossing Vancouver Harbor and into North Vancouver and eventually made their way to Mount Seymour Provincial Park. The couple parked the car and entered the trail system. After approximately thirty minutes on the trail, Mrs. Walter told her husband that she was too tired to continue and went back to their vehicle (Point of Separation). She waited nine hours for her husband and then called North Vancouver RCMP reporting Karl as missing.

The police arrived at the park early the night of the 28th and got onto the trail almost immediately. After a short cursory walk up the trail, North Shore Search and Rescue was summoned.

Search teams arrived in large numbers the morning of June 29. A July 2, 1997 article in the *Vancouver Sun* had this information about the missing hiker, "Walter was not equipped for an overnight stay. For much of the last four days, rains and low clouds have shrouded the popular mountain that's crisscrossed with many unauthorized trails." Rain was inundating the lower elevations of the mountain while snow was falling higher up. Another article on July 2, 1997, this time in the *Surrey Leader* had more details, "At press time Monday the Mounties and North Shore Search and Rescue were still looking for the man, searching the area with the help of helicopters and dog squads. By that time Walter had spent two nights on the mountain. "With the cool and wet weather and this gentleman's age, it' not looking good right now," said North Vancouver RCMP Constable Tom Seaman. Seaman said Walter has Huntington's Chorea, a nervous disorder that causes muscle spasms and physical unsteadiness but did not have his medicine for the ailment with him."

Mrs. Walter told searchers that her husband did have a backpack with him that included snacks and a candle and he was an experienced hiker.

There are dozens of times I have written about people being together on a trail, one doesn't feel well and decides to go to their car or camp and wait for the other. It is during this time that the solo hiker is alone that something happens.

After four days of extensive searching, nothing was located. I did a search going forward several years and cannot find anything indicating that Walter, his backpack or supplies were ever located.

Case number five Mount Seymour.

Brian Douglas Faughnan
Missing 07/12/02–Unk, Whistler, BC
Age at Disappearance: 35 years
Cluster Zone• Weather•

On July 9, 2002, Brian Faughnan left his residence in Montreal, Canada, for a trip to the opposite Canadian coast, British Columbia. On July 11, Brian left a youth hostel in Vancouver and traveled by bus to the vacation resort of Whistler.

Whistler is one of the most beautiful ski and mountain-biking resorts in the world. There is a village at the bottom of Whistler's ski runs that includes some of the nicest hotels and condominiums you

Brian Faughnan

will find anywhere. There is great nightlife in the village during the summer or winter. During the summer, the ski resorts transform themselves into a mountain-biking mecca. You recognize the mountain bikers by seeing many them during the day walking the village in arm and shoulder braces, as so many crash and are injured.

Brian was with a small group (Bigfoot Adventure Tours) that checked into the Shoestring Lodge. The first night Brian was in the village, he talked with tour operators about hiking a nearby peak and asked about trails and directions.

On Friday, July 12, Brian told a roommate he was going climb a peak, and he may not be back until the next day. A security camera near the hotel captured him on video leaving the area with a full pack at 9:57 a.m. He was carrying a yellow daypack with some type of ax attached at the rear and a map, and it was believed that he was headed for the Valley Trail. When Brian left the lodge, the weather was pleasant and comfortable.

On July 13, the tour group was ready to leave the lodge, and Brian was nowhere to be found. A search was made of the area, and many of Brian's personal belongings were found in his room, including his passport. The hotel waited to see if Brian would arrive, and then, at approximately 3 p.m. on July 15, they contacted the RCMP and reported Brian as a missing person. The RCMP waited one more day before contacting the family, explaining the circumstances and asking if they had had contact with Brian. On July 17, the RCMP made a determination that Brian was missing and the following day, they activated local search and rescue.

The effort to locate Brian was initially hampered by bad weather. In fact, the weather turned bad early the first day that Brian was missing, as rain and fog hit the area. The search lasted for three days without finding any significant clue of where Brian may have traveled.

All indications were that the Montreal native had climbing experience and was in good physical condition. He had hiked many times in the New York Adirondacks and knew the associated risks of being in the woods. He was not carrying a sleeping bag, as one was found in his room. This is a puzzling point. Brian did tell his roommate that he might not be back till the following morning, yet he didn't bring a bag to sleep.

Summary

I have been to Whistler many times. I personally feel it is one of the nicest and most beautiful resorts in the world. I've seen bears on every trip to the region, even though on a few of the trips, I spent the majority of my time at the hockey rink for a tournament or at the hotel sleeping. There is a significant wildlife in the region, and the weather can change very quickly.

When I read the name of the tour group (Bigfoot Adventure Tours) that Brian was with, it reminded me of one of the first trips I took to Whistler with my kids for one of their tournaments.

We had a free afternoon with no hockey games, so I decided to find a fishing guide to take us up into the Canadian Rockies for a day of enjoying nature and fishing. The guide we had was a coach during the winter months for the Canadian national ski team and a fishing guide in the summer. We took a dirt road from the valley floor for about an hour up into the wilderness. The road was very rough, and we slowly made our way with the four-wheel drive.

I was asking the driver general questions about his background and experiences in the woods as we drove on. About fifty-five minutes into our trip, I asked him what the wildest thing he had ever seen out here was. The guide told the kids and me that he was once on a road very similar to the one we were traveling, forty-five minutes outside of Whistler, when he saw a Sasquatch run from behind a bush across the dirt road in front of his car. He said it was unmistakable. It ran much like a man but was covered in hair and very fast. He said that he couldn't believe what he had seen, and he had never seen one again.

This guide reeked of credibility and integrity. We never prodded him about any topic related to Sasquatch prior to his claim; this was a totally voluntary statement that definitely shook up my kids the remainder of the day. This information about the guide isn't to insinuate in any way that what he saw had anything to do with Brian's disappearance, but it does go to show what people who regularly visit the woods sometimes claim to encounter.

Grizzly bears are a reality in British Columbia, and I have seen several. Many people believe that moose are beautiful and passive. Moose can be some of the most dangerous mammals in any community, and extreme caution should be maintained when you see one in the area.

There are so many ways to die in the mountains that the worst decision anyone can make is to hike alone. Always carry a personal transponder. As well, I always carry a firearm when the law allows.

Richard Milner
Missing: 09/29/03, Strathcona Park, British Columbia
Age at disappearance: 43
Cluster Zone• Water

Strathcona Park is in the center of Vancouver Island, British Columbia. It is a large area with rugged mountains, lots of water and located on Vancouver Island. Much of the park reminds me of something you'd find in Olympic National Park in Washington. You will read about two disappearances at this location where hikers were never found, now making this a geographical cluster zone. On page 287 in Missing 411- Off the Grid, I wrote about a female hiker that also vanished in this park. Searchers found a trail of clothing and supplies belonging to her high on a ridgetop; she was never found.

On July 29, 2003, Richard Milner was a single mechanical engineer from Edmonton, Alberta vacationing on Vancouver Island. He had vacationed and hiked the island many times, with Strathcona Park being his favorite spot. Richard had been staying at the Ralph River Campground; he drove his white 1998, Dodge Dakota Pickup to the Price Creek Trailhead. This trail would take you to Cream Lake. It's a four-hour hike to a dead end and a four-hour hike out. Two days after the truck was first parked there, the local campground host noticed something was wrong and called SAR on July 31.

RCMP ran the license plate number and determined the missing hiker was Richard. The police contacted Tad Milner, a Simon Fraser University Professor and brother of Richard advising him of the disappearance. Tad immediately left for the park.

The Campbell River RCMP took control of the SAR. They mustered over fifty searchers, three helicopters and one plane to look for the hiker. Once Tad arrived, he told SAR commanders that his brother was very athletic, extremely knowledgeable of trails and backpacking and would not take unnecessary chances. RCMP advised Tad that the path that his brother had chosen was not dangerous and it shouldn't have been very challenging.

A five-day search effort found nothing associated with Richard. This is another example of a mundane hike, alone, turns into a tragic account of a missing hiker.

Juaqueline Bob
Missing 07/06/04, Alexis Creek, BC
Age at disappearance: 41 years
Mushroom Picker• Canines• Weather•
Point of Separation

Juaqueline Bob

It should be noted that the first name of the victim in this event is spelled correctly. She was a First Nations member of the Stone Reserve and left on July 5 and drove with her friend and others to Alexis Creek (Central British Columbia) for Mushroom picking. The group camped the first night and then headed into the forest early the next morning. This area was prime for mushrooms, in 2003 a forest fire-scarred the region and one of the first signs of vegetation returning are mushrooms.

The group got together at lunch and then separated going back into the woods, this was the last time Juaqueline was seen. When she failed to come back to camp the night of July 6, the friends went into the woods calling her name and not getting a response. The following morning the Alexis Creek RCMP was notified of the disappearance and asked to assist in a SAR.

The exact location of the search was called Nemiah Valley and the Brittany Valley Wilderness. Prince George is approximately 140 air miles north of Alexis Creek.

The RCMP was notified that Juaqueline was carrying a lighter and a pocket knife. She knew how to make fire, but weather conditions were starting to change rapidly. A July 13, 2004 article in the Nanaimo Daily News had this information, "Rain and cold night have been obstacles, and lightning struck a satellite repeater, zapping a key communications system." A July 13, 2004 article in The Tribune had more details of the SAR, "In the cold and wet days that have followed the numbers of searchers looking for the Stone Reserve woman have swelled to as many as 140 people using a fixed-wing aircraft, an RCMP helicopter, several private helicopters. Williams Lake Dog Services as well as more than seven SAR personnel from across the area."

Friends advised SAR personnel that the Bob was last seen wearing a red coat with blue lining and a red ball cap. SAR informed the press that the group of mushroom pickers were in an extremely remote area that took searchers almost a day to travel to the location. One RCMP searcher admitted in the July 14, 2004 edition of the 100 Mile Free Press, "She admits that it is unusual that not one clue regarding Bob's whereabouts was uncovered during the massive search. "It is puzzling that a person would disappear without any trace," Armstrong said."

The RCMP estimated the 14 day search cost over $200,000 and was one of the largest ever in the area. Family members and friends stayed in the region for weeks continuing to look for the woman, still not finding a clue.

Juaqueline Bob was never found.

The disappearance of a Native American or First Nations woman under these circumstances is rare. I have documented several missing mushroom pickers in the past, predominantly from Washington and Oregon, many have not been located.

Jared Stanley
Missing: 01/10/05, Mount Seymour, British Columbia
Age at disappearance: 25 years
Cluster Zone• Missing Clothing• Weather• Intellect

It's an unfortunate fact that law enforcement makes mistakes. Sometimes those mistakes can lead to a death or a significant delay in an investigation. In this disappearance, it's vague as to what the error may have caused.

One of the categories I have identified in the profiles of the missing people I have researched is individuals with high intellect. In January of 2005, Jared Stanley was a twenty-five-year-old Physics graduate student from Longmont, Colorado studying at the University of British Columbia (UBC) in Vancouver. Jared was specifically studying Meteorology and avalanche behavior. He was an athlete, running 4-5 miles per day in the mountains and also completing in several marathons, including the Breckenridge Marathon. When the student was in high school, he was a member of the school's soccer team, he was the optimum student athlete.

On January 10, 2005, the UBC student drove his blue, four-door Subaru sedan from school to the parking lot on Mount Seymour. Friends knew he was going to study on the mountain, but few had concerns because of knowledge of the woods and great common sense attitude. On January 13, the Mount Seymour lodge called RCMP about an abandoned vehicle in its parking lot. Officers arrived, ran the registration of the car and determined it was Jared's. They called his residence at the university, did not get a response and towed the vehicle.

Nine days after the physics major parked on Mount Seymour, a friend called the Vancouver Police and reported Jared as a missing person. Jared's friends tried to get the university to release the contact numbers for his family, they refused citing privacy issues. As the information of a missing Colorado resident studying in British Columbia hit the online news sources, Jared's brother living in Arizona read the story and contacted his parents. Jim Stanley got the news about his son and jumped the next flight north.

News of the search was included in this January 24, 2005, article in the *Vancouver Sun*, "During a helicopter search Friday, two days after a friend of Stanley's called Vancouver Police to report him missing, the body was found. An earlier search on Thursday had to be called off because of heavy rain and low cloud cover. Searchers initially thought he was lost in the western part of the mountain away from the Mount Seymour recreation area, possibly in a popular area known as Suicide Gulch. But his body was found on the east side of the mountain." More details about the body recovery are found in the January 25, 2005 edition of the *Colorado-an*, "Ron Royston, a North Shore Search and Rescue manager, said a headlamp was discovered on the body, possibly an indicator that Stanley was trying to hike out of the area after dark and fell into the creek. It's our assessment that he died on the day he went out, " Royston said. It was unclear whether he walked or skied into the area because he was wearing ski boots, but no skis have been found. Rushing water in the creek tore off some of Stanley's clothing and swept away much of his gear, Seaman said." I read this paragraph and just shook my head. There is nobody alive that is going to cross a creek with rushing water wearing skis. The skis would've come off and be on the bank. If the water was flowing as fast as searchers claim, why didn't it tear off his headlamp, especially if he suffered head injuries. There is also nobody that has ever worn ski boots would contemplate hiking in them, they are not comfortable for walking or hiking.

There was this article in the January 28, 2005, *Coloradoan* that had details from the coroner, "His body was found in Shone Creek, an area of rugged terrain that all but experienced moun-taineers and skiers avoid. B.C. Coroner Nic Snyckers said Thurs-day that Stanley died from drowning after disorientation due to hypothermia had set in." More details are found in the January 24, 2005 edition of the *Vancouver Sun*, "It would appear that he fell down an embankment, was severely injured and succumbed to his injuries, " Royston said., adding it is likely Stanley was knocked unconscious and died the same day as hypothermia would have quickly set in." What physical element did the coroner review for him to be able to state that Jared was disoriented before hypother-mia setting in?

Sometimes it's more important what's not in the coroner's re-port rather than what the coroner states caused the death. There was never a mention of broken bones, fractured skull or severe injuries. From what the coroner reported, Jared was not debilitated from a physical injury. The cause of death was drowning with an associ-ated factor of hypothermia, something I devoted an entire book to the topic, Missing 411- A Sobering Coincidence. Readers need to remember, if someone falls in water, they will fight for their lives to get out, if you are young and healthy and there is an avenue to safety, you will probably make it. After you are out, you need to get the wet clothes off the body and get a fire started to get warm. Shone Creek is by its definition, a creek, not a river. If somebody accidentally went in, they should have the ability to get out, but Jared was located in the water. Jared was in top shape at an age where the body is resilient, strong and pliable. If anyone should have made it out of that creek, Jared should have done it.

In Missing 411- A Sobering Coincidence, there were a series of healthy young college men that all disappeared (An exact profile match to Jared). They were eventually located in a body of water. There were never logical answers about how they got in, or why they never got out. Autopsies never showed anything unusual until a group of families started to perform a second autopsy with a secondary, more advanced drug screening. The screenings found levels of GHB (Date rape Drug) in the body that were exceptionally high. It could never be explained how these levels got into the victim's bodies. GHB paralyzes the body but allows the victim to understand what is happening and continues their breathing. If you fell into the water with high levels of GHB in your system, you will drown. If you were in icy waters, hypothermia would set in, then drowning. The vast, vast majority of all coroners do not routinely screen for GHB.

Jared Stanley disappeared in a geographical cluster that includes many people that were never located. There is something about this region that is different than any other set of mountains I have researched in Canada.

It was to the benefit of the police that the coroner and SAR commanders make a statement that Jared died the day he left his car or the day after.

Jared's parents had his cremated remains spread near Breckenridge, Colorado.

Case number six Mount Seymour. The amount of disappearances coupled with the number of people that are never located on this mountain make this location one of the most dangerous I have ever documented. This is not a technical climb that takes advanced skill. Why the people disappear here is a true mystery.

David Koch
Missing: 05/25/05 at 8:00 p.m.—Grouse Mountain, BC
Age at Disappearance: 36 years
German• Canines• Weather• Area Previously Searched• Water•
Cluster Zone

The location of this incident is approximately fifteen minutes north of the city of Vancouver, Canada. Sometimes called the "Peak of Vancouver," it is a ski resort in the winter months and a destination for hiking and dining in the summer. Various locations on the mountain boast giant wood carvings, and the area gets very desolate very quickly.

The first summit of the mountain was documented in 1894. It became a noted destination for travelers wanting a wilderness escape and later became a very popular ski resort. The first double chairlift was placed there in 1949.

In 1998, Mertland, Wisconsin, couple Suzanne and David Koch traveled to Vancouver on vacation. They made their way to Grouse Mountain and viewed the mountains and lush atmosphere that surrounded the area. They didn't get a chance to hike that day but told themselves they wanted to tour the mountain if they ever came back.

In 2005, thirty-six-year-old David was the sales manager and associate publisher for a magazine, *DM Review*. On May 25, 2005, David was taking a business trip from Wisconsin to Vancouver, Canada. David couldn't get a flight directly into Vancouver, so he landed in Seattle, rented a car, and drove into Canada. It was late in the day when he arrived in the Vancouver area, and he decided to drive to Grouse Mountain and see if he could tour it before dark.

David drove his rental car into the parking lot of the mountain, parked, and left his cell phone, computer, and luggage inside. It was 8:00 p.m. when he used his credit card to purchase a tram ticket up the mountainside. There were between twenty-four and twenty-eight people on the tram with David when he disembarked at the summit.

When David didn't call his wife and didn't make his business appointments, he was reported as a missing person. David was last observed wearing sandals and not dressed for a lengthy hike. He was seen leaving the tram and taking a brief ten-minute walk and then returning to the atrium at the top of the mountain. Two minutes later, he left and wasn't seen again. It was the opinion of everyone involved that he was just going up for a quick visit.

The official search started on May 27. The RCMP and local police committed significant resources to finding David. There were multiple canine teams used, as well as several helicopters; hundreds of professional and volunteer searchers scoured the mountain and the surrounding area. David's wife, Suzanne, arrived at the search location on May 27 and monitored searchers' activity.

At one point, ten canine teams were on the mountain trying to find David's scent. Weather cooperated with search efforts for a while, but the skies opened up on June 5 with heavy rains. After ten days, officials terminated the search effort to locate David. A June 7 article in the *Milwaukee Sentinel* had these details: "The search was the longest ever conducted by North Shore Rescue, a Vancouver based volunteer group that's considered the leading search and rescue operation." This was not a quick search. A June 6 article in the *Daily Globe* had these additional details: "'After ten days of searching and not turning up any clues whatsoever, no tracks, no broken branches, no articles of clothing, no threads of clothing, there's no tangible likelihood we will find Mr. Koch,' Royal Canadian Mounted Police Constable John MacAdam told the Associated Press." Imagine you are the family and get this notification from the head of the search effort. How devastated would you be?

The formal search was terminated, but volunteers from throughout the area stayed on the scene and continued to look for David. To the shock of every searcher on the scene, David's body was found on June 7, one day after the formal search ended. This June 8, 2005, article in the *Capitol Times* had extensive details: "'where he was found was not where he perished,' MacAdam said. 'He might have been underwater at some time,' he also said. George Zilahi of Vancouver's North Shore Search and Rescue said the area is one frequented by expert hikers. The body was at the base of two cliffs where waterfalls are located, he said. 'We searched that [area] extensively the first couple of days of the search,' he said, adding that heavy rainfall Sunday may have washed the body out of pools of water in the steep drainage of the area." I'm sure the police were shocked by the find, especially because it was in an area that had been searched previously. Initial reports stated that the body showed no obvious signs of trauma. As if this information wasn't disturbing enough, the coroner's report was about to shock the community.

An October 6, 2005, article in the *Daily Tribune* exposed some disturbing facts: "A Hartland man who died while hiking in a Vancouver Canada suburb was alive for several days while rescuers looked for him, according to a coroner's report. David Koch, 36, the son of Merrill resident Ardell Koch and the late J. Stewart Koch; was found dead by a searcher June 7, in a creek bed on Grouse Mountain 10 days after employees discovered Koch's rental car in the parking lot at the bottom of the mountain." Later in the same article was this: "Koch had been the subject of an intense search using helicopters, search dogs, infrared devices and trained personnel. According to the coroner's report, he died of hypothermia around May 31, six days after he was last seen."

This is one of the rare times I have found coroners, police, and other legal sources to be surprisingly honest and straightforward. It was absolutely shocking news. The family and the search–and-rescue team must've asked themselves where David was for six days.

There were no significant injuries to David's body. He didn't die from blunt trauma, broken bones, or a fractured skull. There was also no mention of David being in water for an extensive period of time.

In a truly amazing coincidence, many of these cases were also from Wisconsin.

Coroners and medical examiners in the public spectrum are given a budget they must follow. That budget includes screening for drugs and alcohol but restricts the number of drugs that are screened for. One drug that is almost never screened for is GHB. I have no idea how the victims were given the GHB.

I am not stating that David Koch was given GHB; I am stating that to understand what is happening in these cases, we need to explore all scientifically proven avenues.

It's a fact that David didn't lie in the water for the entire time he was missing. If he had been in that creek, his body and skin would exhibit obvious signs. If search-and-rescue personnel combed the area as they stated (and I believe they did), and search dogs were combing the same area, I do not believe they would've missed him.

David wasn't incapacitated. He could've walked, talked, or yelled for help. Searchers regularly call victims' names as they search, and no one ever heard David. Finally, the victims I write about are never found by helicopters with FLIR (heat-seeking radar). When I was a police officer, I spent a night as the observer in our helicopter and saw firsthand how well FLIR works. If someone is alive in the woods, you should be able to see their heat, especially if he or she is moving and staying out of the canopy. All these facts lead to only one conclusion: where he was found was not where he died. How did he end up in the creek bed? The formal search ended, and the following day, he arrived in the water. Where was he for six days? This case is a stellar example of how to methodically show the facts surrounding these disappearances. There are only a few conclusions that can be drawn.

Tom Leonard
Missing: 10/02/2005, Spatsizi Provincial Park, BC
Age at disappearance: 40 years
Weather• Hunter
Spatsizi Plateau Provincial Park is the location of this incident and is one of the more remote places in British Columbia. It is located in the far northwestern section of the province. Here is what the BC Parks Department states about their property: "Spatsizi Plateau Wilderness Park is one of Canada's largest and most significant parks. True wilderness at-

Tom Leonard

mosphere, outstanding scenery and varied terrain make this park an excellent place for quality hiking, photography, and nature study. Lands within the park have an excellent capability for supporting large populations of wildlife."

This park is noted for big game and lots of bears. The terrain is steep, difficult with outstanding wildlife viewing.

Tom Leonard loved the outdoors and knew the risks of wilderness travel. He applied and received a limited-access sheep hunting permit for the fall. On September 11, 2005, Tom drove his truck to the Eaglenest trailhead, parked, and put his backpack, tent, food for three weeks, sleeping bag, and other supplies in his pack. He had a large and heavy pack and left for his three-week expedition to the high altitudes associated with sheep.

On October 2, Tom was scheduled to leave the park and contact his family. He never did. The wife contacted the parks department and notified them of an overdue hunter. They found Tom's truck exactly where he had parked it, and it appeared as though it had been there for three weeks. A search was immediately started.

SAR workers found one campsite that they thought might be something Tom had used. Under a rock at the site, they found a granola bar wrapper they thought might be his. On October 8 bad weather moved into the area, and the search had to be terminated. Local authorities put posters up and tried to contact hikers and other hunters. Nobody saw the man.

In June 2006, Tom's family mounted another search to find his remains. Again, poor weather moved in, and after a short time they had to terminate their effort. In July 2006 the RCMP mounted a five-day air search of the area of the park they believed he'd hunt. They found nothing. In 2007 the family went back and searched the Waterfall Trail area. They again found nothing. In July 2008 there was another search of the Cartmel area. They found nothing.

The number of times that weather stopped a search effort is notable. What is even more surprising is that it's been over ten years since Tom vanished. There have been hundreds of hikers and hunters that have tromped the ground where Tom traveled. Nobody has found a backpack, rifle, canteen, pots, pans—nothing. Where can all of this be hiding? The area of travel for a sheep hunter is at the high elevations that really have no trees or significant ground cover.

There is another story of a missing sheep hunter in the Alberta section. What's even stranger about the two sheep hunter disappearances is that they vanished within twenty days of each other, and they are back-to-back on the missing hunter list at the back of the book. They are the only two hunters who made the list for 2005. Is that a coincidence?

John Kahler
Missing 11/04/07-4:00 A.M. Great Stave Lake, BC
Age at disappearance: 22 years
German• Unknown Cause of Death• Canines • Water• Cluster Zone
        The insertion of this case in the book may not make much sense to new readers. I would encourage you to read Missing 411- A Sobering Coincidence. There are over 100 stories of young men who had been drinking alcohol, generally with friends in a social environment and became separated. Canines could not track them from the scene, trackers could not locate their tracks, and if they were located, they were found in an unusual location in a body of water. There was never any explanation of how they could've ended up in the water, and many times a cause of death could not be determined. Almost all of the men were young, in excellent condition, intelligent and had been drinking alcohol. Many of the families did not believe the explanations given to them by law enforcement and coroners and paid to have second autopsies completed. It was the result of the additional coroner's participation that the truly unusual is revealed. The case of John Kahler is a match for the disappearances in Missing 411- A Sobering Coincidence.
        John Kahler was raised for a time in Manitoba, and then the family moved to Langley, BC. John's dad was an ironworker and had his own successful business. After graduating from high school, John joined his dads business and quickly reached the level of a journeyman ironworker.
        During the weekend of November 2-4, 2007, The King of The Pit celebration was occurring at Great Stave Lake in the southern part of the province. John drove his white Ford F-150 pickup over to the event to join friends. John was last seen at approximately 4:00 A.M. on November fourth drinking around their primary camp. Shortly after he was last seen, a friend discovered the following that is described in the October 24, 2008 edition of the *Langley Advance*, "His White Ford F-150 crew cab truck was found 200 meters from

the main campsite, stuck in a sinkhole, still running and with its wipers on and music playing. His cellphone and other belongings were in the truck." Initially, John's friends didn't think much of the incident and got his truck out of the hole. The rear wheels were low in a gully with the front end up higher. It wasn't until late Sunday that friends started to get concerned. They eventually called John's parents at 9:00 P.M. Sunday.

Mr. and Mrs. Kahler responded to the lake and searched for days. Kahler was camping 15 kilometers up Burma Road on the lake. His truck was located on the mudflats of the lake. The RCMP responded in mass with a helicopter, canine units, and seventy search and rescue personnel. The search was extensive and could not locate anything that pointed to where John may be found. The canines could not locate a scent to lead to Kahler.

There was nothing new on this disappearance until October 21, 2008, almost a year later. A Kayaker was on Stave Lake approximately 5 kilometers from Kahler's truck when they came across a body in the water. The RCMP was called. The remains were recovered and sent to the Royal Colombia Hospital in New Westminster for an autopsy. It was stated at the time that the BC Coroners Service was investigating.

One day after a body was pulled from Stave Lake, the RCMP announced it was John Kahler. There was no announcement on the cause of death.

On February 7, 2012, the *Vancouver Courier* ran an article that had this notation about John Kahler, "Kahler's body was found in 2008 in Stave Lake, one year after he went missing. As far as I know, the cause of death in Kahler's case has never been determined."

Investigators need to start thinking critically on these incidents. Ask yourself, how many twenty-two-year olds leave their phone in a truck with the engine running and walk away? Why weren't the RCMP able to track John's through the mudflats from the truck? Why couldn't the canines track his scent from the truck? What would cause a young man to leave his truck running with the wipers going on a mudflat with his phone and other personal belongings on the front seat? I don't believe that the scene represents normal behavior for a young man.

The number of missing and unusual disappearances in southern British Columbia represents some of the most significant numbers that I have seen anywhere in the world. In John Kahler's case, it is easy to discount the death as a drunk guy vanishes, falls into the water and drowns. If drowning was the cause of death, the coroner hasn't said it.

John's family believed something unusual, and maybe criminal occurred, I concur. Just as I described in Missing 411: A Sobering Coincidence, the similarities in these deaths is off the chart.

It is almost a guarantee that the coroners in British Columbia screen for the same standard drugs and narcotics in all deaths that the same medical professionals do in the United States. It wasn't until families in the states paid for their own second autopsies that they started to see an unusual finding within the scope of toxicology testing. I can almost guarantee that there are many other cases in this province that mimic John's death; people are just ignoring them.

William Pilkenton
Missing: 02/15/08, 10:00 a.m.,
Tofino, Vancouver Island
Age at disappearance: 7
Water• Point of Separation

William Pilkenton

David and Camilla Pilkenton left their home in Bellingham, Washington, for a leisurely vacation at a bed-and-breakfast on the west coast of Vancouver Island. The couple chose the city of Tofino to bring their sons, Timothy and William.

Tofino is a somewhat isolated community at the end of a long peninsula sitting to the south of Vargas Island Provincial Park and to the west of the giant Strathcona Provincial Park. The small city is surrounded by dozens of small islands and is known as a city where many First Nations People reside.

Cable Cove Inn, the bed-and-breakfast, is near Duffin Cove, which is at the far western side of the city. It sits just to the north of the cove and has a commanding view of the water and nearby islands.

On February 15, 2008, David awoke early and decided to take a walk on the beach. His son William asked to join him. The boys walked to the street and then down a set of steep stairs to the rocks and beach area of the cove. The two were in the area of Tonquin Beach. William stayed at the bottom of the stairs as David walked the rocky beach area. William wanted to get a little closer to his dad. David was approximately thirty-six feet from his son when he took his eyes off of him for just a few minutes. William vanished. David frantically searched the beach area and the steps. He found nothing. He went back to the inn and notified his wife and the inn operators, who notified the RCMP.

The RCMP supplied a huge response to the disappearance of William. Land, sea, and air units responded. Canine units also responded the first day and tried to pick up a scent. A very lush and thick forest borders the beach, and that was searched as well.

On the second day of the search, a steady rain hit the area and hampered efforts. The search lasted three days and involved scuba divers, helicopters, and two hundred volunteers that included people from a local First Nation tribe. Nothing was ever found of William Pilkenton. RCMP forces believed the body and parts of clothing and shoes would wash onto nearby beaches in the following days, but nothing appeared.

There are no more than twenty streets in the tiny city of Tofino; everyone knows everyone else. When people come to town, there are only a few places to stay. There were only two places for William to be: the ocean or the forest. Neither location offered any clues. William and his clothes have never surfaced.

Michael Raster
Missing: 08/08/08, Tuchodi Lakes, BC
Age at disappearance: 43 years
Water• Point of Separation• German

This is the second case in the same area, Tuchodi Lakes. You have read about missing hunter, Raymond Krieger, a 43-year old German who disappeared from his hunting camp on August 28, 1992. Mr. Krieger was never found.

A September 19, 2008 article in the *Vancouver Sun* had a statement from Wayne Sawchuk, a trapper from the region of Tuchodi Lakes describing the country where Michael Raster vanished, "It's rough country," said the backcountry horseman, noting any old outfitter trails that may exist in the area are likely to be littered with deadfall. "He had to traverse what could be called the pole of inaccessibility, as far as you can get from access by road in the province."

Michael Raster

You now have a clear picture in your mind where this story takes place.

Michael Raster, 43 years old, traveled from his native Germany to British Columbia and made his way to the northern Rockies. He made his way to a lodge on Muncho Lake where he found a pilot to fly him to his starting point, Tuchodi Lake.

The same newspaper noted above has this information on Michael's pilot, "Lodge owner and pilot Urs Schildknecht said the hiker showed up the day before the flight and claimed to have backcountry experience for such an expedition. To Schildknecht's knowledge, the hiker carried neither a gun nor pepper spray. He had maps of the area and a GPS unit, but no satellite phone or other form of communication. "I was a little bit worried about him, but he said he had done these things before," he recalled of their brief conversation. "To tell you the truth, I didn't want to know much because I felt he didn't ask for my advice and I didn't want to give him the advice," due to liability concerns." Michael was dropped at Tuchodi with Urs agreeing to pick him up September 10 at Frog Lake, a vast 155-mile hike.

Urs had weather issues on September 10 and couldn't get into Frog Lake until September 12. He waited for Michael for several hours and then flew back to his base. Once home he notified the local RCMP that there was a missing hiker, Michael Raster.

Law enforcement knew that the backcountry would soon be filled with hunters and that would lead to the possible recovery of Michael's backpack and other articles or the finding of him.

The Fort Nelson RCMP committed a helicopter, two fixed-wing planes, and multiple ground teams into looking for the German hiker. They obtained assistance from the local SAR teams and the provincial emergency services program. Twenty Four SAR members made their way through dense brush, deadfall, creeks, and rivers searching for anything relevant to the missing man. A four-day search found nothing and was terminated.

There was nothing new on Michael's status until later in September and explained in this September 26 article in the *Whitehorse Daily Star*, "Since then (search), a Tumbler Ridge hunter found a backpack that belonged to Raster on a sandbank 1.5 KM upstream from Terminus Mountain, which he turned into police on September 16. Four days later, on September 20, search teams returned to the site to find waterlogged documents, including copies of Raster's identification papers. The same day another hunter found a waterproof bag with his diary, passport and other papers on a log jam on the Gataga River. In a diary, Raster carefully plotted his route and marked down campsites until August 8, when the notes abruptly end."

Michael's body was never found. A September 24, 2008 article in the *CBC News* had these statements from RCMP, "We're assuming something happened to him, and he lost his life," RCMP Staff Sgt. Tom Roy said Tuesday. "He either fell in the river or befell some other misfortune. There's an abundance of people out in the backcountry right now," Roy added. "It's very unusual; to have someone just vanish."

I don't like to send guess people who make life-ending decisions, but I will here. To enter an area where there are Grizzly Bear without bear spray or a rifle is craziness. Every time I go into a new wilderness area, I am always seeking out an expert to tell me where the potential land mines are located. Every wilderness area is different. Some regions are easy to walk in and out of, others are easy to get lost. Sometimes looking at a map doesn't tell you enough about the area to be safe. If you are bushwhacking cross country in a remote region, you are playing loose with your life by not carrying a satellite phone or personal locator beacon. As someone who has broken their leg on a backcountry trail, it can happen. If you break your leg, you aren't walking anywhere. Without an emergency communication device, you will lay there, and day, nobody is going to find you. If you die in the wild, it won't be long before animal predation will occur and scatter your remains throughout the region. The chance that any SAR team will even find the bones is minimal.

The fact that two German men in their forties both were lost and never found in the same wilderness area has not bypassed me, it's odd.

Raster may have drowned, it's possible. From the way, Sgt. Roy spoke of the area, and it seems that he believed they should have found the body. The local RCMP knows the region better than I.

One of Michael's biggest mistake was not engaging Urs Schildknecht in a lengthy conversation at his lodge the night before he departed. I've known several Canadian bush pilots. The ones I have met are smart, knowledgeable, cautious, and make sound recommendations about the area they fly.

The chances that Michael's body will ever be found is almost zero. The wilderness has a very efficient manner of disposing of carcasses. I only hope that Michael's last days on Earth were gorgeous, peaceful, and full of some joy.

Tyler Wright
Missing 08/10/10, Boise Creek Trail, BC
Age at Disappearance: 35 years
Cluster Zone•

Tyler Wright was a big man. At 6'4" and with a size-fifteen foot, Tyler was very recognizable. On August 10, 2010, Tyler embarked on a six-day solo hike from north of Squamish to Coquitlam. Reports indicate that Tyler was taking the Boise Creek Trail toward Pitt Lake through Mamquam Pass, and eventually he would be picked up. He never came out of the mountains.

Tyler had a history of taking hikes alone and always prevailing. He was in very good physical condition. An August 30, 2010, article in the *Squamish Chief* had the following descrip-

HAVE YOU SEEN TYLER WRIGHT ?

Tyler Wright (*goes by Ty*)
Male, Caucasian
35 yrs old, 6'4"
shoe size 16
Blonde hair, shaved head
Blue eyes
green toque and t-shirt
black backpack, black
fleece
experienced hiker

If you may have seen
Tyler, please contact
Squamish RCMP
1-604-892-6100
or 911

Ty is believed to be hiking Boise
Creek Trail near Mamquam Pass and
heading towards Pitt Lake .
Coquitlam Lake . or Indian Arm.
Last seen 4:30pm August 10, 2010 at
the beginning of the Boise Creek
Trail. He was expected home on
August 16, 2010.

For more information, photos, maps:
www.MissingTylerWright.blogspot.com

Tyler Wright

tion of Tyler: "'Ty is a competent outdoorsman, and extreme-ly fit. He is an incredibly resourceful and determined person,' said close friend Evian Macmillan. 'His determination fuels our search.'"

RCMP and Comox Valley search and rescue spent nineteen days searching trails and flying hundreds of hours of helicopter time all in the efforts to find Tyler. At one point they did find what they believed was a track left by Tyler's big foot. They also found a fifteen-foot slide area in a creek bed, where it appeared that Tyler tried to climb out and slid down. On August 23, searchers found an area in the grass where they believed a person was lying down and sleeping.

On August 29, Squamish RCMP terminated what they called one of the largest searches in British Columbia history. It was not only a huge effort by RCMP and search and rescue personnel, but Tyler's parents had also incurred huge expenses by paying for additional helicopter flight time.

Summary

Even though the area that Tyler was in was just fifteen miles from Vancouver and ten miles from a significant population base, this area is extremely wild. The area around Pitt Lake is very steep, very wild, and dangerous. This is another one of those areas where there is no way I'd hike alone.

As of the publication of this book, Tyler was not found.

Rachael Bagnall, age at disappearance: 25 years
Jonathan Jette, age at disappearance: 34 years
Missing: 09/08/10, Pemberton, BC
Intellect• Canines• Weather
Significant research went into this case. It was one of the missing incidents that struck me as even more unusual than the majority

Bagnall-Jette

I've documented, if that is possible. In *Missing 411-North America and Beyond*, I documented a series of double disappearances. This incident would qualify for that section of the book. When I first started to read about the background, education, climbing history, and love of the outdoors that this couple had, I knew this story was going to be unusual. Just prior to this book being published, I was contacted by Jonathan's mother and asked if we were looking into her son's disappearance. I reassured her that we were and that this case would be getting significant press by our organization.

Rachael Bagnall was raised in Prince George, British Columbia. She was a brilliant student in her third year of medical school residency at the University of British Columbia in Vancouver. She loved the outdoors and had hiked in the United States and throughout Canada and always read books about the areas before she traveled. She knew the dangers of the outdoors and took appropriate equipment.

Jonathan Jette was raised in Quebec and was also a lover of the outdoors. His parents owned a restaurant. They knew their son's love of Canada's mountains and endorsed his interests. Jonathan was a governmental attaché for the Canadian government in Quebec and living in Vancouver.

Rachael and Jonathan initially met at a climbing gym, and their relationship blossomed. They both were in outstanding physical condition and seemed to thrive off each other's interest and intellect. They had planned a two to three day trip into an area north of Pemberton. The couple knew that this was going to be their last weekend together before they had to separate for a year. Rachael was going to South America to help the underprivileged utilizing her medical background, and Jonathan was staying in Vancouver.

They had purchased the book *Scrambles in Southwest British Columbia* by Matt Gunn. They had brought climbing helmets, an ice ax, backpacks, and food, but no ropes. The couple left early in the morning of September 4, 2010. Credit card receipts show they stopped at Tim Horton's in Squamish at 7:42 a.m. and purchased coffee and hot chocolate. The couple continued driving north through Whistler, Pemberton, and toward their destination, the Spetch Creek Forest Service Road, 8.7 miles from Mount Currie. At this point they parked their car and started a five-hour hike, presumably toward Valentine Lake. The hike would take them into the shadows of Cassiope and Saxifrage Mountains. The trail was large and well maintained, and it would be obvious to all what direction you were supposed to travel.

The Labor Day weekend trip was supposed to be two to three days. On September 8, 2010, Rachel had not returned to her sister's residence, and her sister called the RCMP.

Two days after the initial missing person report, RCMP found the couple's vehicle. They saw cups inside from Tim Horton's.

There were no other clues found with the vehicle. The police asked Rachael's sister to search her room in an attempt to determine what she had and had not taken. They then went on to search Jonathan's residence looking for clues as to how long the couple would be gone and what he had taken. All indications pointed to the couple taking a two to three day hike.

The RCMP put a major effort into locating Rachael and Jonathan. Bloodhounds were brought to the vehicle, and they did not pick up a scent leaving that area. News articles did state that rain and clouds hampered searchers; this may have been a contributing factor in the disappearance. Dozens of search teams from Pemberton, Whistler, Vancouver Island, Ridge Meadows, and more all converged into the area to assist. A commercial and an RCMP helicopter took to the sky when the weather permitted to look for traces of the two. The initial search was for ten days and nothing was found. There have been no less than four additional searches that were initiated by family and friends. The family actually hired professional guides from the area to search for the pair. Nothing was found. Over 2000 search hours went into the effort to locate the couple.

Jonathan's family did state that he had an injured knee and they believed there was a possibility that he injured it further and the couple may be stranded somewhere. This statement was found in one article and seemed to be a side note of the family looking for answers.

The lead investigator on this case is Steve LeClair, staff sergeant from the Whistler/Pemberton RCMP Detachment. I sent the sergeant a series of e-mails inquiring about specific facts surrounding the case. The sergeant confirmed that canines never found the couple's scent at any location. He also stated that they didn't find any of the pair's cookware or used campsites. I asked if anyone on the trail or at the lake reported seeing the pair. LeClair stated that there was nobody else in the Valentine Lake area when Jonathan and Rachael walked in. He said that this would not be unusual based on the area's remoteness and the bad weather at the time. Imagine walking into a massive forest and not having anyone in the area—it sounds heavenly but apparently turned deadly.

Summary

I've read too many search and rescue reports to not know that there is something very wrong with this case. The parents have stated that they believe there may be foul play involved in the disappearance. They have also questioned whether their children are actually still in the area.

Bloodhounds could not locate a scent. Rain and clouds restricted search operations. People intimately involved in the search effort talked about foul play. There are too many commonalities with other cases I've researched for this incident not to be included in this book.

There are posters in the area of Valentine Lake about the disappearance of Rachael and Jonathan. There hasn't been one clue found regarding their whereabouts.

Darcy Brian Turner
Missing 06/20/11, Stein Valley Park,
Lytton, BC
Age at Disappearance: 55 years
Cluster Zone

Darcy Turner

The disappearance of Darcy Turner occurred in a park with multiple names. The location has been called Stein Valley Park and Stein Valley Niaka Pamux Heritage Park. It is located seventy miles southwest of Kamloops and eighty miles northeast of Vancouver in deep and rugged wilderness. The word "Stein" comes from a Canadian First Nations word "stagyn," meaning "hidden place." This is a location that has significant meaning to the First Nations People of British Columbia, as it has petroglyphs and other locations that link the people to their past.

Darcy was a very experienced outdoorsman that told friends he was going on a "vision quest" trip, one that he had taken each of the last five years. He left on June 4 and had planned to have a ride pick him up on June 19. Since the time he was reported missing to RCMP, Lytton Volunteer SAR Team and Lytton First Nations Band Members have spent considerable time in the bush looking for the hiker. On June 24, SAR members found boot prints in an area they suspected to be Darcy. SAR did a massive search of the area around the tracks and could not locate Darcy or his equipment, he has never been found.

Matthew Huszar
Missing: 12/16/2011-p.m., Vancouver, British Columbia
Age at disappearance: 25 years
Water•

Matthew Huszar

Matthew Huszar was an outdoorsman and applied that interest to his academic studies. He studied biology at the University of British Columbia and graduated with honors. He was a very smart young man who enjoyed the Oceanside atmosphere in Vancouver. He was originally from Lethbridge, Alberta, and came to Vancouver for college. In December 2011, he was involved in the restoration of a forty-nine-foot sailboat. He wanted to sail the world.

On December 16, 2011, in the evening hours, Matthew was at the Lamplighter Pub at 92 Water Street in the gaslight district of northern Vancouver, called Gastown. There are several streets that sit close to Vancouver Harbor with a gorgeous harbor view. He was with work colleagues for a holiday celebration; they later stated that he had been drinking alcohol but was not intoxicated. The group decided to leave at some point, and Matthew went his own way. It was the last time anyone saw the geologist alive. He was reported missing by his family after he failed to meet his mother on Vancouver Island the following day. He also missed a meeting with his girlfriend, who had traveled from the United States. He was the type of son, brother, and boyfriend who kept in contact with the people he loved. All contact stopped.

The Vancouver police searched all known areas around Gastown for Matthew. They brought in Bloodhounds, searchers, planes, and helicopters and found nothing. Yes, there were the normal claims by people who stated they saw him on buses, trains, etc. Nothing came of these claims. The police stated early in the investigation that they did not find any indication of foul play.

In one of the longest stretches of searching for a missing person, police found Matthew's body more than two years after he vanished. He disappeared on the north side of Vancouver adjacent to the harbor. His body was located on the opposite side of the city, on the south side in False Creek Harbor. The Canadian press had this statement: "Coroner Barb McLintock says it appears Huszar died shortly after leaving a Gastown pub on December 16, 2011. She says it's still unknown how and why Huszar reached the marina, two kilometers away, and in the opposite direction from his home." Anyone who has dealt with dead bodies knows that if Matthew had been in the water for over one year, nobody could determine within months how long he had been in the water. For the coroner to state that he had been in the water since shortly after leaving the pub is a stretch. Just as the coroner stated, nobody knows how he got into the False Creek Harbor or why his body wasn't seen months prior to when it was discovered. If the claim is that he was in the water for two years, then his body went through two summers of warm water and never rose to the surface.

David Christian
Missing: 03/17/2012-11:30 p.m., Whistler, British Columbia
Age at disappearance: 27 years
Cluster Zone• Water

As we make our way through life, we remember those times when we needed someone to be our friend—someone to keep our mind active, make us feel special, and hang with us. David Christian would've been that person.

David was born in Ireland but had an affinity to travel the world. He was smart and very friendly. He went to college and obtained a three-year degree in bioinformatics and went on to earn a graduate degree. In June 2008 he moved to Toronto with his best buddy, Matt Walsh. The pair wanted to move to the West Coast, and they found a job listing for Whistler Blackcomb Resorts. They were both interviewed and immediately offered jobs. David enrolled in a ski area management class at Selkirk College and was granted his third diploma. The buddies arrived in Whistler for the start of ski season on October 11, 2011.

Every person in every article I reviewed stated that David was a happy person and was kind to everyone. Each person made a special point to state this. He was enjoying a stellar career in Whistler when the night of March 17, 2012, rolled in. David went with his friends to Merlin's Bar and Grill in town. They hung out, and he stayed till 11:30 p.m. David went his own way, and this was the last time anyone saw him alive. On Sunday morning, March 17, David sent a text to a friend at 2:30 a.m. The message in that text was never disclosed and the recipient was never identified, but David was alive at that point. David was supposed to be on a flight Sunday morning to

Vancouver for Sunday mass; he never made it. He wasn't reported missing until Monday morning.

The police brought out canines, helicopters, search and rescue personnel, and the resort's ski patrol. They searched the area around the employee housing and the region outside the bar. Nothing was found. The search continued Monday, Tuesday, and Wednesday. It wasn't local police or search and rescue that found anything of relevant value; it was a member of the community who was walking through the Whistler Fairmont's golf course who found two blue Van skate shoes on the fifteenth fairway. The police were summoned. They were David's shoes.

It's reported that there was a short trail around the shoes that was intermittent. They continued to search and found David's body in several inches of water in Horstman Creek near Lost lake. There were no signs of violence.

The police indicated that all signs showed that David died of hypothermia. They theorized he got disoriented, took the wrong bus, got on the wrong trail, and wandered into the creek after removing his shoes. A March 23, 2012, article in the *Pique News Magazine* had one very important sentence: "It's unknown how Christian ended up in the creek."

David had lived in Whistler for over five months. I've been in this community several times. It's not that large. Anyone would have a very clear understanding of the landscape after a few weeks. David would've known he was on the golf course. The police's description and theory of how David ended up in the creek is as viable as every explanation you will hear about these men disappearing. It doesn't hold water.

David's body was flown back to Dublin, where he was buried.

I could not find an article describing any toxicological results from the autopsy.

Searchers stated that the majority of the trails and campsites had been covered, and the idea of going off trail to search was a near-impossibility because of the rugged and thick terrain.

As of the publishing of this book, there is not one clue as to where Darcy may be. None of Darcy's equipment, nor his campsite, has ever been found.

Raymond Salmen
Missing: 05/28/2013, Harrison Lake, BC
Age at disappearance: 65 years
Water• Canines• Missing Clothes/ Shoes•

This will be recognized by longtime readers as an unusual case. I have stated that I will not include stories in the books that deal with the possibility of drowning. I probably would've excluded this story early in the study, but not now. Canadian officials state they believe that Raymond drowned. I don't think so.

Raymond Salmen was an experienced outdoorsman, camper, and hunter. He left his home with his two dogs and told his wife he'd be camping at Harrison Lake and he'd be back in two weeks. He was going to be spending time in the outdoors, a place he loved. He drove his pickup with a camper to an area west of the lake where there are no established campgrounds. Nothing was heard or seen of Raymond after May 28. There was no cell-phone reception in the area.

On June 9, Agassiz RCMP responded to the area of Raymond's camper on the report of shots fired. Officers found Raymond's camper with his two dogs inside, but no Raymond. They started an intensive search of the area. RCMP called for search reinforcements in an area known as the "48 kilometre mark." Several search groups from

Raymond Salmen

throughout British Columbia responded and started a grid search of the area around the camper.

Four days after the initial call of shots fired, an unusual discovery was made, as is described in the June 18, 2013, edition of *The Province*: "On Thursday, just after 3:00 p.m., crews on board an RCMP chopper spotted balloons about 400 meters north of the abandoned campsite at a secluded beach. Police then uncovered what's believed to be Salmen's clothing, as well as a rifle and spent casings nearby." What they found exactly was the man's backpack in the bush, his shoes, socks, rifle, and shell casings on a small beach. His knife and belt were not found (although there is no absolute proof he had them).

The RCMP believed that Raymond had gotten down to the beach, gotten stuck, and started shooting to draw attention. If he did shoot his rifle, he hit parked cars, and this was reported. The RCMP stated that they think he ditched almost everything he owned and then tried to swim across the lake and drowned, at night. They did put divers into the lake and found nothing. Raymond's wife hired a recovery team with a robotic camera that had recovered over ninety bodies. The recovery team covered every inch of the lake bottom and found nothing.

Raymond's brothers don't believe the RCMP's theory. They think it's possible that Ray ran into foul play. They stated that he had seen odd things out in this area on past trips.

If Raymond were well enough to get down to the beach, why wouldn't he be in good enough condition to get himself out? There is one huge wild card in this mystery. Raymond wouldn't go anywhere without his dogs, and they were found locked in the camper. A June 12, 2013, article on CTV.com had this: "'It's all these mysteries. My mind keeps thinking what could have possibly happened that he would go without the dogs,' his wife Daniela Salmen told CTV News." My question: what if the dogs refused to leave the camper? Raymond obviously went looking for something dangerous and went prepared. He had his backpack and supplies and took his rifle with extra ammunition. He got to the beach, and something deadly confronted him—otherwise, why would he be shooting at cars trying to attract attention?

Summary

The RCMP believes that Raymond drowned. The officers' dive team searched the area, and this was followed up by a specialist in recovering bodies. Nothing was found.

The RCMP wants to close the case and ignore all other outside possibilities. There is a reason that Raymond didn't have the dogs with him. Remember, canines play a role in many of the disappearances I've chronicled. I don't believe that Raymond would strip his clothing, shoes, and rifle and leave them behind as he swam. If there were a choice, he would've waited for daylight and then shot rounds to draw attention. I don't think he believed he had that choice.

Update

In the winter of 2016, a man who worked for search-and-rescue in British Columbia and had been assigned the Raymond Salmen case contacted me. He said there were several highly unusual things that happened while he was there. He first stated that when he arrived with a group of other searchers, they saw a RCMP SWAT team walking out of the woods and getting ready to leave. I asked him why they would be there? He said they were told that the victim had apparently shot at something in the area the previous night, and they were there to ensure it was safe.

Thinking this scenario through doesn't make sense. They found the victim's rifle. All indications suggest that Raymond was trying to get people's attention for some reason, not trying to kill anyone.

The SAR worker also stated that if a SWAT team had already searched the area and ensured the region was safe and nobody was in the grid area, why would a SAR team go back in where they'd just been? As it turned out, the SAR worker stated that they had them confined in a small area near the campsite and vehicle; they never went into the woods or searched a two-mile radius where statistics say the victim would be found. This person also said that there have been many unusual disappearances around this lake.

I appreciated the SAR volunteer reaching out and supplying the fascinating information.

Sylvia Apps
Missing: 07/13/14 at 4:00 p.m.—Strathcona Provincial Park, Vancouver Island, British Columbia, Canada
Age at Disappearance: 69 years
Canines• Provincial Park•
Loss of Clothing•

Sylvia Apps

Certain headlines grab and hold my attention. On July 22, 2014, the headline on CBC Canada was this: "Search for missing hiker Sylvia Apps baffles searchers in Strathcona Park." The park is located on Vancouver Island, a gorgeous and wild location off the coast of British Columbia. I've been to the island several times and am constantly amazed how wild it gets when you move slightly outside of any city. I've documented several highly unusual disappearances from this location.

This case got my attention for several reasons. I had just completed researching the disappearance of Karen Sykes, an extremely fit seventy-year-old outdoor writer, from Mount Rainier National Park. As unusual as Karen's case was, this case would challenge the best search-and-rescue folks in Canada.

Sylvia Apps, like Karen Sykes, was a fit older female out on the trails. Her sons commented that Sylvia was "tough as nails" and would walk for fifteen miles if the situation called for it.

On July 8, 2014, Sylvia left her North Courtenay home on the east side of Vancouver Island near the geographical center and went to the Paradise Meadows Trailhead approximately ten miles west of her residence. She had called her relatives and told them of her plans, the date she would be out, and the place she was going. She did everything right.

Many hikers make critical mistakes in not being adequately equipped for their journey. Sylvia had two cell phones with extra batteries, a navigational trail guide, and more. A July 26, 2014, article in the *Huffington Post* had a statement from the head of the Comox Search and Rescue group, Paul Berry, who said Sylvia had been properly equipped for her trip.

Nobody really knows where Sylvia was from the day she left, July 8 at 11:00 a.m., until she summited Castle Crag in Strathcona Park on July 10. We have confirmation she did summit, because she signed the logbook at the top, and officials have a confirmed sighting of her in the area of the mountain on July 11.

I encourage readers to get on the Internet and look at YouTube and Google images of the Castle Crag. This is a gorgeous but extremely rocky, boulder-ridden crag. The area can be very desolate, but the views are breathtaking.

Sylvia's trip was supposed to end on July 13 at 4:00 p.m. When she didn't contact friends and relatives, the RCMP was called, and she was listed as a missing person.

The Comox SAR group was one of the primary organizations that started the effort to locate Sylvia. The RCMP put their search dogs, as well as search-and-rescue dogs, on the mountain. The effort rallied six different SAR teams from throughout Canada. Two helicopters equipped with FLIR flew the skies for several days.

The seven-day search effort did produce some very intriguing evidence. A July 22, 2014, article on CBC Canada had this information: "Searchers found her backpack in one location, her walking sticks and camera in another, and her name in the logbook on one of the peaks, but not Apps herself." On July 26, 2014, CBC Canada reported, "Paul Berry, president of Comox Valley Ground search and rescue said it was the first time they had failed to find someone despite finding all of their belongings."

I've had several discussions with people about the fact that the backpack was in a different location than the walking sticks and camera. It's possible she put down the backpack to take a few photos. It would make sense that she would have walking sticks in her hands with her camera. For Sylvia to drop all three items simultaneously indicates complete incapacitation, but articles indicated that she was an extremely fit and experienced hiker and backpacker.

As I wrote this story, I was thinking about the disappearance of Karen Sykes from Mount Rainier National Park. Both ladies were older, highly experienced, fit, and extremely knowledgeable of hiking protocol. Both vanished. Coincidence? There are 285 air miles between the location where Sylvia vanished and the one where Karen disappeared. Two hundred and eighty-five air miles and twenty-five days separate two women and their stories.

If search-and-rescue workers were able to find Sylvia's property but not her, was she there? Here is a partial list of the groups that searched:

- Royal Canadian Mounted Police (RCMP) Canine
- Port Alberni SAR
- Parksville SAR
- Nanaimo SAR
- Lake Cowichan SAR
- Comox Valley RCMP
- Grizzly Helicopters
- West Coast Helicopters

- RCMP Aircraft
- 442 Squadron CFB Comox
- Provincial Emergency Air Support

Where is Sylvia Apps?

Sukhjeet Saggu
Missing: 06/05/15 at 4:00 p.m.—Lindeman Lake, Chilliwack Provincial Park
Age at Disappearance: 20
Canines• Boulder Field• Water• Point of Separation

I receive thousands of e-mails a year. Many readers send me their thoughts and ideas about cases. One of the most common responses I get is that many of the victims are dropped into their positions. Some say this is blatantly obvious, and others are subtler.

When you read this story, I want you to read the statements of the searchers and people involved carefully. It is rare in the world of SAR or law enforcement that you get them being upfront and straightforward with their comments.

Sukhjeet Saggu was a recent graduate of Enver Creek Secondary School in Surrey, British Columbia. Surrey is almost directly west of Chilliwack Provincial Park, a location he visited on June 5, 2015, with a few friends.

Sukhjeet was walking from the parking lot of the trail to Lindeman Lake with two friends. For a reason that has never been made clear, the following happened and is described in the June 7, 2015, article in the CBC.CA: "Chilliwack Search and Rescue was called to the area early Friday after a young man went jogging ahead of his two friends on the trail to Lindeman Lake. When the friends arrived at the lake, the man couldn't be found. They searched up and down the two kilometer trail, but turned up nothing."

Chilliwack SAR arrived on scene, searched till dark, and found nothing. Doug Fraser, the SAR manager for the group, made several appearances on local channels, expressing his shock that the young man couldn't be found. Nothing about the incident made sense.

SAR arrived early on June 6 and started to cover all areas on the ground. An RCMP helicopter arrived on the scene later in the day and started their search. At 2:00 p.m., they made a very unusual discovery that shocked everyone. North from Lindeman Lake is the trail to Greendrop Lake. The pilot was flying along this path. The *Van City Buzz* of June 7, 2015, had these details: "An RCMP helicopter spotted the man's body within a boulder field Saturday afternoon. At this time, the cause of death has not been released, but circumstances of the disappearance have been deemed highly unusual as he was found away from the meeting point with his friends-far away from the lake and any trail."

Several articles showed the boulder field, and the gradient looks very slight and appears to be hard to fall from.

The June 9, 2015, edition of the *Now* newspaper had these additional details: "Liana Wright of the BC Coroners service said Saggu's body was found 'at the foot of a loose rock incline.'" She made it clear he hadn't fallen down a cliff.

Doug Fraser was interviewed for the June 7, 2015, edition of the CBC.CA: "'It was very, very strange and difficult to explain why he ended up where he did,' said Fraser, adding that the boulder field is quite a bit of elevation above the lake, and a fair distance from the trail."

I actually saw two of the interviews with Doug Fraser. He looked upset. The wording he used to describe what happened was much the same as is used above. It appears that everyone involved in this incident had a difficult time trying to explain away the odd circumstances under which Sukhjeet vanished and where he was found. I searched for hours to see if the British Columbia Coroner's Service ever released a cause of death; I could not locate one.

If Sukhjeet ran off and continued running, as some may believe, why didn't canine teams follow the scent to the body? Why would a young man who was having a fun afternoon with friends run off miles down the trail, go off trail, climb up in elevation, and end up in a boulder field?

This incident is just eight air miles southeast from the disappearance of Gordon Sagoo. Look at the size of British Columbia and think about what an odd coincidence it is that these two cases happened to be so close in geographical terms. Is this mere coincidence?

Doug Fraser knows his mountains like you know the neighbor-hood where you live. If this professional is confused about how this happened, you should be concerned.

Neville Jewell
Missing: 09/12/15—6:00 p.m., Cy-press Mountain, British Columbia,
Age at disappearance: 52 years
Weather • Cluster Zone

Cypress Mountain located in West Vancouver, British Columbia is a gorgeous spot. I can remember taking the lift to the top of the hill and hiking into the countryside. It is lush, thick, green and you can quick-ly get into a very rural area. People vacationing in all regions of British Columbia have to understand that it rains there a lot during all seasons, dress accordingly.

Neville Jewell

On Saturday, September 12, 2015, 52-year-old Neville Jewell, a native of Ireland and now living in White Rock, British Columbia decided to take a hike into Cypress Mountain of West Vancouver. He was in decent shape but didn't have significant hiking experience. Neville parked his car in the parking lot of the Cypress Mountain ski resort and hiked into the mountains. At 2:00 p.m. he sent his girlfriend a text message stating that he made it to West Lion and told her it was a strenuous hike and all was good. This is the last communication.

The 52-year-old hiker had told his girlfriend in days prior that he was thinking about going back to Ireland to see his mom. When the girlfriend didn't hear from him at the end of his hiking day, she thought he had gone overseas. As the days moved forward, workers at Cypress Mountain saw Neville's car in the lot and got increasing-ly uncomfortable with the possibilities of why it was there. Seven days after Jewell left on his hike, Cypress Mountain contacted the West Vancouver Police and reported the car as suspicious. The police tracked down Neville's daughter, and she confirmed that under the circumstances that he is missing. She explained that she has a good relationship with her dad, they didn't communicate much. The police called North Shore Search and Rescue, and soon they had people on the mountain.

The effort to locate Neville was challenging as they were almost a week behind his track. There were multiple notes in various articles that SAR faced wind and rain off and on for the entirety of the search, which culminated in just 3 days. This December 27, 2015, article in *The Province* had these crucial details, "After the search was called off, Jewell's cell phone data was further analyzed, and North Shore Rescue searchers pinpointed some areas they wanted to go back and re-examine. However, attempts in October and November were foiled by bad weather."

Rescuers believed that Neville had taken the Howe Sound Crest Trail and had made it to West Lion. The hike was slightly over 6 miles, a significant effort for someone who hadn't had much mountain experience. The route of the trail was directly north, paralleling the coast and staying predominantly on the ridgeline. The mountains in this area are very steep and seem to almost swallow up people. The number of individuals missing in the West Vancouver area is significant and rarely discussed. The one item that sets this area of British Columbia apart is that the coast, rivers, creeks are all close by; water is almost everywhere.

There were additional search efforts on more advanced cell phone data. There was some belief that he might have wandered in the Capilano watershed, at a lower elevation, very thick and lush. Searchers went in the Capilano and found nothing.

Neville's case is one of hundreds and hundreds I have documented where the people would probably have been found if they would've had a PLB. Sometimes I think there should be a national campaign, probably by the NPS or the USFS to educate the public that these devices exist and they are not that expensive, cheaper than a smartphone.

I have documented other disappearances from British Columbia in *Missing 411: The Devil's in the Details*, *Missing 411: Hunters*, *Missing 411: Off the Grid*, and *Missing 411: A Sobering Coincidence*.

Deanna Wertz
Missing: 07/19/16—Salmon Arm, British Columbia
Age at Disappearance: 46 years
• Canines• German Ancestry

    I almost dismissed this case for its association with two other women missing from the Okanagan region. Deanna Wertz lived on Yankee Flats Road in Salmon Arm, the same road from which thirty-one-year-old Ashley Simpson disappeared on April 28, 2016. In the Simpson case, RCMP went through the residence the victim shared with her boyfriend and took many personal articles from each person. The Mounties stated that the cases were not related, and it would appear they are treating the Simpson case as a crime and the Wertz case as a missing person. The RCMP made an incorrect statement when they said there is nothing to link the two cases, however. How about two women missing off the same rural road? In spite of the coincidence, I think there is much on the Wertz incident that deserves to be here. The third woman missing from Salmon Arm in that same six-month cycle took a ride from an individual and was never seen again.

    Deanna Wertz was a wife and sister. She and her husband lived on Yankee Flats Road, between Vernon and Salmon Arm, British Columbia. Vernon is the northern edge of the giant Okanagan Lake, and Salmon Arm has the equally large Shuswap Lake.

    The Wertz home sits in a beautiful area on a dirt road that crosses a rough mountain region known for its beauty. On July 19, 2016, in the morning hours, Deanna's husband was going to work, said goodbye to his wife, and asked what she was going to do with her day. She said she was going to take a hike. After Mr. Wertz left, Deanna called friends, discussed local issues, and again told them she was going for a hike. This was the last contact anyone had with the forty-six-year-old Salmon Arm resident.

    Mr. Wertz came home, found his wife missing, and made some calls to friends and family. She was eventually formally reported missing on July 22.

    The *Saint Catherine's Standard* of January 14, 2017, ran an article that included a segment about Deanna's disappearance. Here are some details about her heritage: "The First Nations label wasn't an issue. Deanna Wertz carries aboriginal and German blood in her veins." This is important to our research, as an unusually large number of Germans seem to go missing. Considering this area of Salmon Arm has a high concentration of First Nations people, finding someone with German blood would seem like finding a needle in the haystack.

The RCMP mounted a huge search for Deanna, which is described in the *Salmon Arm Observer* of August 18, 2016: "Many areas were searched again, by ground search and rescue teams, RCMP Police Service Dogs and RCMP aircraft resources." They also put up roadblocks on Yankee Flats Road and interviewed drivers. They found nothing, and canines never found a scent trail. RCMP search managers stated they were focusing their efforts on Spa Creek, Spa Lake, Williams Road, Lionel Road, and Watson Road.

Deanna was known to take many long hikes. One of the unusual facts of her disappearance is that she usually took her dog. When her husband returned home, however, the dog was in the house.

Three women missing in a six-month cycle is an outrageous number, and law enforcement would be fools to not look for an association. Two women missing off the same road within three months of each other is almost a slap in the face. As I stated earlier, you need to dig into the facts. I find these three cases incredibly odd. In case readers do not know, one of the biggest cases in British Columbia history is still ongoing with the "Highway of Tears." This is a series of murders and disappearances on a section of Highway 16 extending between Prince Rupert and Prince George. Many of the victims were First Nations Women. Some investigators estimate that there are as many as twenty victims, while First Nations communities say that number could be over forty. Two suspects have been associated with two cases; nobody has been arrested for the majority of the cases.

Gordon Sagoo
Missing: 08/14/16 at 2:00 p.m.—Baby Mundy Peak, Chilliwack, BC
Age at Disappearance: 50 years
• Runner, Canines, Wilderness

I don't think I've ever written about someone who went through such a profound life change as Gordon Sagoo did. When Gordon was in his forties, family members said he knew he was obese and took up running. He turned into an outstanding trail runner who posted great times. It was during this life transformation that he left his job as general manager of Apollo Signs in Vancouver and became a life coach and personal fitness trainer. He made his new passion for fitness his career.

MISSING

Gordon Sagoo last seen Aug 14th Cheam Mountain Range – Baby Munday Peak

If you have any information please contact:

Chilliwack RCMP: 604.792.4611   SAR: 604.792.3414

Gordon Sagoo

Gordon spent significant time in the mountains running trails and enjoying his passion with family and friends. On August 14, 2016, Gordon; his friend, Sherril Budai and another unidentified friend went hiking in the area of Baby Mundy Peak in the Cheam Mountain range. This location is just ten miles north of the US border and Northern Cascades National Park. The website desibuzz-bc.com had the following details from an August 18, 2016, article: "Sherril Budai was hiking the trail with Sagoo and another hiker at the time. She said Sagoo separated from the group to explore some other peaks, and planned on meeting them before returning to the trailhead, reported CBC News. 'We thought that Gordon was ahead of us on the trail, we could see him in the distance,' said Budai. 'When we got to the trailhead he wasn't there, so the other hiker went back looking for him.'" From other sources, I gleaned that the other mountain he might have been exploring was Mount Knight.

It was the night of August 14 that Gordon was reported as a missing person to RCMP. There were officers on-site the first evening.

The following morning started an all-out blitz to look for the trail runner. Friends told RCMP that Gordon had at least three liters of water with him and a cell phone.

The RCMP obtained SAR assistance from Chilliwack, Coquitlam, Surrey, and Lions SAR Units. They received air support from the RCMP Comox 442 Transport and Rescue Squadron and from Talon and Valley helicopters. They had canine ground searching done by the Lower Mainland Integrated Police Dog Service and the Canadian Search and Disaster Dog Association. The RCMP also put up a specially designed radio-controlled plane to search. SAR commanders met and decided there was nothing else they could do to find Gordon. The search was terminated on August 22.

Gordon's family started a GoFundMe that earned more than $30,000 to extend the search, but the extended effort found nothing of value.

When you review the facts of this case, the classic elements are present. Gordon is fine until there is a separation point between him and his friends. Something very unusual happened that we might never understand. Gordon had his cell phone with him.

If he were down the side of the mountain or in a gully, the phone transmission would not hit a cell tower. Gordon was a trail runner; he wasn't using ropes and pitons and was known to be in phenomenal shape. Trail runners usually stay on trails and aren't taking extraordinary risks, such as hanging off the sides of ledges. Even if Gordon was in a precarious area, one of the helicopters used in the search effort was equipped with FLIR. He would have put off a profound heat signature, which would have led to his being located.

Everyone who commented on Gordon's personal traits stated that he was mentally and physically strong. I hope Gordon's family members possess those same personal attributes.

Do you believe in coincidences? I think it is highly strange that the only names close to Gordon's last name I have ever documented in a disappearance is Sukhjeet Saggu, just miles from where Gordon vanished, weird.

Debbie Blair
Missing: 09/29/16 at noon—Cypress Mountain, North Vancouver, British Columbia
Age at Disappearance: 65 years
• Weather, Canines, Wilderness

In the last few years, I have started to pay close attention to reports from the media on people missing with dementia or early onset dementia. In the times I hear from a friend, emergency services worker, or relative about

Debbie Blair

one of these cases, 100 percent of the time they state that the reports are completely false—the person never had dementia.

On November 3, 2016, I received an e-mail from a close friend of Debbie Blair. She stated that Debbie had disappeared off the Baden Powell Trail in Cypress Provincial Park north of Vancouver. She said a continuous and almost nonstop series of storms had hit the area and asked if I would look into it. When I did research on

Ms. Blair, I found that she was a clown and dancer for a local band and enjoyed performing.

Every article I researched on this case said Debbie was an active hiker who met friends to hike Cypress Mountain Provincial Park on September 29, 2016. The friends split into two groups, one fast and one a bit slower. Debbie went with the faster group as they headed into thick woods.

It was approximately noon when Debbie realized she was having difficulty keeping up with the faster group. An October 1, 2016, article in the *Vancouver Sun* explained what happened, as told by SAR leader Mike Banks: "He said Blair had been traveling with a faster group of hikers but had hurt her knee so she went to find a slower group to continue the journey. He believes while looking for the other group, Blair hit a junction and went off trail." Many of the stories I've documented involve a person that who gets ill or has an injury. The person decides to leave the group (point of separation) and disappears. Banks went on to say that SAR was confronted with heavy rain on Saturday. My contact that sent me the e-mail wrote that it rained twenty-eight of thirty-one days in October in this area.

It was confirmed that Debbie was last seen on Donut Rock Trail junction on Cypress Mountain, leading toward Eagle Bluffs at noon on September 29. There was a three-day search for Debbie. Officials found tracks in the Dick Creek area, where searchers had to push their way through extremely thick brush; they never confirmed if the tracks were from her.

SAR commanders stated that the three-day search effort utilized one hundred searchers, multiple dog teams, and two helicopter searches with FLIR, and volunteer searchers went back multiple times in October. They said Debbie was in very good physical condition but wasn't dressed for subfreezing temperatures.

One of the last items in the e-mail sent to me was an interesting note. Debbie's friend said a West Vancouver Police detective has this case and told friends of the victim that this is one of the strangest cases he has seen in his twenty-year career.

The area around greater Vancouver has a significant number of unusual disappearances in its mountains. Where are these victims going?

Alison Leanne Raspa
Missing: 11/23/17- 1:15 A.M., Whistler, BC
Age at disappearance: 25 years
Previously Searched• Water• Missing Clothing

I can remember the first time I wrote about a strange disappearance at a ski resort. I could not believe that someone could disappear so quickly and oddly as the number of times I have documented such a case. I have read about similar matters in Vail, Colorado, Lake Tahoe region of California and others.

In May of 2016, Alison Raspa was living in Perth Australia when she decided to take a job at the Westin Resort and Spa in Whistler. She moved to the ski area and immediately liked the outdoor feel, definite change of seasons, and the young people that are the majority of the labor in the city.

On the night of November 22, 2017, Alison went with friends to the Three Below Restaurant and Bar on Blackcomb Way in downtown Whistler. She had a few drinks, socialized with those friends, and decided to head back to her room at approximately 11:30 P.M. She caught the local bus that travels up the highway and was dropped at the southern edge of town about five kilometers from the bar she was drinking. At 1:15 P.M., Alison sent a text to a girlfriend stating she was lost. It was later confirmed through an investigation that she was seen exiting the bus at Highway 99 and Lake Placid Way. This location is north of Alpha Lake Park and in an area of several businesses. The 1:15 P.M. text was the last time anyone heard from Alison. When she didn't appear for work at the Westin the next morning, friends went to check her room and then called the local RCMP.

The RCMP started a search at the area where they pinged her cell phone, the area of Alpha Lake Park. Her backpack and wallet were found in an open field north of the lake. A citizen walking through the area the morning she disappeared saw a women's coat and turned it in to police, this was Alison's. The coat was found in the same general area as her wallet and backpack. Her cell phone was located in Alpha Lake Park.

Once the RCMP started to see that Alison appeared to be dropping items, they began to spread a rumor that she probably had hypothermia. This seemed to be a believable excuse to the press, and it was something that was talked about in the community.

Details about the search for Alison were documented in the December 6, 2017 edition of the *News.au*, "Rescue workers and RCMP divers equipped with sonar technology searched the lake and surrounding areas but failed to find any further trace of her." The search of the lake is critical. Not only did the RCMP put divers in the water, but they also used sonar. Divers can only see as far as visibility allows, sonar goes through the murkiness and shows everything solid in the water. There was a second search of the lake weeks after the first, and again nothing was located. After the second search, the RCMP did not look in the lake again.

Alpha Park Lake is located at the far southern edge of Whistler below Mount Sproatt. It sits on the edge of the wilderness in an area of the city that would not get a vast amount of foot traffic or witnesses in the early morning hours.

The profile on Alison was that she was an athlete; she had a black belt in martial arts; she was friendly and happy. She was a stable person that did not drink to excess, and her friends stated that the night she vanished she was not intoxicated.

The SAR for Alison was comprehensive and included hundreds of ground searchers, a helicopter and two weeks of on-scene investigation.

Ms. Raspa's brother and family flew to Whistler when they learned of her disappearance and carried on the search efforts long after the RCMP terminated their efforts. I encourage everyone to go onto Google Maps and look at the size of Alpha Lake, and it is not huge.

There were no new developments on this incident until 7:30 P.M. on March 16, 2018. A resident was walking along the northern end of Alpha Lake Park and thought they observed a body in the water and called emergency services. Law enforcement and Whistler Fire Department recovered the partially frozen body of Alison Raspa. The body was sent to autopsy.

Several groups understand that this case does not make sense and some media outlets have pickup up on this fact. The United Kingdom's *Cosmopolitan Magazine* ran an article on March 27,

2018, that had these details, "The fact that Alison's jacket was found discarded led investigators to believe she likely suffered from hypothermia. Temperatures in Whistler can plummet to -5 degrees Celsius, and one of the symptoms of hypothermia is hot flashes, which can trigger sufferers to remove their clothes in the belief they're too warm. However, it's thought on that night in November that temperatures in the area were nearer to 8 degrees Celsius, which isn't necessarily keeping with the hypothermia theory. As it stands, Brit Hill remains in the dark about what actually happened to her friend. "Whistler was still a new place to her, so maybe she took the wrong path and got lost," she told the Australian. "I'm still trying to work it out in my head, and it just doesn't make sense." " I also watched a report on Canadian television that stated at 10:00 P.M. the night Alison left the bar, and it was 10 degrees Celsius in Whistler.

Alison was riding on a heated bus; this is confirmed. She was dropped north of the lake approximately four miles from the bar she had left. She left the bus warm, wearing a coat. Eight degrees Celsius equals 46 degrees Fahrenheit. It would take someone quite a while to develop hypothermia at that temperature.

I want people to think through this logically. Why would a young woman drop some of the most valuable items in her life, her wallet, and cell phone? The facts in these cases almost always have the victim leaving their cell phone behind; it's almost as though they need to separate themselves from the phones tracking ability. One of the critical profile points I have documented hundreds of times is bodies being found in a location that has been previously searched. I have never alleged that SAR teams had not done a thorough job, quite the contrary. All indicators are that the body was never in the location when searchers were looking. In my other books, bodies have been found in places that were searched dozens of times. Do I believe that Alison walked into onto the lake or into the water, no? There are far too many instances where this exact scenario has replicated itself dozens of times and there is no satisfactory answer.

I cannot find a cause of death that was listed by the coroner's office in Alison's incident. Many of the cases that mimic this incident can be found in Missing 411- A Sobering Coincidence. In many of the cases I wrote about, the coroners could not determine a cause of death.

Travis Thomas
Missing: 08/07/18, Bartlett Island, British Columbia, Canada
Age at disappearance: 40 years
Water• Point of Separation

Bartlett Island is a small piece of land just off the south-central shore of Vancouver Island. It is approximately 4000 feet long and 2500 feet wide with very rocky shores and a few nice beaches. The interior of the island has a lush and thick forest that is so thick; it makes it difficult to travel through the center of the land mass.

In August of 2018, Travis Thomas was a member of the Ahousaht First Nations group that lived in Ahousaht, approximately eight miles northwest of Bartlett Island. Travis was a lifelong member of the community, played and coached basketball and was also a marathon runner in excellent physical condition. Early in August, Travis told his elders that he wanted to take a spiritual journey of cleansing and a plan was put into place where he would go to Bartlett Island, fast, live in isolation and reach spiritual enlightenment. This was a common practice of his group and a location they regularly went for the cleansing. Travis was taken to the island by elders, dropped off and would be checked on every two days. One other group member was staying on the other side of the island. Travis was last seen on August 7, 2018.

On August 9, family members came to Bartlett Island to check on Travis and could not locate him. They searched the island for two days and then called for additional assistance. The Canadian Coast Guard, Ahousaht RCMP, RCMP air services and volunteers scoured the island for 30 days. The September 12, 2018 edition of the Hashithsa had these details of the search, "The RCMP has been to the island with RCMP Dog Service. On August 30 the RCMP dog team returned to the island to search the beaches, with negative results." There were numerous comments from searchers explaining the difficult the search of the small island had been because of the thickness of the forest in the center of the island.

The RCMP determined that Travis and the other person on the island had never interacted. Neither man had access to a boat, and there was no other way to leave the island. Family and friends have returned to the island multiple times since the search efforts terminated and have not found Travis.

The southeast portion of Vancouver Island and the northern shore of the Olympic Peninsula in Washington has a series of puzzling disappearances. All of the cases involve males, and the majority are young boys.

Chapter Conclusion

There is no other province in Canada that comes close to the number of missing people matching our profile points as British Columbia. There is no other city in Canada that has the number of people missing within an eighty-mile radius as Vancouver, 31. The numbers of missing in this province are staggering.

There are so many people missing in British Columbia, there are clusters within clusters (Refer to map). The standard United States cluster is eighty miles in diameter. Within the Vancouver cluster, the most obvious secondary cluster is Mount Seymour. There are six confirmed disappearances in the immediate area of this mountain:

Arthur Tibbet	11/19/53- 29 years- Never Found	
Michael Bryant	11/14/70- 32 years- Never Found	
Charlie Musso	09/07/87- 61 years- Never Found	
Steven Eby	11/14/93- 29 years - Found Headless	
Karl Walter	06/28/97- 65 years- Never Found	
Jared Stanley	01/10/05- 25 years- Deceased in Creek	

The percentage of people missing on Mount Stanley and never found is high at 66%. The finding of Steven Eby's headless body is troubling to me. I cannot ever remember reading any case of a missing person where the body was located without a head. All of these cases happened within twelve air miles of downtown Vancouver.

Within a fifteen-mile radius to the west of Mount Seymour, there are four additional disappearances. Of the eight missing people, 25% are females. I have been to Vancouver and Northern Vancouver area several times. The mountains to the north are steep and rugged, but the numbers of missing are mind-boggling. I doubt that the residents of the metropolitan Vancouver area have any idea how many people have vanished, some within the eyesight of the city.

Vancouver Island could be a missing person study by itself. I have twelve documented cases on the island and five on the southern side. I have always found the Strait of Juan De Fuca, a fascinating place. This body of water separated the northern peninsula of the Olympic Peninsula in Washington from the southern side of Vancouver Island. Three missing boys on the northern side of the Olympic Peninsula vanished on the beach under very suspicious circumstances. There were two different incidents separated by one hundred miles where the boys disappeared. All of the cases on the southern side of Vancouver Island are all males. I don't know of any other body of water that has the number of missing on both sides of the strait.

I'd be remiss if I didn't address the disarticulated feet found in tennis shoes found in the general area of the Salish Sea. The vast majority of these have been located in the greater Vancouver area and approximately five in Washington. I know of one other case in the last ten years that was found on a northern California beach. The number of incidents in recent times is probably near 20. Various articles written about this issue have interviewed people employed by the coroner's office in Vancouver. These experts have stated that there is nothing suspicious about these cases, and the vast majority have been identified, and the explanation is that the victims were suicidal.

I did an extensive multi-day archive search from 1900 until 2019, looking for cases of feet found in shoes on coastal waters. I found a total of four instances in 119 years, none in the same area, all in different locations throughout North America. Other than the cases in Vancouver that were identified in recent times, I could not locate any in years prior. If this is a common trait of the water and currents, why weren't there any cases from 1900-1960 in the Vancouver area? If disarticulating feet are so common, why aren't there feet washing up in San Francisco, San Diego, Long Beach, Miami, Pensacola, Sarasota, Tampa, New Orleans, Washington DC, Boston, and Biloxi? These are locations that have bridges, bays, and currents and fit the description supplied by experts.

If you couple the fact that the greater Vancouver area has more disappearances matching our profile that any other urban city in the world with the unusually high numbers of disarticulated feet found, you have a highly unique region.

Manitoba

Population: 1,362,000
Capital City: Winnipeg
   The majority of the province of Manitoba sits over the top of North Dakota with approximately one-third of the southern border sitting over Minnesota. The western boundary is next to Saskatchewan, and the east is Ontario. The Northern border is with Nunavut. The northeastern section of the province sits on the shored of Hudson Bay. This area of Canada is known as the province with 100,000 lakes. Here is a list of some of those freshwater lakes and their square miles:

Lake Winnipeg	9,416 square miles
Lake Winnipegosis	2075 square miles
Lake Manitoba	1785 square miles

   The word, "Manitoba" comes from the First Nations saying, "The God Who Speaks." The Native American and First Nations people have a significant portion of the Manitoba population with the Assiniboin and Ojibwa's in one region and the Cree, Chipewyan, and Inuit in another. The Inuit are known to United States residents as Eskimos.
   The agricultural economy is vital to Manitoba with the short growing season the favorite crops are flaxseed, rapeseed, oats, rye, sugar beets, sunflower, and corn. The livestock industry has continued to increase in size in the last decade, and growth is expected to continue to rise. The one sector that has gained significant momentum is manufacturing and technology, and both centered in the Winnipeg area.
   Because Manitoba stretches from the states to the frigid north, animal life is quite diverse. Visitors can expect to see deer, moose, elk, black bear, foxes, and coyotes. If you travel to the Hudson Bay area, you might also see a polar bear.
   Our geographical cluster map of North America has almost no disappearances in North or South Dakota. If you travel directly north into Manitoba, there are several missing that are identified on our map that forms a cluster zone. One of the main differences between the Dakota states and the province are the two vast bodies of water in

Manitoba. Lake Manitoba and Lake Winnipeg are both within fifty miles of the United States border with our identified cluster of missing people within twenty miles of Lake Winnipeg. We encourage everyone to go to our website (www.canammissing.com) and purchase a copy of our cluster map and stick it on the wall you pass by daily. The more people that look at this map and attempt to understand the cluster distribution, the better chance we have of solving this issue.

Manitoba Missing Person List by Date

Missing Person	Date Missing• Age• Sex
T.H. Vigfusson	05/04/34-1:00 A.M.• 70• F
Betty Wolfrum	05/15/34•4•F
Florence Spence	08/05/34 at 3:00 p.m.•3•F
Frank Goy	08/07/34 •7•M
George Wanke	07/27/35•58•M
Jack Pike	09/05/35•5•M
Simon Skogan	07/02/40•9•M
James McAmmond	10/05/41•19•M
Alex Thorne	10/04/58–Unk•44•M
Madeline Grisdale	07/06/86-Unk •49•F
Marcus McKay	07/15/00–PM•8•M
Mark McKelvey	07/24/17-8:30 A.M.• 36• M

Mrs. T.H. Vigfusson
Missing: 05/04/34-1:00 A.M., Weedy Point, Manitoba
Age at disappearance: 70 years
Water• Previously Searched• Point of Separation

During my time investigating missing people, I have seen mistakes on top of errors which eventually lead to disappearance or death. In this incident, many factors led to a woman leaving the presence of a neighbor and then vanishing.

As you read this narrative, you are going to see that is not like the majority of the stories in this book, but it is like several other stories I have documented in the nine books.

In early May of 1934, Mrs. and Mrs. T.H. Vigfusson and their son (Stoney) lived on the northeast shore of Lake Manitoba. This was Mr. Vigfusson's second wife. His first marriage had a very odd ending in 1884. They were living in Iceland when his wife went on a shopping trip, and was returning home when an avalanche caught the woman, swept her into the sea where she drowned. Keep this story in mind as this disappearance continues to evolve.

On May 3, 1934, Mrs. T.H. Vigfusson left her blind and sick husband with her son and took her buggy to Steep Rock (12 miles north of Weedy Point) on a shopping trip. On the way back home, the shafts on her carriage broke, and she was picked up by a storekeeper from the same city, F.E. Snidal. The storekeeper got the woman within a mile and a half of her home when he saw that his gasoline was dangerously low and let her out of his car. The area where she was dropped is thickly wooded and goes straight towards her home. She was let out at approximately 1:00 A.M.

On May 4, 1934, a cousin of Mrs. Vigfusson stopped by their residence and realized that she never made it home. The cousin contacted other relatives and friends, and a search was started. The Gypsumville RCMP arrived and organized 70 people to search the area from where Mrs. Vigfusson was last seen and where her home was located. All of this was happening near Lake Manitoba.

Mr. Vigfusson gave an interview after his wife disappeared, and it was posted in the May 9, 1934 edition of the *Winnipeg Tribune*, "At the home of Mr. and Mrs. Gislason, Tuesday, this story was told by Mr. Vigfusson that early Friday morning he fell asleep while he waited for his wife to return from Steep Rock. Suddenly he awakened, he said and saw his wife before him. She was calling for help, but as he moved toward her, she disappeared. He declares that the visitation was not a dream, but that his wife stood before him."

At the time of this event, Lake Manitoba was still partially frozen, but it also had large blocks of ice breaking up. Mrs. Vigfusson was a very wise traveler and lived in the area for decades. A May 9, 1934 article in the *Winnipeg Tribune* had these details, "They (fellow residents) point out that she was thoroughly familiar with the district surrounding her home. Her friends do not believe it possible that she could have become confused in the bush during such a short walk." The six-day search did find one footprint near the lake that searchers believed may have belonged to the missing lady. Nothing was 100%, but that was the only item that was close to pointing towards finding the victim.

Nothing new happened on this incident until May 11, 1934, and is explained in the May 12, 1934 edition of the *Windsor Star*, "Stoney (son of the victim) had lain down to rest just before noon yesterday when he fell into a fitful sleep. Without heed to others, he jumped from his cot and raced to a spot on the beach. There he found his mother's body. With the dream fading from memory, Stoney said that voices kept telling him to, "go to the beach. There is a letter for you." Mrs. Vigfusson's body had $36.55 on it, the right amount she would've had after going shopping. The RCMP surmised that she wandered onto the ice at dark, drowned and was later washed ashore. There was never any explanation of how searchers on the water and beaches failed to locate the lady.

Several articles said that this area around Lake Manitoba are superstitious and found this disappearance eerily similar to the loss of Mr. Vigfusson's first wife. Both women were coming back from shopping, and both supposedly drowned.

I have documented approximately five different incidents where people had dreams about a disappearance and then were spoken to in the middle of the night about where a friend or loved one was located. In each incident, the recipient of the dream was able to go to the described location and find the body. From the facts explained in news archives, the finding of the remains cannot be luck or happenstance. In past disappearances, I have documented that parallel this case, and I am always trying to understand where these voices that are heard are coming from and who made them.

There was never an autopsy done on this death. We don't know how long Mrs. Vigfusson was in the water or on the beach or if she drowned or died of possible exposure.

Betty Wolfrum
Missing: 05/15/34, Moosehorn, Manitoba
Age at disappearance: 4
German• Weather• Missing Clothes-Shoes•

When considering the thousands of missing person cases I've researched over the years, the Betty Wolfrum disappearance has a special place on my list as one of the most unusual.

Moosehorn, Manitoba, is approximately 160 miles north of the United States border and 120 miles northwest of Winnipeg. The town is located on Highway 6 just north of Dog Lake and just south of Lake Saint Martin in an area surrounded by large bodies of water and wetlands. A large farming community predominantly supports the region.

The Wolfrum family owned a small farm on the outskirts of Moosehorn just southwest of Spearhill. On May 15, 1934, Carl Wolfrum put sleeping four-year-old Betty in a small carriage in front of the farmhouse and went into the field to do spring seeding. Betty Wolfrum disappeared.

The Wolfrum farm is in a very remote area of Manitoba that is dotted by small family farms. It has very few visitors, and it's rare to see a neighbor traveling the roadway. Where there is not farmland, there is significant tundra and wetlands with swamps. The day Betty disappeared, Carl did not see anyone near his home or hear anyone driving on the roadway. He also didn't see any dust clouds on the roads near his farm, which appear when someone is traveling the roads.

Carl discovered his daughter was missing and promptly searched the yard and farm before he contacted neighbors for assistance. After a lengthy search, a neighbor left to contact the RCMP. The searchers were aware that Betty was young, and she didn't speak English. Mrs. Wolfrum was from Germany and had only taught Betty basic words in German.

The first five days of searching were very uneventful. Over one hundred police officers, farmers, and other volunteers scoured the farms and swamps surrounding the Wolfrum farm without finding any trace of Betty. On Saturday morning the clouds dumped heavy rain in the area, and this convinced the RCMP that Betty would not survive. The nights had been brisk, and the general feeling was that searchers had covered every possible area where Betty could be and they hadn't found anything.

On Sunday at approximately 2:00 p.m., Spearhill farmer Roy Rosin left his farmhouse and took a walk, hoping to find Betty. Approximately two miles from the Wolfrum residence, Roy found Betty walking in a swampy area. She was semi-conscious and calling for her dad. Roy picked the girl up and carried her home. A doctor was summoned and examined Betty.

A May 21, 1934, article in the *Saskatoon Star* had the following interview with the doctor who examined Betty, Physician Frank Walkin:

> This is to certify that today I examined Betty Wolfrum. The history of the case is that this child has been lost 110-120 hours. Examination of the child reveals very little loss of flesh and no evidence of dehydration. Furthermore, in view of the fact there have been so many mosquitoes present, it is significant that there are no bites or scratches present. In my opinion this child has had food, water and some shelter for the past 3 to 4 days as I do not believe that a child who has always been delicate could have withstood this long exposure and show so little trace.

It was also noted in many papers that Betty was found completely dry (even though it had rained heavily the previous day and night), and that her clothing and shoes were fairly clean considering the time she spent in the bush.

A May 22, 1934, article in the *Montreal Gazette* had the following headline: "Girl is Terrified." The article states that Betty had hardly spoken once she arrived home. The family stated that Betty was "whimpering softly" and sleeping a lot.

Another interesting and intriguing part of this case was brought forward by a neighboring farmer, George Romein. He told authorities that the last three days prior to Betty being found, one of his cows had returned from deep in the bush milked on each of those days. He stated that this had never happened before but that it was obvious to him that someone had been milking the cow.

The RCMP interviewed Roy Rosin at length about his ability to find Betty when everyone else had failed. A May 23, 1934, article in the *Winnipeg Free Press* understood the importance of Roy's actions and covered it in their story. Roy did admit that he went almost straight to the exact spot where he found Betty. You can read a lot into some styles of writing, and you could tell that the reporters believed that Roy knew more than he was telling. It wasn't a belief that Roy knew the kidnappers, but he did know more facts of the story. Here is the last paragraph in the article: "Furthermore, when queried by the newspapermen on the scene Monday, he [Rosin] admitted that he had not told all. He did say that when he went on his successful quest for Betty, 'I did not expect to come back alive, or if I did come back I would be all broken up.'"

Roy's statement is one of the most baffling I have ever read from a searcher. It's understood that the RCMP debriefed Roy at length; however, they refused to clarify what they learned from their interview. Why? What could he have known that was so sensitive that he couldn't tell the family, the press or public? The only other clue that was given to the family was that Roy left the Wolfrum farm Sunday afternoon at 1:00 p.m. and found the girl two miles away at approximately 2:00 p.m. The RCMP did state that the area where he found Betty was searched several times during the five days she was missing.

The RCMP went back into the bush and swamps to the area where Betty was found. When she was found, Betty was missing her coat, hat, and one shoe, items that were never found by the RCMP or searchers who continued to scour the area.

Three days after Betty was found, she started to talk with her mother in German. She told her mom that she had met a mother and daughter while she was gone, and that she had seen a cat that had scratched her. She explained that on the morning she was found, a man had pointed for her to walk in the direction that would lead to her farm, which she was doing when she was found.

After hearing Mrs. Wolfrum retell Betty's statement, the RCMP again scoured the area for shelter and evidence of food consumption and sleeping areas. Nothing was found. Remember, the night before Betty was found, it rained extremely heavily, yet Betty was found dry and clean. How can that be?

There is no feasible way that anyone could have gotten in or out of the Moosehorn region without other farmers noticing a vehicle or coach. The RCMP were completely stumped by this case. They were reluctant to speak with the press about all the facts surrounding the incident, and their reasons were never fully disclosed. The police did confirm that they believed Betty had been kidnapped.

Conclusions

This is another case where a small child goes missing under highly unusual conditions. It does not appear that international borders mean anything in these cases; the similarities between Canadian and U.S. cases are obvious.

Somehow and somewhere Betty Wolfrum was sheltered while she was missing. The RCMP could not find a shelter, and they didn't believe that anyone traveled in or out of the area while Betty was missing or during their search. This area isn't like a metropolitan area; it is a remote area where everyone knows their neighbors, their vehicles, and their wagons. The million-dollar question is, where did Betty obtain food and shelter?

Betty was fed and hydrated while she was missing. How was this happening? The answer to part of this question is the milking of George Romein's cow. Betty was too small to milk the cow, and her parents confirmed she didn't know how. Someone milked the cow and probably supplied Betty with the fluid. If someone was milking the cow daily, that means that someone stayed in that immediate area and didn't leave the region with Betty. How were they able to avoid searchers? Remember, it wasn't just one person avoiding searchers; there were four people avoiding the search parties—Betty, the girl and mother, and what was probably a father.

It would be inappropriate not to acknowledge the efforts of Dr. Walkin and the RCMP working the Wolfrum case. Even though this incident occurred miles from a major metropolitan area and there resources were limited, the professionals investigating this disappearance were able to recognize factors that many jurisdictions working the cases in this book were unable to comprehend. The indicators of suspicious circumstances are present in many of the abductions. Sometimes, though, local law enforcement officers are too occupied with the fact that they found the victim to properly examine the circumstances surrounding the disappearance. It should also be noted that without spending years researching missing people events, the chances of recognizing recurring factors are slim.

The person who could probably answer almost every question about this disappearance—Roy Rosin—is reluctant to talk. Roy knew exactly where to look, when to look, and to go alone. Why would he say he knew there was danger associated with going to the location where he found Betty, and state that he knew he might come back battered? If Roy had these feelings, why not take a battalion of RCMP to defend you and ensure the release of Betty? It was Roy's knowledge of his property and the region that gave him the knowledge that led to Betty's discovery.

Farmers know their land like you and I know the insides of our homes. The farmer is on his land every day of his life; it's his job to know what's on it and when there are threats to his livestock and crops. I believe that Roy was a very, very smart man. He knew that taking other people to get Betty would cause further harm and disruption than going alone. Roy was probably seen daily by the person or people who had Betty. Anyone seeing Roy on the land wouldn't be surprised or shocked, and if Roy had an agreement with whomever occupied that location, he probably knew he was either going to easily retrieve Betty or die trying.

I believe that Roy was a good man, a man who probably told the RCMP an incredible story. The reluctance of the RCMP to share a witness/hero's story is not just unusual but something I had never seen or read.

In the articles I found, there is no mention of whether or not the Wolfrum's stayed on their property and continued to farm.

Florence Spence
Missing: 08/05/34 at 3:00 p.m.—Central Manitoba
Age at Disappearance: 3 years
• Distance• Missing Clothing

Manitoba had something highly unusual happening in August 1934. Two small children disappeared in a span of forty-eight hours and weren't immediately found.

Florence Spence was a First Nations member. Her family lived in the Central Manitoba mining area in a log cabin. On August 5, 1934, Mr. and Mrs. Spence went to the Oro Grande mine three miles from the cabin to do shopping. They left the three kids at the cabin, and Florence was last seen playing in the front yard.

The Spence's returned from their trip in a few hours, and nobody knew where Florence was located. The kids said they had just seen her in the front yard, and she couldn't be far away. The family went into the bush calling for the girl and didn't get a response. It wasn't long before neighbors and the RCMP were contacted. Constable Carswell responded from San Antonio and took charge of the search.

The region around the Spence's rallied, and they received neighbors' assistance from far away and got up to one hundred searchers looking for the young girl. They also got the assistance of a man named Roy Brown, who was president of Wings Limited. He flew his plane low over the countryside looking for any sign of the girl and found none.

Ground searchers saw what they stated were large bear tracks around the residence. They never found anything that would indicate that Florence had been attacked but were at a loss to explain why they found no sign of her for many days.

I have written before about miraculous recoveries of missing people made by individuals they never knew. The people claimed they had a dream that told them where the victim was located, and they headed out to find them. This is what happened with Florence and is described in the August 13, 1934 edition of the *Winnipeg Tribune*: "M. Blair, diamond-drill setter who found the child Friday on a hunch following a dream that night before, discovered her lying almost naked and semi-conscious between two rocks. As soon as he was able to arouse the child, she moaned, 'water.' Blair immediately gave her a small drink and sprinkled her face with ice-cold water from a nearby pool." Blair picked up Florence and carried her for forty minutes until he could get her to a mining-company physician. Later in the same article was this: "Experienced Bushmen of the district shake their heads in wonder. They cannot understand how the little girl survived. They would not have believed it they said, had they not seen the proof." Articles vary on how far away Florence was located by Blair. The common number was three miles from her cabin. It was said she was found in an area with no trails and no easy way in, and nobody thought she'd be there.

In the same *Winnipeg Tribune* article were these interesting facts: "The night before she was found, wolves and coyotes were heard howling in the vicinity of the mine. Residents shook their head and felt sure there was no chance of the child being found alive."

The day Florence was found, this headline ran in the *Winnipeg Tribune*: "Searchers Abandon All Hope For Child Missing Five Days." The article stated that everyone believed a bear had consumed the girl and there was no hope she was alive. This was claimed even though there was no evidence she had been attacked by a bear.

There have been several instances I have written about a victim being found semiconscious. It seems strange that Florence asked for water almost immediately, but fresh water was within reach. You have to ask the question: Was she there the entire time, or had she just arrived somehow at that location? There have been too many times I have written about people getting some type of subconscious signal telling them where the victim is located. How does this happen? I know some readers will discount this and consider it unethical to even write about, but I don't believe so. Blair told friends of his dream, and they laughed at him. He was so confident in his dream that he took a day off work without salary and walked directly to the girl. Something is at play in these cases that we don't understand.

Frank Goy
Missing: 08/07/34—Dallas, Manitoba
Age at Disappearance: 7 years
Distance Traveled• Water

On August 7, 1934, seven-year-old Frank Goy somehow managed to wander away from his home in Dallas, Manitoba. Peter Goy, his father, searched for the boy for several hours before contacting authorities and asking for assistance.

The small community was able to muster only twenty searchers. An August 11 article in the *Winnipeg Tribune* had these key details: "Seven-year old Frank Goy was found at 3:00 p.m. Friday wandering in the bush 13 miles from his home. He was found by a search party of some 20 men organized by Constable S. Hull, RCMP of the Hodgson District." It went on to say that Frank was suffering from exhaustion and hunger and had been taken to a local clinic. He was in good condition.

Articles stated that the searchers were going through swampland looking for the boy, making his thirteen-mile journey truly remarkable and shocking. This area of Manitoba is very flat. SAR manuals state that a seven- to nine-year-old child lost in a flat environment will be found 95 percent of the time in five miles or fewer. Frank was found outside the established search grid by more than double the distance. It was a miracle the boy was located.

Is it only a coincidence that a boy and girl went missing in the same region, on close to the same day, and then were missing for three days in common and found on the same day? In this instance, both kids were found and lived, another coincidence. I could not find a similar disappearance in this region for an entire decade.

George Wanke
Missing 7/27/35, Brightstone, Manitoba
Age at Disappearance: 58 years
Berry Picker•
On July twenty seventh of 1935 the *Winnipeg Free Press* ran an article regarding Mr. Wanke's disappearance. The article stated that Wanke was from Beausejour and was traveling with 24 other residents from their city to Brightstone, an area known for berry picking. The group arrived and then agreed on a specific time to meet for the ride home. The entire group did arrive at the designated meeting location except Wanke.

Residents initially returned to Brightstone and then next morning they drove back to their berry picking spot with three truckloads of searchers. The search effort was in vain, Wanke was never found.

Jack Pike
Missing 09/05/35, St. Norbert, Manitoba
Age at Disappearance: 5 years
Berry Picker• Point of Separation
The Pike family took a trip from their residence in St. Vital Manitoba to the area near St. Norbert to pick blueberries. The family exited the car and started toward the patch. Jack Pike ran through the bush and was out of sight only a few minutes when his mother heard something very unsettling. Mrs. Charles Pike gave an interview on September 7, 1935 to the *Leader Post* and she stated: "He screamed as if he were terrified, the scream seemed to be choked off in the middle." The mother ran the 100 yards towards the scream

and found nothing. The husband arrived and they both scoured the area and didn't find the young boy.

The family was on the grounds of the Trappist Monks Monastery and somewhat near the Red River. The family called the police and a search was initiated.

The search for Jack Pike lasted four days and was called the largest search in the history of Manitoba at the time. Over 2000 searchers went through the river, riverbanks, bush, trees and the grounds and they found nothing.

On the fourth day a man was searching on the opposite river bank and found Jack Pike under a bush, unconscious but still alive. The boy was rushed to the hospital where the doctors gave him stimulants and his father gave him blood. At one point the boy awoke and stated, "Hi daddy." It was felt that Jack was going to survive but in a strange turn of fate, Jack died hours later.

Searchers were confused how Jack could have made his way across the river to hide under a bush, a bush they felt was way too far from where he disappeared. Many were amazed that they boy had made it that far and survived that long. It had appeared that after four days without water or food Jack had died of either exposure or dehydration.

Authorities were concerned about the fact that it sounded as though Jack had been abducted but they could not find any additional evidence or suspects.

Simon Skogan
Missing 7/2/40, 55 Miles North of Winnipeg, Manitoba
Age at Disappearance: 9 years
Water• Berries• Cows Milked (Unusual)• Point of Separation

In early July of 1940 Simon Skogan traveled 55 miles north of Manitoba to visit the rural home of his grandparents near Tuelon. The area around the home was very wet, swampy with farmland surrounding the vicinity.

On July 2, 1940 Simon went berry picking with his grandpa and disappeared. Local law enforcement was immediately called along with military personnel. Eighty soldiers from the Canadian Third Division Ammunition Company stayed on the search for over thirty days.

During the search for Simon, Indian Trackers found some very unusual facts. A July 29, 1940 article in the *Windsor Daily Star* had the following:

"A few days ago, however Indians of the district reported traces of someone living on berries and sleeping in the woods. They even reported someone who ran away at the sight of them. Nearby residents said they often found their cows milked almost dry in the morning."

The search for Simon lasted over one month. There was even some conjecture that Simon was the one running from the searchers and living off the land. Over two hundred searchers assisted on the effort to find Skogan including 80 soldiers. Professional soldiers could not locate the boy or whoever was living in the forest off the berries.

On Sunday, October 27, 1940, approximately 4 months after Simon vanished, a local farmer was looking for lost cows and located Simon's remains in dense bush. It took Simon's dad and the farmer over four hours to work their way back into the location to locate the body. There were no details on the condition of the body or the exact location.

James McAmmond
Missing: 10/05/41—10:00 a.m., Rennie, Manitoba
Age at disappearance: 19 years
Weather • Water • Canines • Hunter
The location of this disappearance is in an area that's had several suspicious missing cases. Just 30 miles to the west is a geographical cluster zone, and there are other unexplained disappearances in the region surrounding this incident.

The McAmmond family lived in Winnipeg and owned a summer home at Brereton Lake, 60 miles to the east and near the small town of Rennie. The

James McAmmond

cottage was used during the warm Canadian summers and was an excellent duck hunting location. The surrounding area was very wet, marshy, and rural and was also the home to the Whiteshell Reserve.

James McAmmond was a 19-year-old apprentice for the Canadian Railroad in Winnipeg. On Friday, October 3, 1941, he invited three other students to join him at his parent's summer home for a weekend of duck hunting. The foursome made the 90-minute ride to the house and established a weekend retreat. James was an experienced hunter and knew the region around the house as he had hunted with his dad many times. The young man was always armed with a 22-caliber rifle.

On Sunday, October 5, the group of four had driven the roads around the reserve looking for ducks and had stopped a few times to get out and scan the water. At approximately 10:00 a.m., they stopped at a promising location and agreed to spend 30 minutes searching the area and then would meet back at the car. All of the young men went in different directions alone, as did James, point of separation. An hour passed and all of the guys were back in the car but McAmmond. There was a search of the area, and nothing was found. It was at this point that the local ranger was notified that there was a missing person.

The word that their son was missing quickly got to the McAmmonds in Winnipeg. The group of apprentice railroad workers suspended their classroom teaching for the week, and all went to Brereton Lake to assist in the SAR. The local chief ranger believed he would need more resources and made a call to the southern Saskatchewan military regiment and had a platoon of soldiers respond to the search. The military also dispatched two teams of dogs and two helicopters. Trains that were traveling just to the north of the lake were directed to blow their whistles continuously as they passed the search zone to give James an idea where the tracks were located.

The effort to locate James was one of the most massive I have ever read in a small Canadian town. Hundreds of people were on the ground; there was a constant buzz of planes and helicopters coupled with the whistles of passing trains. Searchers claimed they found some grass that appeared to be pushed down and areas where large patches of the grass were forced down. Some of the locals claimed that animals caused the grass to go down and others said it might have been James. According to multiple articles, the center of the search was Whiteshell Road and the local Whiteshell Reserve.

Searchers not only dealt with a marshy, rural environment, this October 10, 1941, article in the *Winnipeg Tribune* explained more details, "It was bitterly cold and wet again Thursday night, with temperatures near freezing and old-timers fully expecting another heavy rain or even snow." Weather was working against the SAR effort.

The RCMP was in charge of the search and worked closely with the military. An October 11, 1941, article in the *Winnipeg Tribune* had these claims, "Constable G.E. Lenhard, RCMP, Whitemouth, fully endorsed that statement Friday evening. "If it had not been for Captain Watt's (Military) company of industrious men, most of the land would have to go unsearched, and our minds would never be at ease." Seven days of nonstop looking for James had found nothing. The search was over.

I can't imagine that the McAmmond family was ever able to enjoy their summer cottage again. Memories of a family member going missing in a specific region will always cast a dark shadow, even if the place had great memories. The family went back to their home in Winnipeg and soldiers returned to southern Saskatchewan. I doubt that anyone living in this region today knows of the events of October 1941.

Alex Thorne
Missing 10/04/58• Wanless, MB
Age at Disappearance: 44 years
Hunter/ Trapper• Canines

Wanless, Manitoba, is approximately five hundred miles northwest of Winnipeg and ten miles from the Saskatoon border. This small city sits between Grass River/Wekuso Falls Provincial Park, Clearwater Lake Provincial Park, and Rocky Lake Provincial Park. The region is thick with wet and swampy ground and hundreds of small lakes.

The missing person in this case, Mr. Alex Thorne, was identified in archives with two different first names, Alex and Alec. For ease of documenting this incident, I will call him Alex.

Alex lived on the outskirts of Wanless with his wife and eight children in a small home. Alex was a trapper by trade and was able to support his family through his ability to live off the land. On October 4, 1958, in the morning hours, Alex grabbed his .22-caliber rifle and told his wife he was going out to check his traps and he'd be back in a half hour. In my years of writing about missing people and trappers, going out only that short of distance to check trap lines really doesn't sound realistic; it is normally an all-day or several-day trip. Whatever the case, Alex didn't return, and his wife told the kids to start the search. Two days later, the family gave up their search and notified the Royal Canadian Mounted Police (RCMP).

The RCMP responded with canines, helicopters, and ground searchers. Dogs couldn't find a scent, and the helicopters found nothing from the air. Special canines were transported from Dauphin; they also failed to find Alex.

Alex's father-in-law knew of an Amactek First Nations Indian that was a specialist in finding missing people. A call was made to Louis Prince, and he responded to the Thorne residence. Reporters watched as Louis sat on a blanket on the floor of the Thorne residence and drew figures in charcoal on the floor. Louis stated that Alex was across the railroad tracks northeast of the settlement and that an animal had killed him. RCMP sent dozens of searchers into the area described by Louis and found nothing. Louis told them to go further out into the bush in a southerly direction. The RCMP found nothing again.

It appears that reporters started to make a mockery of Louis's efforts even though he had never failed to find a missing person up to this point. An October 16 article in the *Winnipeg Free Press* explained the feeling of the family: "Mrs. Thorne has told her sons and daughters that there is to be no information given to the press at present. Whether this is Prince's instructions, is not known."

Summary

I searched three years of archives on the Thorne case and could not find any articles declaring that Alex was found. I did find one article in November 1958 explaining that searchers were making one last attempt to find the body. They found nothing.

I do believe that if I were the Thornes, I would've tried just about anything to find my father. I probably would've tried Mr. Prince first, just because of his track record. I think it's interesting that he told the RCMP that Alex had been killed by an animal but failed to say what type. I find it doubtful that Alex was in the area where Louis stated to look, as a standard animal attack would've been a gruesome scene and one that canines would find. No locations were found that could be attributed to Alex or an animal attack.

The far north of Canada has consistently produced unusual disappearances, including the bizarre. The amount of small lakes, ponds, swamps, and areas of vast desolation make this area very intriguing.

Madeline Grisdale
Missing: 07/06/86-Unk, Fort Alexander Indian Reservation, Manitoba
Age at disappearance: 49 years
Berry Picker• Canine• Disabled• Previously Searched
This disappearance happened on the Fort Alexander Indian Reservation, which is located at the southeastern end of Lake Winnipeg in Manitoba. It sits approximately thirty miles west of the Ontario border.

On July 6, Madeline walked into the bush to pick blueberries with her small puppy. Friends knew the woman wouldn't go far because of a stroke she had suffered ten years earlier, which left her with a severe limp. Madeline was also considered disabled because she was a mute. When the woman didn't return to her resident care facility, the RCMP was called.

There was an initial response by thirteen officers followed by fifty-five members of the Canadian armed forces. The search was intense and nonstop. The area of the search was swampy, wet, and thick with bushes.

Six days after Madeline vanished, she was found 2.1 miles from where she was last seen. Searchers found her lying under a tree adjacent to a trail, dehydrated, weak, and alive. Her puppy was sitting by her side. Searchers described her as very scared. She was airlifted by helicopter to a medical center in Pine Falls and declared to be in stable condition.

A July 14, 1986, article in the *Leader Post* described how Madeline was found: "A group of 20 searchers, including McKenzie and two other of Grisdale's children went into a previously unsearched area around 10am and were lost for some time before they discovered the woman. 'We went one direction and then we came back along the trail and we found her,' said Willy Grisdale. He added he didn't know how his mother got to the spot, why she couldn't return home, or if she had eaten during the ordeal."

Summary

Madeline was found just off a trail that had been searched just prior to her being found. Even her family couldn't understand how she had gotten to where she was found or why she hadn't made it back home.

Because of Madeline's disability, she couldn't explain details of what happened while she was missing.

Marcus McKay
Missing 7/15/00–PM, Waterhen Lake, MB
Age at Disappearance: 8 years
Hunter• Point of separation• Weather• Canines•

Waterhen Lake is located approximately two hundred miles northwest of Winnipeg in a very remote, wet, and desolate area of the far north. There are thousands of small lakes, ponds, creeks, and rivers within one hundred miles of the lake. Articles about this incident identified the exact location as one hundred kilometers northeast of Dauphin.

Riley Chartrand was the stepfather of Marcus McKay when the two decided to go deer hunting on the eastern side of Waterhen Lake. It was July 15, 2000, when the two left their residence in Mallard and drove a lonely road up the eastern side of the lake, stopped, and headed into the bush. The two guys were also meeting other friends in the area and would split up to hunt the region. It was a fairly warm day, and both were wearing only T-shirts and blue jeans, and Rilley was carrying a rifle.

MISSING PLEASE HELP

MARCUS MCKAY

Missing Since: Jul 15, 2000

Missing From:	Mallard, MB
Date of Birth:	Feb 6, 1992
Gender:	Male
Height:	4'2"
Weight/ Build:	70 lbs
Hair:	Dark Brown
Eyes:	Brown

Marcus McKay

As Rilley and Marcus were in the bush, Rilley shot and killed a deer in the afternoon. Both tracked the deer through very thick and swampy vegetation that was tiring even for an experienced man. Marcus was exhausted. The two did locate the deer. Rilley knew the deer was large, and he would need help. He realized it was necessary to go back to the vehicles and get the other men for assistance. Marcus stated that he was tired, and he'd wait with the deer for Rilley to come back.

Rilley went back to the vehicles and returned in one hour. The weather had turned bad, and it had started to rain. When Rilley returned to the deer, he found that Marcus was gone. He frantically searched the area, yelling for the boy, but didn't get a reply. More men were summoned, and soon the area was crawling with hunters and friends. On July 16, in the area where Rilley shot the deer, sixty Royal Canadian Mounted Police (RCMP) and their search dogs responded and covered a five-square-mile area looking for Marcus. The landscape in the area of the search was extremely thick vegetation, swampy ground with small ponds and lakes.

Darlene Dumas was Marcus's mother. She had just moved herself and her two boys to Mallard from Winnipeg two weeks earlier. She was on the scene daily asking for additional assistance from volunteers and getting it.

As the search moved into the third and fourth days, the weather would continue to worsen with heavy rain and lower temperatures. Searchers were constantly being challenged at some level in their effort to find Marcus.

As the search was ongoing, RCMP officials were conducting background checks on Rilley. Newspapers at the time indicated that the armed hunter had a conviction that prohibited him from possessing firearms. Rilley did not back down. He admitted to possessing the firearm and the facts surrounding the event; he was not shying away from the truth. The RCMP did focus on Rilley and his background but appeared to back away from naming him a suspect, even though there was a Manitoba law stating that adults cannot leave children unattended under the age of twelve. Rilley was right there with every other searcher in his effort to find Marcus.

The RCMP was into its fourth day of the search and managing eleven different search organizations trying to find the boy. It was felt that Marcus could not survive the elements in the T-shirt and jeans he was wearing with the rain and cold that was present in days following his disappearance.

The RCMP flew in a specially designed helicopter with forward-looking infrared radar (FLIR) to look for heat signatures on the ground. But the FLIR unit broke, and it was never utilized. Forty soldiers from Base Shiloh of the Canadian Armed Forces searched the area for two days and didn't find anything. Elders from a local First Nations tribe sat in the bush at night listening for indicators; they heard nothing. At one point, one hundred searchers joined arms at the point of the kill and walked a line directly to the roadway; they found nothing.

Agnes Beaulieu was Marcus's great-grandmother and only slept intermittently during the search, but she had a dream as is explained in the following July 20, 2000, article from the SARINFO. BC.Library: "The little boy was laying down beside a bear to be warm."

In total there were six hundred people during the official search for Marcus. The RCMP brought in divers that cleared every lake, pond, creek, and water source in the area. A new FLIR unit was brought into the search, and they found only rabbits. A famous seventy-one-year-old tracker, Joe Anderson, was brought into the search. He had found two children lost in the bush before, along with a variety of other successes. At the end of two days of nonstop searching, Joe stated that this was the first time he had ever failed to find the lost person.

Five days after the search started, it was terminated. The RCMP felt that Marcus could not have survived, and they didn't know of any area that had not been covered, even though they had expanded their search to eight square kilometers.

The search for Marcus continued even after the RCMP officially called an end to their work. Marcus's mother made a public cry for additional help, and even more volunteers responded. The RCMP felt the public pressure, and they continued with limited manpower. There were three additional cadaver search dogs brought into the search zone to see if they could find a scent; nothing was found. There were over twenty people on the search for an additional two months after the RCMP terminated the effort.

Marcus was never found.

Summary

The area where Marcus vanished matches areas where other children have disappeared almost to perfection. The elements of the search almost seemed to be scripted, as they match many, many of the failures seen in other searches for children who disappear in the wild. Bloodhounds cannot find a scent, the weather turns to rain and cold, and no evidence of the boy being in the area is ever found. There was a very brief statement in one article about searchers finding a different "footprint" in the area, but nothing more was ever said about it.

There were other hunters and friends in the area besides Rilley, and considering the fact that everyone knew the boy was with him, I don't believe Rilley purposely harmed the boy. The area was searched for over two months, and Marcus was never found, meaning he somehow got out of the region. Rilley admitted to another felony: carrying a rifle while hunting. I understand the RCMP's interest in Rilley, but him harming his stepson doesn't make sense.

The dream of Marcus's grandmother struck a memory with me. There have been several cases where children were abducted and later claimed they were cuddled and kept warm by a bear during the nights they were missing. The behavior of a wild bear is not consistent with cuddling a child.

Readers of my past books will immediately recognize Marcus's age as a number that continues to show its ugly face on cases of boys that disappear and are never found. For some unknown reason, boys around eight years old that vanish are very rarely ever found.

The search for Marcus was one of the longest and most intense in the history of Manitoba. The RCMP, soldiers, local volunteers, and family members never wanted to give up on finding Marcus. My personal prayers are with everyone in that community.

Mark McKelvey
Missing: 07/24/17-8:30 A.M. Duck Mountain Provincial Park, Manitoba
Age at disappearance: 36 years
Point of Separation• Water• Injury/ Disability• Lack of Tracks

Mark McKelvey

Duck Mountain Provincial Park in Manitoba is located approximately 225 miles north of Minot, North Dakota and fifteen miles east of the border of Saskatchewan. The park is 550 square miles in size, is in an extremely remote region of the province and has hundreds of small bodies of water in the area.

Mark and Paul McKelvey are brothers and in July of 2017 both worked for Trisum Logging. The men were assigned to a project fifteen miles northwest of Roblin, Manitoba in Duck Mountain Provincial Park.

On July 21, 2017, Mark was working and was stung by a bee. The logger reacted to the bee and was taken to the hospital by his brother. Mark was given treatment and a prescription for drugs to help treat his reactions. Both guys returned to camp and resumed working. On July 23, Mark was again stung but continued to work and did not seek treatment. The night after the second sting, Mark wasn't feeling well. A July 25, 2017 edition of the CBC News had these details," Bobby Sue Mckelvey, said her uncle had complained of feeling dizzy and faint the morning he went missing. He told the workers he didn't feel good that morning, and his brother actually works up there with him, too," she said. "He went wandering into the bush and nobody has seen him since." Mark did not go to work the morning of July 23 and stayed behind. He was last seen walking into the woods at 8:00 A.M. and not seen again.

At 1:30 P.M. on July 23, the Prairie Mountain Division of the RCMP was called, and Mark McKelvey was reported as a missing person. The police responded with 50 ground searchers, an airplane and logistical support. An August 17, 2017 edition of the CBC had these search details, "RCMP located his hat and sunglasses not far from his camper, family said. Several different agencies pitched in as aircraft performed surveys from above, but RCMP called off the search effort on July 28." Details from other articles clarified that police located Mark's hat and sunglasses in a small hole twenty feet from his camper, nothing else was found. Later in the same CBC article was this statement from Mark's brother, Paul," There are no leads, there are no footprints," he said. "We're in desperate need of searchers out there because the bush is just way too big and way to thick."

The McKelvey family continued the search long after the RCMP pulled out of the area after four days. There were efforts even during the winter months to find some evidence of where Mark might be located. All of the search efforts produced nothing other than the hat and sunglasses.

The McKelvey family made several comments to the media upset that the RCMP did not bring canines to the scene in an attempt to find a scent. Law enforcement officials stated that there had been too many people in and around the area and this disrupted any scent trail used by dogs.

One year after the disappearance, Mark's mom, Debra McKelvey, was interviewed the CBC on July 24, 2018, and made the following statement, "He just can't vanish off Earth." The number of times I have read similar comments from families and searchers are into the hundreds. This type of speech is so common, I made a list of them in, Missing 411: Off the Grid.

In many cases of the missing people identified in my books, the victims report being ill, not feeling well, or being tired. These people become separated from others later disappear. Mark was stung by a bee twice in three days, stated he didn't feel well, was observed walking into the woods and vanished. Articles report that tracks cannot be located leaving the area.

The heartache that the McKelvey family had endured is palpable. They continued to go to the location and search for their loved one. The mystery is what happened to Mark Anthony McKelvey in Duck Mountain Provincial Park?

New Brunswick

Population: 772,000
Capital City: Fredericton
There are three regions in Canada that are considered maritime provinces; New Brunswick (NB) is one. It shares its western border with Mains and the northern area with Quebec and the Gulf of St. Lawrence. The southeastern landmass of the New Brunswick shares a twenty mile stretch with Nova Scotia.

The University of New Brunswick was the first university in Canada and was established in Fredericton. The majority of the population in this province, with 28,150 square miles speaks English. This is the only region of Canada that considers itself the only official bi-lingual province, speaking French and English.

This province has over 3000 farms, and it has 20 percent of the landmass that is suitable for agriculture. The most common crop for the farmers is potatoes and dairy.

There are two distinct seasons in NB, winter, and summer. The winter months have people playing hockey, skiing, and curling. The summer has locals boating, fishing, and swimming. The rivers have salmon, trout, and bass.

If you like going to national parks, this province boasts two. The Fundy National Park has the world's highest tides. These massive movements of water cause the St. John River to reverse flow two times a day that also causes massive current changes. You may also want to visit the Kouchibouguac National park on the Northumberland Strait.

I could find two notable NB natives, Louis B. Mayer was a co-founder of MGM Studios was raised in this province along with horse jockey Ron Turcotte called the province home.

If you enjoy driving, you'll enjoy the forests and open space on NB. A large amount of timber supports many sawmills and the lumber industry. There has also been a surge in oil refining and technology employment throughout the province.

The most common large mammals roaming NB are moose and white-tailed deer.

New Brunswick-List of missing by date.

Name	Date Missing • Age • Province
Robert Comeau	06/28/74• 42•M
Matthew Sloan	09/17/2006-11:30 p.m.•26•M

Robert Comeau
Missing: June 27, 1974, Moncton, NB
Age at disappearance: 42 years
No Memory

There are several stories I have discovered over the years that deal with people making lengthy trips across the country and seemingly not knowing how they arrived. In this segment, I will present two cases of Canadians that disappeared and were later found in areas that don't make sense. This first case involves a man who vanished in Canada and was then found in the United States. This is the one case that will be included in statistics of missing from Canada. The second case involves a Canadian vacationing for the day in the United States and vanished. This incident will not be included in the statistics but will be documented here.

In February of 1974, Annette and Robert Comeau lived in Moncton, New Brunswick, approximately fifteen miles from the North Umberland Strait. The family-owned a launderette that burned to the ground that month. Nothing of notoriety happened after the fire until June 27, 1974. Moncton Police found Robert's vehicle was parked next to the Shediac Bridge and adjacent to the river abandoned. Other reports state that the car was off the side of the roadway near the river. After finding his automobile, Annette reported him as a missing person.

There is one bridge in Moncton on the Shediac River. The area on the city side of the bridge is a swampy, undeveloped area where they located Robert's car. The Shediac River flows into the Bay of Fundy.

Annette Comeau and the police searched the area and dragged the river around where Robert's vehicle was located. The extensive effort to find a body or evidence proved useless. There was no news on this incident until July of 1974.

On July 13, 1974, Robert Comeau surfaced two hundred miles south of Moncton, in another country. The incident is described in the July 20, 1974 edition of the Lebanon Daily News, "Last Saturday, Comeau walked into the St. John's Catholic Church and told Rev. Jack O'Haire that he didn't know who he was or where he was from. O'Haire called police and Comeau was taken to Eastern Maine Medical Center here to undergo tests. The case broke Thursday when Bangor Police received a call from Comeau's wife, Annette. Her description of her husband, down to small marks and a scar, matched the man without a name." Detectives said that the man was using the last name of Comeau and a possible first name of Bob, but knew little else about himself. Annette read a story about a man in Bangor who had amnesia and called Bangor Police to see if it was Robert, it was. Robert told police that he walked around Bangor for two weeks going to a local library and looking at newspapers trying to determine who he was. He stated that he found $80 in his pocket, but no wallet or other papers.

On July 20, 1974, Annette arrived at the Eastern Maine Medical Center and met with Robert. She stated that he didn't remember her or their children but was happy to be with someone who loved him. Detectives later noted that Robert had recognized items about history and politics but almost nothing about his personal life.

The first issue I considered was how Robert crossed the border into the United States without a passport? He was found without a wallet or paperwork, and he would not have been allowed into the United States without identification. Bangor Police and the United States Customs never commented on this part of the story. I could not locate any other details about Robert Comeau's life after he returned with Annette to Moncton.

Case #2
Danny Filippidis
Missing: 02/07/18-2:30 P.M., Whiteface Mountain Ski Resort, Lake Placid, NY
Age at disappearance: 49 years
In early February of 2018, a group of eight current and retired Toronto Firefighters planned a trip into the United States to go ski-

ing. On February 7, Danny Filippidis was a current Toronto Fire Captain skiing with a fellow firefighter on the slopes of Whiteface Mountain Ski resort in Lake Placid, New York. It was approximately 2:30 P.M. that Danny's friend told him that he was fatigued and was going down to the lodge to meet with the group. Danny stated he was going to stay on the slopes for one more run.

As the ski lifts closed and the firefighters were waiting for Danny at the lodge, he never arrived. The resorts ski patrol kicked into high gear and started to search the mountain for the 49-year old fire captain. Local police and resort officials went into high gear when Danny was found that first night. One hundred Firefighters from Toronto responded to assist with the search while an additional one hundred firefighters voluntarily covered the shifts of the fireman who traveled. There was also a large contingent of local police and firefighters all looking for the man. There was no evidence found on the slopes that Danny was there. The New York State Police Investigative Unit was also at the resort and looking into the disappearance. It was estimated that 7000 hours were spent searching the area.

There were no additional details on this disappearance until February 13 when Sacramento, California Police were called by a man identifying himself as Danny and asking for assistance. He had just purchased the phone. The police found Danny, still dressed in his heavy ski coat, ski pants, helmet, and goggles saying he had some head trauma. When he was asked how he got to Sacramento, he said he thought he was in some type of transport truck. It was stated that he had a difficult time remembering anything about the past several days. The last thing he remembers was skiing. A February 14, 2018 article in the Globe and Mail had these details, "Officers found Captain Filippidis wearing snow pants, a ski jacket, and winter boots, as well as carrying a ski helmet. Sgt Hampton said the sight of a man clad in winter attire was nearly as striking as the "odd" story he told officers. It's a bit chilly here, but it's not that cold,"he said."

Danny had a credit card and no identification. He told officers he purchased a new cell phone and called his wife. Officers felt that he might have some sort of medical condition and was transported to a local hospital and later released. At the request of New York State Police, Danny returned to Lake Placed and answered questions about what happened. New York State Police have not released details of that interview.

A CBC reporter did get an interview with Danny in August 2018. At that time he did state he remembered a trucker saying they were in Utah. He also stated that he might have remembered trying to get his cell phone from his car. Doctors theorized that Danny may have suffered a head injury on the slopes. He is now back to full duty at the fire department.

In many of the cases I document, the victims have severe head trauma. It's fascinating that Danny claimed to have had a head injury and even had a ski helmet with him. This incident had international press, yet nobody has ever come forward claiming to have given Danny a ride.

The disappearances of Robert Comeau and Danny Filippidis have several similarities. Both men were Canadian and were found in the United States. Danny was located 3900 miles from where he vanished, on the opposite side of the continent. It is peculiar that each man cannot remember details of their trip from where they disappeared to where they were found, a consistent part of each story. Both men were in their forties, Danny, 49 years and Robert, 42 years and both had a wife and children. Danny is from Greek heritage, and Robert is French.

There have been too many cases that I have researched that have this familiar theme to the stories, loss of memory, lengthy travel without memory, and credible people. Something very unusual happened to Danny Filippidis and Robert Comeau.

Matthew Sloan
Missing: 09/17/2006-11:30 p.m., Fredericton, New Brunswick
Age at disappearance: 26 years
Water• Canines

This incident occurred at the far northeastern area of Canada, thirty miles north of the Bay of Fundy and the Atlantic Ocean. Fredericton sits on the Saint John River.

Matthew Steven Sloan was a well-rounded young man involved in sports and community. He had a degree in kinesiology from the University of New Brunswick and followed that by attending the educational program at the University of Maine at Presque Isle. Throughout his years in school, Matthew played and coached sports. He committed several summers to the Fredericton District Soccer Association where he coached summer soccer camp. After his formal education, Matt went on to teach at Nashwaaksis Middle School, Leo Hayes High School, and Bliss Carmen Middle School.

On September 17, 2006, Matthew went to the Harvest Jazz and Blues Festival in Fredericton. His exact activities during the day are vague. Either late at night on the seventeenth or early the following morning, he disappeared. There was a search that looked at the Saint John River and the surrounding neighborhoods. Search dogs and ground personnel found nothing to point in any direction.

In the early morning hours of September 23, a young lady crossing the Thorpe Walking Bridge saw something unusual in the water. She called the police, and they recovered the body of Matthew Sloan. Very few details are available about the condition of the body.

The coroner in Fredericton did an analysis of Matthew's body and came to a somewhat unusual conclusion. They could not determine a cause of death. This is a conclusion reached in several cases I have highlighted over the years through my previous four books. This means that Matthew did not drown, wasn't assaulted, etc. They made no mention of any toxicology testing.

This case matches dozens of cases documented in Missing 411: A Sobering Coincidence.

Newfoundland and Labrador

Population: 519,000
Capital City: St. John

One of the immediate impacts, when you visit St. John in New-foundland, is the colorful building in the city. It reminded me of waterfronts in some Caribbean countries. Don't let the buildings fool you, and the weather is nothing like the Caribbean. It can get to -40 Degrees Fahrenheit in the winter and 50 degrees Fahrenheit in the summer. This town of 180,000 people is the capital of Newfoundland and Labrador.

Newfoundland and Labrador are the newest province in Canada, being added in 1949. The population of this most easterly landmass in North America is 515,000 and is predominantly English speaking. The highest point in Labrador is in the Torngat Mountains, Mount Caubvick at 5,420' in elevation. The highest point in Newfoundland is in the Long Range Mountains and is 2,670'.

The government introduced moose to this province in the twentieth century. The mammal has multiplied quickly and is one mammal that has large numbers. Other large mammals you may see include black and polar bear and caribou.

Labrador and Newfoundland have four gorgeous major parks, Dungeon Provincial Park and Terra Nova, Torngat Mountains and Gros Morne which are the three National Parks. Many of these areas are in remote regions which do not get large numbers of visitors. If you want isolation and great views, you might want to visit these locations.

Newfoundland and Labrador list of missing by date.

Name	Date Missing• Age• Sex
Anne Abraham	08/05/76 at 3:00 p.m. • 22 •F
Andrew Sexton	02/25/06 • 21 • M
Cleon Smith	04/02/11-p.m.• 30• M
William Oberkiser	10/09/11• 65• M

Anne Abraham
Missing: 08/05/76 at 3:00 p.m.—Torngat Mountain National Park,
Ramah Bay, Newfoundland
Age at Disappearance: 22 years
•National Park• Weather• Intellect

When you read a description of the location where someone disappears and it's as follows in this August 13, 1976, edition of the
Morning News, you pay attention: "The Royal Mounties searched
yesterday for a 22- year old woman archaeologist from Washington,
DC, who has been missing 6 days in an area of Labrador prowled by
polar bears and described as 'so bleak it's called the land God gave
Cain.'" How could someone disappear in a landscape so bleak?

Anne Abraham was a twenty-two-year-old archaeologist for the
Smithsonian Institute in Washington, DC. She was exploring an area
in the far northern region of Labrador in Torngat Mountain National
Park, specifically the region around Ramah Bay. This was Anne's
eighth year making the trip north for the summer. The teams were
looking for five-hundred-million-year-old fossils.

Anne's partner for the journey was thirty-year-old geologist
Richard Gramley, a professor at New York University at Stony
Brook.

Anne wouldn't be lonely during this trip; her boyfriend, Stephen
Loring, had made the journey with her. On August 5, 1976, Anne
and Gramley had traveled twenty-five miles north of the other expedition team members and were working an area near Ramah Bay.
The August 13, 1976, edition of the *Schenectady Gazette* had these
details (Point of Separation): "'Gramley told police that last Friday
that he and Miss Abraham had split up and taken different routes to
a campsite occupied by another team of diggers. The last he saw of
her she was climbing the face of the mountain to go across the top.
When he returned there was no sign of her and he presumed she had
gone over the top,' Halloran said. 'She hasn't been seen since.'"

During the initial hours after Anne vanished, the teams had a
difficult time rallying resources to assist. They were finally able to
get the RCMP to send a Sea Ranger helicopter hundreds of miles
north to help. During those first few days, only four members of the
team were looking for the woman, including her boyfriend. Later

in the search, two civilian helicopters were added, along with Eskimo searchers from Sagick and two Canadian military choppers from Labrador. Here is one detail about the search that was in the August 13, 1976, edition of the *Schenectady Gazette:* "Dense fog and rain hampered the search Thursday."

In the middle of the search effort, Anne's brother, Edward, flew in from attending Harvard Medical School. He was later interviewed and was devastated by the loss of his sister. He made statements about how desolate and bleak the region was.

There was no significant ground cover in this area. Helicopters could see for miles. The mountain Anne was last seen climbing was described as very rocky. She was not using ropes and carabiners, as it wasn't a cliff-type climb. This was Anne's eighth year in the great north. She was very experienced and well aware of the dangers associated with being in that area. She knew that if you took unnecessary risks, help probably wouldn't arrive quickly. Gramley even believed that Anne had gone over the top of the mountain easily and told investigators as much.

There were a few theories on what happened to Anne. One article stated that a polar bear had been seen in the area in the days before the incident. Polar bears are known as killers of people, and great caution needs to be exercised around them. The other theory was that Anne fell off the mountain and into the water. There was never a mention of any of her belongings being found and no evidence she fell off the mountain. Articles stated that the bay was filled with frozen ice at the time, meaning there should've been a break in the ice sheet.

There were some rumors of foul play, but I couldn't find anything to validate the claim. Anne was never found.

Andrew Sexton
Missing: 02/25/06—Goose Cove, Newfoundland
Age at Disappearance: 21 years
Canines• Weather

There is an old saying in the world that we study history for a reason. If you have read my past Missing 411 books, this story is going to sound very reminiscent of another disappearance.

The location of this case is St. Anthony in Newfoundland. The town is located on the big island at the far northeast tip. It has a city population of 2500 people with a regional of 25,000. The city has cruise ships that visit during the summer with local highlights of a very large moose population and visits by polar bears. During a specific time of the year the coast has outstanding whale watching opportunities. The city may have attractions that pull visitors, but it has a dark side. There are four people missing from this small town, two of which match our profile. This is case number one.

Andrew Sexton was a twenty-one-year-old native of St. Anthony, Newfoundland. The location is northeast of Maine and sits on the Atlantic Ocean. Andrew was born and raised in community, loved the outdoors, and knew the area extremely well.

On February 25, 2006, Andrew and his friends got onto their snowmobiles and planned a trip to a cabin in Goose Cove. It would be a short four-mile trip with everyone knowing the route well. The group left at 10:00–10:30 a.m. with Andrew by himself on his snowmobile. It didn't take long to reach the cabin, and the group didn't stay long. They realized there was a big incoming storm, and they needed to get back.

Two other teenagers were traveling on snowmobiles with Andrew. They arrived in St. Anthony at approximately noon. They thought their friend would be behind them, but he wasn't.

The St. Anthony RCMP was notified, and a search was started. The storm that hit the area was strong and hindered search efforts and their ability to keep aircraft in the sky. The effort to find Andrew didn't get started until the following day.

The search-and-rescue effort to find Andrew included multiple canine teams, helicopters, Newfoundland Rangers, RCMP, multiple fire departments, and volunteers. Teams did find Andrew's snowmobile. The vehicle was pointed in the wrong direction to get home, yet had half a tank of gas, had keys in the ignition, and was operable.

The May 5, 2006, edition of the *CBC News* had these details about what the RCMP did with Andrew's companions: "He said they were both interviewed multiple times by RCMP, and even took a lie detector test. RCMP Constable Mike Babstock said the two men accompanying Sexton were never considered suspects in his disappearance. The two men maintain that Sexton got lost in the storm. The RCMP said they believe the same."

After the RCMP closed down their five-day search because they stated there were no possible leads to follow, Andrew's family got two additional bloodhounds to look for the man. None of these efforts produced Andrew.

There were many claims that his body would be found during the following spring and summer. Nothing was ever found.

Let's review the basic elements of the case:

- Man traveling with friends on snowmobile alone
- Group was visiting a cabin
- Man gets separated from group
- Snowstorm hits the area
- Search efforts inhibited by bad weather
- Snowmobile is eventually found
- Vehicle is pointing in a direction away from their intended destination
- Man is never found

In *Missing 411: North America and Beyond* (page 422), I document the case of an Alaska man who disappeared under circumstances identical to those identified above. When news agencies contacted SAR coordinators about what may have happened to the snowmobiler and asked why he wasn't found, one of the SAR leaders at the time stated, "He says that he is sticking to his original alien abduction theory because he cannot come up with another scenario."

Andrew grew up in the outdoors in this area of Newfoundland. The cabin was approximately four miles from St. Anthony, and he would have known anything within a four-mile radius of his house very well.

The RCMP did everything possible to find the man; they even put divers in the water in the middle of the winter to clear any possibility that he had been accidentally submerged. People who live around snowmobiles know that these vehicles can save your life. They provide a big target for helicopters to find. They can offer shelter and warmth, especially if they're operational. Why would

Andrew have left the security of his vehicle? Why wasn't his body found? You could ask the exact same questions about the Alaska incident. After ten springs and summers, Andrew hasn't been found, and nothing associated with him has ever been recovered.

Cleon Smith
Missing: 04/02/11- p.m., St. Anthony, Newfoundland
Age at disappearance: 30 years
Weather• Water
    This is the second case from St. Anthony. This is a remote town at the end of the northern edge of Highway 430. To have two profile hits in a distant, Canadian village may seem very odd to some, not to me. The city sits on the ocean, a significant contributor to many Missing 411 cases, the closer to water there seems to be more missing.
    I have always had a special place in my heart for ice hockey players. I coached my son and daughter at the highest levels of youth hockey, and eventually, my son played defense in Division 1 for Miami University on a scholarship. Hockey players are always hard-working (or they don't play), generally very polite and don't get into much trouble; there are still exceptions.
    By every account I could locate, Cleon Smith was an extraordinarily talented and committed ice hockey player in Newfoundland. He played on a provincial AAA midget championship team from 1996-1997. He went on to play for the Ontario Hockey League for the Sault Ste. Marie Greyhounds and then went on to play college hockey in Canada for two years with the University of Prince Edward Island.
    Cleon was raised in St. Anthony and lived there on April 2, 2011. A *CBC News* post of April 4, 2011, explained what happened, "Dozens of volunteers raced across freshly fallen snow on Newfoundland's Northern Peninsula Monday, looking for any hints that would lead to the whereabouts of a missing hiker. Cleon Smith, 30, went out for a walk in St. Anthony on Saturday afternoon and has not been seen since. Blizzard conditions on Sunday hampered the search." Searchers did find footprints that they belonged to Smith, and they were heading to an area that he was known to frequent. An April 11, 20122

article in the *CNA Journalism* had additional details, "The hiking trail off Goose Cove Road is a lengthy trek through hills and wooded terrain behind St. Anthony. It leads out as far as the crumbling foundation of the former American military base. Cleon Smith routinely walked the path, and was often seen by locals walking along Goose Cove Road from North Street on his way to the trail. On a snow-covered day in early spring 2011, the 30-year old would take this familiar walk. It would be the last time he was ever seen.

Friends stated that Cleon was still in great shape the day he vanished. His hockey career was cut short by a severe shoulder injury, but that didn't stop him from playing recreationally. The search for Cleon was massive, 150 volunteers, the Canadian Rangers, RCMP, St. Anthony Fire Department, Roddickton Search and Rescue and student from the College of the North Campus all participated. Four days into the search, rescuers thought they found tracks that might have been Smith's heading toward the ocean, this was not confirmed.

The region that Cleon vanished has dozens of small bodies of water and water seems to be one consistent item that surrounds St. Anthony.

Articles written about the disappearance of the people from this small community all state the population is stunned. The loss of residents where there are no answers and no recoveries bother this far northern town.

William Oberkiser
Missing: 10/09/2011, Buchans, NL
Age at disappearance: 65 years
Weather• Canines• Hunter

Even people who think they are familiar with Canada probably are not keenly aware of Newfoundland. It is a relatively small island off the northeastern coast of Canada. If you look at a map, it's just northeast of Maine and Nova Scotia.

William Oberkiser

William Oberkiser was a seasoned and experienced hunter and outdoorsman. In 2009 he shot a world-record black bear in New-foundland and had it recognized as such. He had made numerous trips there hunting moose and bear.

William was a retired American Power electric linesman that had been enjoying the good life. He lived on Big Turkey Lake in Indiana. He loved the woods and forests, and the lake view gave him that constant reminder of the great outdoors.

On October 5, 2011, William left his home en route for Canadi-an hunting. He drove his Ford F-150 pickup and took an eight-hour ferry ride to Newfoundland. He was seen driving his truck off the boat and toward his hunting camp. William had taken a few days to eventually reach the end of his ferry ride. It was October 9 when his truck drove off.

On October 9 and October 10, another hunter had seen William's abandoned truck on a remote road and began to be concerned. The hunter contacted RCMP. The vehicle was found on Bottom Brook Road off of the Trans-Canada Highway. The truck was stuck on a stump. RCMP stated that William had taken a wrong turn and drove for six to nine miles on a road that wasn't fit for many ATVs. The po-lice got to the location and found that there was money in the truck, along with his hearing aids. They contacted his home in Indiana.

William's relatives confirmed that it appeared that he took two firearms when he left his truck, one being his shotgun. The family and RCMP couldn't understand why William would've taken the road the truck was found. He had been to the camp several times and wasn't suffering from any mental issue. They described him as extremely fit and smart.

Weather did inhibit some of the search effort. An October 20, 2011, article in the *Telegram* had this information about the rescue attempt: "A cormorant helicopter from the 103 search and rescue squadron from 9 Wing Ganger is also helping with the search and will airlift the police dog unit into the area as soon as weather per-mits. The weeklong search for the 65-year old from Indiana has been scaled back earlier this week because no sign of him had been found."

Several canine units were taken to the scene. None of the dog units were able to find William. Numerous helicopter overflights in the area did not find him. There were two separate searches that started and stopped because of weather issues. In late October the final search was terminated, and nothing was found. William's son and daughter both got emergency passports to travel to Canada and made it to the scene to look for their dad.

It has now been many years, and William has not been found.

Northwest Territories

Population: 44,000

Capital City: Yellowknife

The majority of North Americans do not know that one of the biggest suppliers of diamonds in the United States and Canada are located in the Northwest Territory (NWT). The mines are both located approximately 190 miles northeast of Yellowknife, and both have their offices in the city. The open area mines are in a harsh environment that can be driven to in the winter when creeks, rivers, and ponds are frozen. You can only get there by air during the summer.

When I was working for a company introducing new technology to the diamond industry, I flew to Yellowknife to meet with the general manager of one of the mines. The first reaction I had when landing was the enormous amount of huge mosquitoes. The city had nice facilities, including one of the largest public hockey rinks I have ever seen.

Yellowknife sits on Great Slave Lake, a vast body of water in the territories. The majority of the population lives in Yellowknife, and half the residents in the province are indigenous.

The region has excellent fishing and some hunting to the north. In the far north, the locals still trap for income.

Almost everything in the NWT is flown or trucked. I took a relatively short flight from Edmonton. The plane was odd, it was large, and the front was exclusively for cargo, and the rear half was for homo sapiens.

Yellowknife advertises heavily in Japan that they have the best Aurora Borealis sightings. Over 10,000 Japanese tourists a year travel to Yellowknife to view what they believe is a natural wonder and stare at the sky in frigid temperatures.

The primary industries in the NWT are mining (Petroleum, Gas, Diamonds), tourism, and government employment.

People in the states tend to think about how large the United States is and how much open space is still available, this pales in comparison to Canada. As an example of size, the NWT is almost twice the size of the State of Texas. The 44,000 inhabitants of the

NWT are spread throughout thirty-three main communities stretching from north of the Arctic Circle to the southern border with British Columbia, Alberta, and Saskatchewan.

I was extremely fortunate to take a trip into Nahanni National Park and see Virginia Falls. It meanders through granite outcroppings and falls 315 feet, nearly twice the height of Niagara Falls. The park is one of the most remote locations you can imagine, near the Yukon border. A friend gave me a ride into the region in his helicopter. Seeing the falls from the air was breathtaking.

The NWT is worth a visit in the summer months. Take with you lots of clothing and several bottles of insect repellant, which at times the local bugs seem to thrive on the spray, odd.

Northwest Territory list of missing people by dates.

Name	Date Missing• Age• Sex
Paul Robert	05/07/49• 21• M
Herbert Lafferty	10/08/60-Noon•12•M
Fred Van Duffelen	12/17/78, 4:00 a.m.• 26•M

Paul Robert
Missing: 05/07/49, 30 Miles south of Slave Lake, NWT
Age at disappearance: 21 years
Water• No Tracks

Morinville Alberta is twenty miles north of Edmonton. This region of the province is predominantly farming land and rural. Paul Robert spent the majority of his twenty-one years growing up in the suburb of Edmonton just outside Morinville. He was a young and athletic man and got a job working on oil rigs.

On May 7, 1949, Paul was working for Boyle Brothers Drilling at their site thirty miles south of Hay River in the Northwest Territories. The crew had worked a lengthy stretch, and Paul had a day off. He told his associates that he was going to follow a bulldozer path to another camp eight miles south that he had been to before. He packed some food and a few supplies and started his hike. Nobody in the work crew thought the length of the trek was unusual, and everyone liked to get out of their environment when they had the time.

How the search for Paul started is a story of perseverance and commitment. The following May 18, 1949 article in the Edmonton Journal has the details of how the RCMP and Army were notified of the disappearance, "Fellow workers with the Boyles Brothers Drilling Company started a search as soon as they learned that Robert had not reached his destination. Two men walked the thirty miles to Hay River to notify police."

When Paul vanished, all drilling in the immediate area stopped, and employees were sent into the bush to look for the man. The Army put up two Fox Moth aircraft that searched from the sky. On May 19, Indian trackers were used in an attempt to follow the path of Paul, and they did not have any luck. The Army coordinated with the RCMP and local trappers as two trappers traveled the river, looking for any clues as to where the hiker might be located.

Hay River is on the Great Slave Lake. The Alberta border is approximately 45 miles south of the town and lake. The region around the mining camp that Paul left is very wild and thick with vegetation and small bodies of water. This would not be a place where you'd want to wander from the bulldozer trail.

The search for Paul lasted three weeks. There were over one hundred hours of aircraft time dedicated to looking, and there were dozens of men that took time off work to do nothing but search. There was never anything found relating to Paul or what he might be carrying.

Herbert Lafferty
Missing: 10/08/60-Noon, Fort Resolution, NWT
Age at disappearance: 12 years
Point of Separation• Water• Weather

The Northwest Territories are located in northwest Canada just north of Alberta. I have visited the territories twice. The first time I went to the Cirque of the Unclimbables, a gorgeous granite monolith that is a favorite for climbers. You either fly in by helicopter or take a boat by river and hike into the valley. I was staying at the Inconnu Lodge operated by Warren, and Anita Lafave and Warren flew our family in to paint and refurbish an outdoor toilet. Yes, we were on vacation, but we were also great friends with the Lafaves, so a favor deserved a favor. The Cirque reminded me of a miniature Yosemite Valley.

This disappearance happened on the southeast side of Great Slave Lake in a small community named Fort Resolution. Yellowknife is almost exactly straight north across the lake approximately 50 miles.

On October 8, 1960, twelve-year-old Herbert Lafferty was hunting rabbits with his grandfather, Napoleon Lafferty in a remote region outside of town. An October 13, 1960 article in the *Edmonton Journal* had these details, "Herbert Lafferty disappeared around noon Saturday while snaring rabbits in the bush south of Fort Resolution. He was accompanied by his grandfather Napoleon Lafferty before they became separated. The search is concentrated on an area on the south shore of Great Slave Lake, about 650 miles north of Edmonton. Mr. Lafferty said he and the boy were approximately 10 minutes-walk from the main road, collecting rabbits from snares they had set out previously. Herbert set out for the road, planning to collect some rabbits along the way and wait for his grandfather to meet him on the road."

Napoleon stated that he waited for Herbert for about an hour and then went into the bush calling his name and then fired off multiple rounds trying to get his attention. No shots were fired by Herbert's 22 caliber rifle he was carrying. Napoleon thought at this point that the boy must have gone home, so the grandfather went back to the residence. Once he arrived and realized that Herbert was lost, he called Fort Resolution RCMP. After calling law enforcement, Napoleon went back to the location where he lost Herbert and continued to search late into the night.

The RCMP gathered volunteers with airplanes to search from the air and also found 40 town locals to scour the ground. The area of the search was described as swampy with muskeg and dense bush. An October 17, 1960 article in the *Leader-Post* had these details about the SAR, "Searchers have been hampered by cold weather and snow. RCMP Saturday described the weather as cold and clear." The RCMP had airplanes flying the region and also summoned a helicopter that operated for almost five days.

The massive search for Herbert Lafferty started on October 9 and continued for two weeks with the assistance of airplanes, helicopter, ground teams, and professional RCMP searchers. The effort found nothing. Searchers were surprised that they didn't even locate the rifle the boy was carrying.

This is another disappearance in a long line of cases I have documented where a young person disappears while in the presence of their grandparents, it's odd. I've lost count the number of times I have specifically mentioned this.

Fred Van Duffelen
Missing: 12/17/78, 4:00 a.m., Holman, NWT
Age at disappearance: 26 years
Point of Separation• Equipment Failure•
Water

Fred Van Duffelen

Fred Duffelen was raised in Ottawa and is the son of Frank and Freida Van Duffelen. He had a brother named Michael, a photographer for the territorial government in Yellowknife, Northwest Territories. Yellowknife is one of those cities that you have to visit to truly understand it. The area was frozen, cold, with few people on the streets. Summers in this area are known for great fishing and wildlife.

Michael and Fred grew up with an appreciation of the outdoors and were taught how to hunt. Nobody would claim that Fred was an expert hunter, but his family stated that he knew how to handle himself in the extremes of the north.

Holman is a small community on Victoria Island in the Northwest Territory. Fred ran a small co-op handicraft store in the city of three hundred. At 4:00 a.m. on December 17, Fred left the town on his snowmobile carrying his .243 Magnum rifle for big game and a .22-caliber rifle for small emergencies. He had told others that he'd be gone for one night on a caribou hunt and be back the following afternoon. During this time of the year, this region only gets two hours of partial sunlight per day. It is mostly dark during the winter this far north.

On December 19, the small community got concerned when Fred did not return. This wasn't the first time something like this happened to Fred. The RCMP told the press that Fred had gone out in months past and had his equipment fail only to be saved by the community and his friends that responded. Frank Van Duffelen strongly disagreed with the police stating that Fred's snowmobile only broke down one other time and it was the community that found and saved him.

Without strong survival skills, nobody is going to live long outside without cover in this environment. It can regularly get down to minus forty to minus sixty degrees.

The community and RCMP started the search to find the hunter almost immediately. Fred was headed fifty kilometers north to the hunting grounds. He specifically told a friend he was traveling ten miles northwest of Holman. He had a partner lined up to go with him who backed out at the last minute. A December 26, 1978, article in the *Ottawa Citizen* described the area: "'It is a well-traveled route, but it's treacherous in spots,' said Michael Van Duffelen, Fred's 28-year old brother. 'There's everything from deep valleys to high cliffs, so you've got to be careful.'" This exact area is 440 kilometers inside the Arctic Circle.

Search parties found Fred's camp thirty miles north of Holman and nowhere near the lake where he stated he was going. Searchers found his abandoned snowmobile, rifle, and survival gear. They found his sled held up by a piece of plywood, and it was apparent he had been sleeping under it. beneath it they located a foam mattress, sleeping bag, stove, and food. They even found a tea mug on a slight snow ledge. Fred had also brought along a second snow machine as backup. This was also found at the camp.

The RCMP flew their twin Otter aircraft for weeks looking for any sign of Fred. Local community members took long wood poles and penetrated the snow in the area, looking for a body.

There were many articles written a year after the disappearance calling this the "Arctic Mystery." There was no body. There was no explanation why Fred would leave the comfort and safety of his camp, knowing that the community would be looking for him.

Fred's family stated that he left the big city for the solitude of the great north. He loved the Inuit people and the freedom of movement offered by Holman.

Some people may think that Fred was reckless. I think you need to understand the mind-set of the natives living in the area. When someone goes missing, there isn't anger or any question if you are going to search. Everyone able to search will search. Everyone knew to go. The area can be treacherous, and the Inuit people know they need to count on each other. Fred knew this. The RCMP made statements that were demeaning to Fred. They stated that he didn't follow village instructions to tell the RCMP office when he was leaving and going to return. Well, if you are traveling with others, you supposedly didn't have to. When Fred woke up that morning, he believed his friend was going with him. At the last minute, the friend backed out.

Fred took another snowmobile with him to ensure he had transportation. I do not believe that Fred voluntarily left his camp. There was no reason to walk away from the safety, security and warmth of the structure he built. There are dangers in traveling the far north in the winter, Polar Bears. Nobody travels far in the arctic without a rifle, Fred knew this.

The formal search for Fred was terminated on January 4. Villagers did go back to the area the following spring and didn't find his body. It is truly a mystery what happened to a well-supplied and safety minded hunter.

Nova Scotia

Population: 942,000
Capital City: Halifax: 434,000

If there were ever a province that could be mistaken for an island, that would be Nova Scotia (NS). If it weren't for a narrow ten-mile strip of land that attaches NS to New Brunswick, we'd be talking about an island of 21,400 square miles in size. It is one of three maritime provinces with New Brunswick and Prince Edward Island.

Nova Scotia is one province that sits just fifty miles to the east of Maine and has approximately 3000 lakes and hundreds of rivers and streams. Eighty percent of the landmass is forest, and the government owns twenty-five percent of the forest. If you are in the open space areas, you might see moose and deer. The most prominent language in this area is English.

The capital of NS is Halifax, and the primary industry in this eastern town is shipping. Major oil tankers usually dock at Point Tupper, and other transport vessels often will go to the capital.

If you want an actual wilderness experience, it is recommended you visit Cape Breton National Park at the northernmost extreme point of the province. This open space is going to give you the wilderness experience you thrive for.

The demography you will find on NS is Scottish, 30%, English, 29%, Irish 20% and German 17% of the population.

The major cities in the province and their population:

Halifax: 434,000
Cape Breton: 31,000
Truro: 13,000
Amherst 10,000

One of the odd facts about this province is that it wasn't until 2013 that their flag wasn't officially adopted even though it had been in use for over 150 years. The United States and Canada have been arguing about the ownership of a small island between NS and Maine for hundreds of years. The grounds around the water are known as fantastic lobster fishing. One last interesting note, there has been a treasure hunt ongoing on Oak Island for hundreds of years, made famous recently by a show on the History Channel.

Nova Scotia list of missing people by date.

Name	Date Missing • Age • Sex • Location
Son of John Henderson	11/15/1826• 4 • M
Howard Newell	01/22/55-Noon •6 •M
Harris Hill	11/10/10, 1:00 p.m.• 87•M
Marty Leger	05/29/14-4:00 p.m.•30•M

Son of John Henderson
Missing 11/15/1826, Canadia Marsh, NS
Age at Disappearance: 4 years
Water• Berries

Nova Scotia is a province in Canada just northeast of Maine and along the Atlantic Coast. It is a region that is extremely swampy with large segments of undeveloped land.

A Halifax paper made mention of the fact that the son of John Henderson had disappeared from a rural family residence. The four-year-old was lost in the woods and not located until the following Wednesday. The article stated that four hundred people were searching for the boy, but it was the boy's father and his servant who found the boy as they were walking through the woods, and the boy recognized the servant.

A November 21, 1826, article in the *Indiana Journal* had the following description of what happened when the boy was found: "The little wanderer recognized the servant man and exclaimed 'Will you not take me to mamma?' The father on turning his eyes, beheld his son seated under a pile of hemlock windfall, completely embosomed in a thicket. The little fellow had eaten nothing but a little sorrel, but had drank freely of water."

The interesting part of this story to this point is the location where the boy was found—a thicket in a wind fall—a common location where missing children are found.

The other fascinating issue is what was noted that the boy was eating: sorrel. I have documented three other cases in the past where people have vanished and were found eating sorrel.

One of the more fascinating parts of this story is what searchers found just after John Henderson's son was located. As they were searching, they came across someone who we would describe today as a wildman. In the same *Indiana Journal* article was this description of the individual: "He was discovered in a most deplorable state of exhaustion, having lost the power of utterance; his face was black, his mouth filled with leaves and berries which he had neither the power of swallowing or spitting out—his body exhibited the appearance of a skeleton. He was conveyed to the nearest house—and in a few moments after, he died." This is a fascinating event that happened to occur just as the missing boy was found. Was this a coincidence, or were the two events related? Was it also a coincidence that the man died shortly after he was brought to a residence?

Many, many of the missing cases I write about have berries involved in some way. The man had berries in his mouth.

An October 26, 1826, article in the *Bangor Register* had additional information about the man who was found: "It is said to be a common thing for people to be lost in the wilds of Nova Scotia." I read this line multiple times. It appears that the disappearance of people in Nova Scotia while in the wild wasn't uncommon. A pretty sobering statement that begs the question: why were these people disappearing? I could not locate any additional cases in Nova Scotia that matched the criteria of this study.

Howard Newell
Missing: 01/22/55-Noon, Little River Harbour, NS
Age at disappearance: 6 years
Water• No Tracks• Intellect

Little River Harbour is at the far southwestern end of Nova Scotia in a very rural section of Yarmouth County. Even today the region has few homes and a small harbor. The forests in this area are thick, lush, and pristine. If you drew a line directly east from Acadia National Park in Maine and traveled fifty miles, you would hit

Little River Harbour. The small town is located twenty miles northwest of Shag Harbour, Nova Scotia. This incident occurred ten miles outside the small city in an extremely rural region.

Howard Newell

On January 22, 1955, at approximately noon, Howard was with a group of family members, led by his uncle, who were cutting firewood on a lot near his home. The group was getting ready to head back to their residence when Howard told the group that he was taking a shortcut through the woods. With nobody anywhere in the area but the group, Howard took off by himself, headed in the general direction of the residence. His cousins last saw him running through the snow, putting on his coat.

The group returned to the residence, and family members asked where Howard was. A June 9, 2008, article in the *NovaNewsNow*.com interviewed family members about the day Howard disappeared. The reporter interviewed Howard's sister Zita, twelve at the time, about the incident: "Her uncle said he was coming behind them but the sister didn't hesitate. She ran into the woods calling out her brother's name. There were no tracks. No Howard. What had she missed, she wondered? 'So I started retracing my steps and calling his name, stopping and listening in case he had fallen down.' But there was nothing. 'Then I kind of started panicking. My sister and one of my cousins appeared; we split up to search.' Still nothing."

This point in time started the search for Howard. Brian Newell was Howard's eight-year-old brother at the time and remembers going with others into the woods looking for Howard. He remembers those first moments of the search and explains what he did in the same article as quoted above: "Like the others, Brian went looking for his brother. 'It started to snow just as I got in the woods, big heavy snowflakes. So within an hour any tracks that you could have followed were all covered,' he recalls."

Nova Scotia threw every imaginable resource into the effort to find Howard Newell. Here is a partial list of the groups that were searching:

- Canadian army reserve from Yarmouth
- Naval training recruits from Cornwallis
- Helicopters from Shearwater
- Firefighters
- RCMP
- Bethany Bible College students and staff
- High school students who responded after the school was closed

Over one thousand people from throughout Nova Scotia walked shoulder to shoulder looking for the small boy. They didn't find anything.

Harold Newell was Howard's father. He remembers coming straight home from his construction job after hearing of the disappearance. He stated that he went straight to every water source he knew. He found no ice was broken and that it was too thick for his young son to crack. Harold worked for Kenney Construction. The owner shut down the company for days so employees could search for Howard.

There were rumors about what may have happened to the young boy. One of the biggest claims in the area was that a truck had hit the boy, and the driver had taken his body and burned it. In 1988 the RCMP took this incident as a cold case and looked into all possibilities. They found one of the occupants of the truck and had him take a polygraph test. He passed, proving there was no involvement and the truck story had no validity.

The RCMP reopening this case and handling it as a cold case is fascinating. Every document from them regarding this incident claimed it was a drowning. After the case was reopened and there were no new developments, they still claimed it was a drowning. Why did they have a cold case team investigate the disappearance if they were positive about their findings?

Howard Newell's relatives believed the child was very smart. In the same *Novanewsnow*.com article of June 9, 2008, his siblings were quoted: "Just in grade 1, attending a two-room schoolhouse in Melbourne, not only could he print his name, but he could write it too they say. 'He could do my homework, where I didn't have a clue,' says Brian [eight years old at the time]. Zita calls him 'One of those smart kids. And he was religious,' she says. Yes, he was still the type of kid to play in the dirt, but when it came time for the children to place their Christmas wishes—for that one special gift that they wanted—Howard's special request isn't what you would have expected a six-year old boy to ask for. 'He wanted a picture of Mary and Jesus, he wanted the Immaculate Heart,' Zita says." He hung the photo over his bed so it was close to him at night.

An eleven-day nonstop search failed to find any trace of Howard Newell. A follow-up search the following May also failed to find any evidence of a body floating to the surface or anything on land indicating where the boy may be.

Summary

I don't think I ever recall hearing such an explicit description of a young boy's intellect as I did in Howard's case. His religious beliefs and affiliation also strike a strong chord. It's obvious that Howard was a very smart and happy boy.

I am in Harold and Brian's camp on their beliefs about what happened to Howard. Harold didn't believe his boy went into the water. Brian is the lone sibling still living in the area, and he also does not believe his brother went in the water. The number of options for what happened to Howard is slim. There are no animal predators out moving in the bush in the month of January, when temperatures are near or far below zero. The idea that a human predator is walking in the woods in the middle of an extremely remote region of Nova Scotia seems unbelievable.

This story pulled at my heart.

Harris Hill
Missing: 11/10/2010- 1:00 p.m., West Bay Rd, Parrsboro, NS
Age at disappearance: 87 years
Canines• Water•

In my years researching missing person cases, Nova Scotia has been on my radar on more than one occasion. Considering the population, 942,926, and the relatively small size of the province, many would think there wouldn't be places to get lost. Even though it is one of the smallest provinces based on geographical size in Canada, it has many, many thousands of acres of open land.

Harris Hill

On November 10, 2010, eighty-seven-year-old Harris Hill had just finished his lunch at his home in Parrsboro. This is a small, rural city located near the Minas Basin, which is attached to the Bay of Fundy. Harris enjoyed the outdoors and deer hunting. He had a deer hunting stand on West Bay Road just outside of Parrsboro. After finishing lunch, he drove his truck out toward his stand to deliver apples for the deer.

After a short drive, Harris stopped just off the road and made the three-hundred-yard walk to the stand. At this point something very unusual happened.

Late on the afternoon of November 10, friends and family members contacted authorities and notified them that Harris had not come back from his stand. The alarm went out, and this started a massive four-day search to find the hunter.

The RCMP took the lead on the SAR and subsequent investigation. It was established that Harris had made it to his stand. That was all that was confirmed. Nearly six hundred ground searchers combed the land around the deer stand for four days. The RCMP brought in multiple police canines to look for a scent and five different search-and-rescue teams also committed canines to search. The dogs found nothing. The Canadian Department of Natural Resources put two helicopters into the sky for the four days. They found nothing. A grand total of 7,500 hours of searching produced absolutely no results. The RCMP made

statements that there was no foul play suspected in the disappearance of Harris.

The area around the deer stand was described as boggy. It was
also stated that this area was not heavily hunted, and it was doubtful
that anyone was in the area when Harris vanished.

Harris Hill was a World War II veteran. He had lived a very full
life and was starting to enjoy the fun side of retirement. His health was
described by family members as very good. If he would've had a heart
attack or medical condition that put him on the ground, I believe that
canines would have picked up the scent and led searchers to his body,
this did not happen. If he would have stumbled into a swamp or boggy
area, the helicopters with FLIR would have seen the body. The search
for Harris started early in the evening of the day he vanished. Searchers
were calling his name and listening for a response. They heard nothing.

A November 14, 2010, article on the CBC News website had
these headlines: "Search for N. S. Hunter Called Off": words that
no family wants to hear. The investigation into Harris's disappearance is ongoing, and there were other articles in 2011 stating that the
RCMP was still on the case.

Let's hope that the family gets some type of closure on the case.

Marty Leger
Missing: 05/29/14 at 4:00 p.m.—Spider Lake, Waverley, NS
Age at Disappearance: 30 years
• Weather• Canines

To a casual observer, this land
may look like an island, but it is attached to the mainland. This is also
the same place where the hit show
The Curse of Oak Island is filmed.
What I find fascinating about this
region is that there are far more people missing from this small piece
of land than from New Brunswick,
especially since there are approximately 30 percent more people in
New Brunswick.

Marty Leger

On May 29, 2014, thirty-year-old Marty Leger left his home in Halifax and traveled north to a remote region northeast of Waverley. He drove out Spider Lake Road and parked at the dead end. At six feet tall and 260 pounds, he was a big man. He got out his mountain bike and rode off into the bush. He had told friends when he left at noon that he'd be back by 4:00 p.m. When he hadn't returned, his family drove out to the site and found his vehicle. At 8:30 p.m., they reported Marty as a missing person.

This area is a combination of extremely thick bush, swamps, and lakes that are marked by a one-hour and two-hour circular path.

On May 30, 2014, the RCMP organized a search and started to deploy resources. One of the biggest searches in the history of Nova Scotia was put into motion. Three helicopters, 450 searchers, boats, planes, search dogs—everything was thrown at the effort to find Marty. The June 3, 2014, edition of the *Chronicle Herald* had these important details: "He said the ground search covered more than 60 square kilometers, and a number of helicopters have gone over lakes, which are remarkably clear because of dry weather. Search dogs scoured the area, and helicopters equipped with thermal imaging technology also failed to locate Leger. Dogs and helicopters will be brought back to the site at some point to resume the search, Wells said." One helicopter pilot said to a reporter it was the largest search he'd ever seen in his life. Even the Canadian military sent two hundred soldiers to train and search.

At the end of five days, one of the lead searchers stated that the extreme heat of near ninety degrees had exhausted searchers and dogs. That is an unusually high heat for that part of the world. After a huge effort, search coordinators terminated the effort to locate Marty. They had found nothing related to his disappearance. There were random efforts to search for the man after this major effort; they also did not locate anything.

Sometimes it's difficult to understand how a body the size of Marty's can be missed. If you couple the body with the bike, it makes not finding anything extremely puzzling. If that bike is anywhere in the sun, it absorbs heat during the day and slowly emits it as night moves on. If SAR had put a helicopter with FLIR up at night, that bike should have stuck out. Why haven't they found it?

Ontario

Population: 13,505,000
Capital City: Toronto
The second-largest province in Canada in area is Ontario. It is 1075 miles from its northern to the southern border and 1050 miles wide. It has 415,000 square miles, with 68,490 square miles of freshwater. The province has 250,000 lakes and ponds that includes 1/5 of the worlds fresh water.

Toronto is the capital of Ontario with 13,505,000 and has notoriety at the country's banking and finance center.

Ontario seems to export many of the celebrities that we know and love in North America. The following list represents individuals that all came from Ontario:
Dan Aykroyd
Jima Carrey
Ryan Gosling
Norm McDonald
Wayne Gretzky
Justin Bieber
Paul Anka
Bryan Adams
Shania Twain.

The largest cities in Ontario are listed below:
Toronto (Provincial Capital): 2,732,000
Ottawa(Canadian Capital): 934,000
Brampton: 593,000
Hamilton: 536,000
London: 383,000

Ontario is so large that it has shoreline of four Great Lakes, Superior, Huron, Erie, and Ontario. It also has five notable National Parks that include, Pukaskwa, Bruce Peninsula, Georgian Bay Islands, Thousand Islands, and Point Pelee. One thing that Canadian thrive for is the great outdoors, and this is mirrored in the number of parks in each province. Ontario has over 125 provincial parks within its boundaries.

If you enjoy water, the plains, outdoors activity, you'll relish Alberta.

Eastern Ontario

You will immediately notice that Algonquin Provincial Park dominates this region. Predominantly during the summer months, 300,000 visitors frequent the park. This park has many areas that are wild and remote. With eight rivers and 2,500 lakes, 10 percent of the park is underwater. The park was named after the Algonquin-speaking First Nations People of Canada.

The Algonquin Park is best known for its population of moose and its 2,000-plus black bear, a very large population for the size of the park. The most amazing thing about this region is that there is not one reported missing person inside the Algonquin Provincial Park, not one! Considering the remote nature of the park, ability to get lost, numerous rivers, lakes, and wildlife threats, this is an amazing statistic.

While there are no people reported missing inside Algonquin Park, there are seven reported missing people on the perimeter. It does seem odd that people are missing on the perimeter of the park, yet nobody is missing inside. It sounds like the national park service of Canada is utilizing the same policy as the U.S. National Park Service.

I usually conduct an Internet search of the regions I'm researching to understand any unusual events and current trends. There are two highly unusual events that occurred in Algonquin Park that received long-term media coverage.

In May of 1978 George Halfkenny (16 years) and his brother Mark (12 years) and their friend William Rhindress (15) entered the park to go fishing. The boys didn't return from the trip and a search ensued. The boys were found mauled and deceased. A May 17, 1978 article in the *Windsor Star* stated, "there was quite a bit of mauling and the bodies were partially eaten." The killing of the boys was blamed on an angry male black bear. The article later states that the only known attack in the area occurred in 1881 when John Dennison was killed by a wounded bear. There was one puzzling statement made by Sergeant Tom Parker of the Pembroke RCMP.

In an *Associated Press* Article on May 18, 1978 Parker stated that Dr. R.G. Tasker a pathologist at Pembroke Civil Hospital stated the following, "the youths all bore marks indicating that they had been mauled by an animal." Readers need to carefully understand statements made by officials, "mauled by an animal", not mauled by a bear. Dr. Tasker chose his words carefully and doctors usually are precise about their diagnosis and descriptions, I don't think this was an oversight.

The second incident in Algonquin Park occurred on October 11, 1991, Raymond Jakubaukas (32) and Carola Frehe (48) were camping on Opeongo Lake in the south-central area of the park. This is one of the largest lakes in the park. They had set up their campsite on Bates Island and were in the process of securing the camp and getting dinner ready when a black bear attacked and killed both people. Articles in the *Toronto Star* state that law enforcement officials claim the bear broke each person's neck and consumed their remains. Officials arrived at the site five days after the people were killed and claimed the bear was still on the scene consuming the bodies. A park official called the killings "off the scale" of normal bear behavior.

I have spent thousands of hours in the outdoors and an equal number researching wildlife issues. The killing of a human by a black bear is extremely rare, and I have never heard of a black bear killing two people in one incident let alone three. It's probably occurred before; I just don't know of it. It's equally mind-boggling that the bear was able to break the neck of each person, not an easy injury to inflict. It seems highly unusual that the bear could withstand the fight of one individual while the other was under attack. Maybe a grizzly would maintain the fight, but it's hard to believe a black bear would stay and fight while exposing itself to injury. I have no doubt that both incidents occurred, but this is very, very unusual.

Missing People in Ontario by Date

Missing Person	Date Missing• Age• Sex
Edward Boreham	10/11/26 at 9:00 a.m. • 2 •M
Ralph McKay	10/27/28–2:15 a.m.•21•M
Eva Hall	08/15/32–PM•13•F

Geraldine Huggan	07/05/53•5•F
Eugene Loughlin	11/12/55, 4:00 p.m.• 62•M
Jack Ostrom	05/29/57 •74 •M
Meryl Newcombe	10/29/59• 50•M
George Weeden	10/29/59• 63•M
Sander Lingman	11/01/60•35•M
Diane Prevost	09/17/66•2•F
Adrian McNaughton	06/12/72-PM•5•M
Elizabeth Kant	10/16/72• 45•F
Brian Henry	05/05/74•21•M
Jane Smith	08/09/75•20•F
Raymond Juranitich	10/08/75•48•M
Foster Bezanson	10/25/80• 64• M
Toivo Reinikanen	09/26/84•36•M
Jessica Azzopardi	07/24/85–3:30 p.m.•20 MOS•F
Clayton McFaul	08/15/86•50•M
Michael McIntyre	04/07/94•37•M
William Reed	08/01/95•69•M
Frank Szpak	09/23/96• 69•M
Bernard Champagne	07/10/97• 80• M
Raymond Tunnicliffe	08/26/02•72•M
Joseph Grozelle	10/22/03-5:00 a.m.•21•M
Christine Calayca	08/06/07•20•F
Lachlan Cranswick	01/23/10 •41•M
Daniel Trask	11/03/11–Unk•28•M
Jeffery Boucher	01/13/14-7:00 a.m.•52•M
Douglas Queen	03/17/14-Noon •48•M
Ethan Stokes	01/25/15-1:45 a.m.•20•M
Paul Yelland	10/23/17-12:30 p.m.• 66• M

Edward Boreham
Missing: 10/11/26 at 9:00 a.m.—Eastview, Ontario
Age at Disappearance: 2 years
Weather• Previously Searched

I have documented many unusual disappearances in Ontario, Canada, over the years. This incident happened in the city of Ottawa in an area called Eastview. It appears to have happened right on the border with the United States, and both police departments shared in the search.

On October 11, 1926, two-year-old Edward Boreham was playing in front of his house at 11 Park View with two other boys, Ronald Tomlinson and another boy named Anson. The two boys had to go on to school and claim they told Edward to go home. This was the last time the child was seen. The police were notified, and a search was started. From every indication in the articles reviewed, this area was remote, and some of it was quite wild.

There weren't a lot of details on the search other than an explanation that Eastview and Ottawa Police responded to at least alleged sightings of the boy and a variety of locations throughout the city. On each incident, the police arrived, and the boy wasn't there, or they found the supposed boy, and it was not Edward.

Nothing happened on this case for forty-six hours. On Wednesday morning, October 13, George Allan was leaving for work. The October 13 edition of the *Ottawa Citizen* had these details:

> I was just leaving for work and had entered the path through the bush to get to the street car at the Patrick Street bridge when, about 150 feet from my house, I heard the whimper of a child. I circled around endeavoring to locate where the sound came from and I soon came upon a boy sitting under a cedar tree and holding a Boy Scout belt in his hand. He was crying for his parents and sister, Betty. I picked him up and took him to my house where I called Rev. Mr. Weary of St. Margaret's Church and when he arrived we proceeded to the home of Mrs. Boreham to who I restored the child.

Edward was found just a quarter mile from his home. Later in the same article were these additional details: "An explanation of the course of his wanderings is very difficult. Seemingly he has been on the move most of the time since his disappearance, and it is not thought by any of the searchers that he had been in the same bush in which he was found since he disappeared. The bush was thoroughly combed Monday and last night by Boy Scouts and others searchers without success." The October 13, 1926, edition of the *Ottawa Journal* had these additional facts: "The area around this spot was thoroughly combed last evening by hundreds of searchers, police, residents of Eastview and Clarkstown, Eastview and Ottawa Boy Scouts, school children and others. In addition, children of Mr. Allan had been at the identical spot last evening playing with a dog. If the child was there, it is believed he could not have escaped notice." What is very interesting about the last article is the fact that Mr. Allan's kids were playing on the property the prior night. If a small child is missing and hears other kids, there is a very high likelihood the missing child would approach the other children.

One article did state that it rained in the area of the disappearance while Edward was missing and was raining as recently as fifteen minutes before he was found.

The October 13 edition of the *Ottawa Citizen* had this information about Edward's condition after he was found: "Little Edward, suffering from a severe cold, had lost considerable flesh about the legs and arms, while his cheeks, although rosy had sunk slightly. How he lived through his wandering experience is beyond the comprehension of his parents and friends. He is confined to be and is being attended by Dr. Robert Law." It was reported that Edward did have a fever.

While kids may not be a good indicator of sensing someone in the woods near them, dogs are. If the Allan kids were in the exact area where Edward was found the night prior and the dog never indicated anything unusual, I do not believe Edward was anywhere in the area. I also think it's important to remember Edward was found adjacent to the Rideau River. How he was able to avoid going in the river for two days, we will never know.

If you couple the Allan kids, hundreds of searchers, and a dog, all in the same area where Edward was found, you can come only to the conclusion that something highly unusual happened. His parents questioned Edward in the days after he was found. They said the only thing they could get out of him was something about a car, nothing else. There was no other clarity offered about the incident.

Ralph McKay
Missing: 10/27/1928-2:15 a.m., London, Ontario
Age at disappearance: 21 years
Twin• Water• Unknown Cause of Death

I've always stated that we study history for a reason. I've also stated that there is a historical aspect to the missing person issue that we need to understand. Once I started to research student disappearances in rivers, I checked the historical archives for similar cases and found Ralph McKay.

London, Ontario is situated on the stretch of land that separates Detroit, Michigan, from Hamilton, Ontario, and separates Lake Erie from Lake Huron. It straddles two of the Great Lakes.

Ralph McKay, who had a twin brother, lived in three different cities while growing up. He lived in Medicine Hat, Regina, and Moose Jaw before moving to London, Ontario, and attending the University of Western Ontario. The university sits adjacent to the Thames River. He was studying mathematics and public speaking.

On October 27, 1928, during the early morning hours, Ralph was working at the Penman Factory in London. He had a part-time job where he got off work at 2:00 a.m. Articles state the night was slightly unusual in that Ralph got a phone call at the factory for the very first time. He left work at the regular 2:00 a.m. time and was never seen again alive.

It isn't clear from reviewing the archives what was exactly the catalyst for reporting Ralph as a missing person, but he was reported. Ralph's father from Regina heard the news that his son had disappeared and responded to the campus. There was a strange statement given to university students who wanted to help search for their friend, as was reported in the November 7, 1928, *Medicine Hat News*: "There is another angle to this baffling mystery which is intriguing. It is stated by a member of Western's Student Council that some of the students desired to organize search parties or adopt other methods of locating their missing colleague. The matter was broached to certain members of the faculty and the students were informed that it would be wise not to take any steps in that direction. Many of the students are now wondering why certain of their professors should not wish them to join in the hunt. As far as the police are concerned they are on a blind trail. There has been a voluminous issuance of circulars." It was never clarified why the students weren't encouraged to search.

Police and family members were confused as to why Ralph would disappear. A December 17, 1928, article in the *Medicine Hat News* had the following: "Police have yet to find the 'something' behind the disappearance. At first it was believed that long hours of study in the day time and mill work at night had been responsible for amnesia or loss of memory, but according to university officials, McKay was taking only six lecture hours per week." I always silently chuckle to myself when I read older articles talking about amnesia as a reason for a disappearance. In the early 1900s and late 1800s, I've often read these types of theories. I have never seen a credible allegation in more modern times.

There were few articles or updates on Ralph until December 17, 1928, in an article in the *Montreal Gazette*: "The body of Ralph McKay, University of Western Ontario student, who disappeared on October 27, was found in the Thames River here Saturday." Later in the same article is this: "The body was found in a small cove near a bathhouse by three boys." The article went on to say that Ralph's wallet and a small sum of money was found inside with his identification cards. He was listed as fully clothed. Investigators stated that the body was badly decomposed but that it didn't appear to them that it was anything more than a drowning.

In a December 20, 1928, article in the *Winnipeg Free Press* was a statement about Ralph's cause of death: "A post mortem report produced by Dr. F.W. Luney, failed to divulge the actual cause of death but reported it was not due to drowning." The report stated that there were no marks of violence on the body and there was no evidence of poisoning. They also stated that foul play was not involved.

I believe that this is an important case. The time of the disappearance, the school that he attended being adjacent to a major river, and the finding that the medical examiner couldn't determine the cause of death with a body in the river for forty-eight days are all suspicious. The area just east of this location in Ontario also has had suspicious disappearances.

Eva Hall
Missing 8/15/32, Poverty Bay, ON
Age at Disappearance: 13 years
Water• Berry Picker•

Poverty Bay is an extremely rural community one hundred and fifty miles north of the United States, six miles west of Sundbridge, and sixteen miles west of Algonquin Provincial Park. There are literally hundreds of small bodies of water in the area of the city with the general landscape being extremely swampy.

On August 16, 1932, thirteen-year old Eva Hall went into the bush to pick huckleberries and never returned. A search party was soon organized and spent two days searching for any sign of the girl, finding none. There was much conjecture that she fell into Poverty Bay and drowned, or decided to go into the woods and live, or that she suffered sunstroke and died. None of these answers made any sense.

News articles indicated that over four hundred searchers from the United States responded to the area of Poverty Bay to look for Eva. If Eva decided to walk into the woods and somehow survived, there is no doubt that she would've responded to the searchers looking for her. Rescue personnel did drag Poverty Bay extensively and never found her body.

Summary

I have written extensively about the relationship between berries and missing people. There was an entire chapter written in *Missing 411-Eastern United States* about missing berry pickers. The most dangerous berries to pick are, without a doubt, huckleberries. I have no understanding why huckleberries represent the most dangerous berry, but people picking these berries who disappear are rarely found.

We actually spent considerable time researching Algonquin Provincial Park and were startled by what we found. There have been several savage attacks by black bears in the park, attacks that are out of character for the normally timid black bear. There was one attack at the park where two people died in one event, a highly unusual attack for black bears. I would invite readers to conduct their own

Google search on the park and read about the attacks. It seemed slightly coincidental that we were researching the park and just happened to come across Eva's disappearance.

Geraldine Huggan
Missing: 07/05/53, 10:00 a.m., six miles west of Minaki, Ontario
Age at disappearance: 5
Water• Weather•

Mr. and Mrs. Jared Huggan left their home in Winnipeg for a six-week summer vacation. They brought their three daughters to visit the girls' grandparents at their summer cottage in Wade, Ontario, six miles west of Minaki. The area around the cottage is swampy and has many lakes. There is also a Canadian Railroad line that ran through the territory. This was an extremely remote and wild part of Northern Ontario.

On July 5, 1953, the families were getting their supplies together to spend the day at Fox Lake. Two of the girls were in the front yard of the cabin and Geraldine was in the side yard. At 10:00 a.m. the families were ready to leave but couldn't find Geraldine. She had been left alone for less than ten minutes. The families did an extensive search but couldn't find the girl. A call was made for police in Minaki and they responded.

Once RCMP from Minaki arrived, they also made a call to First Nations trackers who lived in the region. A call was also made to federal army personnel in Winnipeg for assistance.

As the search was starting, heavy rains hit the Wade area and greatly affected the searchers and their ability to follow footprints. Geraldine's father was one of the leaders of the search party. He informed all searchers that Geraldine didn't like the dark and if lost would sit and cry. She didn't wander. This was good news for the searchers as they felt that the search efforts would be brief and she'd be found quickly.

Nobody thought the search would last for three days, but the third day searchers found what they believed were Geraldine's footprints high on a rock ledge above Fox Lake. The search numbers now reached two hundred and included aircraft, First Nations People, and RCMP.

The search started to drag into the seventh day and still searchers had not found the girl or further evidence of where she was located. At this point Kenora prospector Harry Hawes joined the search for Geraldine. He had been credited with finding two lost boys from Kenora two years earlier. He had found the boys very near Long Lake, and Harry thought the girl would be found there too. He never explained why he felt Geraldine would be found at that lake (of the twelve lakes in the area), but he clearly made that statement.

A July 15 article in the *Winnipeg Free Press* stated: "Ontario Police said Wednesday that a newly discovered print was not too old and pointed out that bushes in the area are laden with berries and that the water in the lake is fit for human consumption." The point of the article is that there was food and water in the area to help a person survive.

Nine days into the search, First Nation searchers found a fleck of what they believed was Geraldine's shirt on the eastern shore of Long Lake. The cloth was shown to Geraldine's parents, who confirmed it was from her shirt. The thread from the cloth appeared to have been pulled off the shirt as if someone had walked by and pulled it away.

On the tenth day of the search, Indians (the term used in articles) were at the far northeastern corner of Long Lake. Six hundred feet south of the railroad tracks, they found what they believed were Geraldine's remains. The searchers found the girl's plaid shirt and her blue jeans. In the area near the clothes, searchers also located a small meadow where the ground had been matted down, indicating something large had been dragged there. Near the meadow searchers found Geraldine's blue jeans had one leg turned inside out, an unusual find that was noted. The exact location of the scene was between Catastrophe Lake and Long Lake, at their northern ends. The area was swampy and had the appearance of a brutal scene. There was blood in the area. A July 16 article in the *Calgary Herald* included the following: "'There was not enough left for either a proper burial or an inquest,' said Dr. D. J. Mason, coroner." Further clarity was given in a July 16 article in the *Sarasota Herald*: "There was no indication immediately as to the cause of the child's death. The body had been mauled, apparently by wild animals, but Indian searchers said there was no blood on the clothing." Trackers also stated that they found wolf hair and tracks in the area of the remains, but believed the wolf arrived after Geraldine died.

Several articles made insinuations that the girl may have died from a wolf attack. The Indians (First Nation) apparently heard about this statement and came back making the statement that there was no blood on her clothing. If a wolf had attacked Geraldine, it is generally believed that the clothes would have been torn to shreds and there would have been blood and bite marks on all the clothing. Also, Geraldine's pant leg was turned inside out; this happens when someone removes the pants. Again, the pants weren't torn.

There was other controversy about this case. Seven days into the search, Indian trackers had found what they believed to be an adult-sized track in the moss in the search area. A July 15, 1953, article in the *Winnipeg Free Press* titled "Controversy" included the following narrative: "After discovery of the Sunday clue [footprint] there had been some controversy among searchers as to whether they could have been animal tracks or prints of an adult shrunken in the moss." Indian trackers tend to know the land better than others—period. If the Indian trackers stated that the way the moss reacted indicates the track may have come from an adult, I would tend to believe them.

Case Summary

This case is near the top of my list for complexity and intrigue. No, I do not believe that a wolf killed Geraldine—no way. The scene would have been much more gruesome; blood would be all over the clothing; and the clothing would be shredded. I also believe Geraldine's skull would have been found (it wasn't). The teams didn't even find enough bones to give the girl a burial (per newspaper articles).

I've been in the bush in the far north, and I understand the terrain. It is very quiet up north when the wind is not blowing. If you yell for someone, your voice can easily travel up to hundreds of yards. When Geraldine disappeared, she was only missing ten minutes before her parents started to search. The bush area in the north can be extremely thick, swampy, and movement can be very slow.

The idea that a five-year-old girl could be out of voice range in just ten minutes is very hard to believe.

It was never clarified why prospector Harry Hawes believed Geraldine would be found at Long Lake. It is also not known if the boys he found two years earlier were found alive. The circumstances behind how and when they were found are not available.

I believe geographical landmarks are named for a specific reason. Whether it is a mountain, lake, or stream, names associated with those locations usually have historical significance. I'd like to know how Catastrophe Lake got its name.

One of the most revealing newspaper articles included an interesting quote: "The body had been mauled, apparently by wild animals, but Indian searchers said there was no blood on the clothing." The portion, "apparently by wild animals," doesn't sound like a very firm statement. I don't believe this statement was framed the way it was by accident. I don't think the evidence that an animal devoured the girl was very strong, and this is supported by the Indians' statements.

What happened to Geraldine Huggan? There are many opinions of what might have happened to the young girl, but the answers with the most credibility would probably come from the Indians who were searching because they know their land and its history.

There are many similarities between the deaths of Geraldine Huggan and Bart Schleyer from the Yukon Territory (see the "Yukon" chapter for details).

Eugene Loughlin
Missing: 11/12/55, 4:00 p.m., Saint Pierre Lake, ON
Age at disappearance: 62 or 63 years
Cluster Zone• Water• Point of Separation• Weather• Illness/ Disability

Over the years I have become very familiar with Ontario and its associated disappearances. This specific area of the province has hundreds of small lakes and ponds. As I have stated hundreds of times, water is one of the factors associated with many of the disappearances I've documented. I am not stating that water killed the people. Water was somehow involved.

I have also written about coincidences. It is quite a coincidence that the exact area where Eugene Loughlin vanished is also a geographical cluster that was established through my research years ago. Aside from Eugene's case, there are three other individuals that have gone missing in this exact area. In looking at the area around this region, nothing about it appears different from the vast majority of the province.

Saint Pierre Lake, where this incident occurred, is twenty-five miles south of Renfrew and eighty miles north of Kingston, a region I have written about extensively.

In November 1955, Eugene Loughlin was a technical officer for the Natural Research Council that was living in Ottawa. On November 9, Eugene left his Ottawa home and traveled with a group of friends to his hunting camp on Saint Pierre Lake. Eugene knew this area like the back of his hand. He had been traveling to and hunting this exact area for over thirty years.

On November 12, Eugene left the camp at 10:00 a.m., telling his friends that he was going to hunt alone. He left camp wearing a bright red coat. At 4:00 p.m. he stopped by another camp at the lake and spoke to friends and then left there to resume hunting. As darkness started to fall, Eugene failed to return to his camp.

Eugene's friends started to search for the hunter the night he went missing. They went into the woods, called his name, but did not get a response. They decided to fire three rounds into the air as a signal. They received three rounds fired back. The friends moved toward the rifle shots and thought they got to the exact spot where they heard the shots. The group again fired three rounds into the air and again got three rounds fired back. They again went to the area where they heard the shots and found nothing. They were befuddled and returned to their camp to get more help.

On November 13, provincial police in Renfrew got involved in the search. They attempted to get more resources into the area and were faced with a multitude of issues. The biggest problem was that thieves had stolen telephone wire that was strewn between the lake and Renfrew, and this made phone communication horrible. The other issue was freezing rain and bad weather inhibiting searchers.

On November 17, one hundred fifty tank and infantrymen from Canadian Armed Services at Camp Petawana came onto the scene and scoured the lake region. Boats were put on the lake and told to search the shore, these efforts proved fruitless.

Mrs. Loughlin was contacted in Ottawa and notified of the disappearance and asked for her insights. She stated that her husband rarely wandered far from camp. She did advise that Eugene wasn't feeling well when he left their home and was hoping he'd feel better before he arrived at the lake.

A November 17 article in the *Ottawa Journal* described some of the obstacles that searchers were facing: "Weather today continued bitterly cold with below freezing temperatures and strong blustery winds hampering the searchers. Planes and helicopters said to have been offered by the RCAF rescue service at Trenton still cannot be called in even though the chances of their useful are slight."

The area that Eugene vanished was described by various hunters as wet, boggy, and a forested jungle. Late in the search effort, some believed they found remnants of an old fire that was thought might have been used by Eugene. Many locals in the surrounding communities took time off of their jobs to help find the hunter.

After a lengthy and comprehensive search, the decision was made to terminate the SAR effort. The loss of Eugene left friends and fellow hunters stunned. A man that owned and visited his hunting camp for over thirty years vanished. A man that never wandered far from camp seemingly disappeared, and the Canadian military and locals couldn't find a trace of him. This is the fourth disappearance from this geographical area that I've documented.

I have explained in the past that if disappearances happened one on top of the other with a small period of time between the cases, this would raise a red flag and make local newspaper headlines. If you spread the disappearances over fifteen to twenty-five years, police officers and local officials have retired, reporters forget about other similar cases in the area, and the community will probably never tie the cases together. This is the reason it is important to study history.

Jack Ostrom
Missing: 05/29/57-Unk, Jawbone Lake, Ontario
Age at disappearance: 74 years
Water•

    I've written about a series of unusual disappearance that happened in Ontario in a one-hundred-mile radius of Timmins. Jawbone Lake is located seventy-three miles south of the city and twenty miles north of the Trans Canadian Highway. It is surrounded by hundreds of small bodies of water and very rugged terrain. The majority of the articles researched for this event listed the man's name as Ostrom; one article spelled it Ostrum.

    Jack Ostrom had taken his son, Harry, and fellow prospector, Ivan Anderson, by floatplane from South Porcupine to Jawbone Lake. Ostrom had a prospecting claim in the area and was going to work the zone for two weeks. On May 29, 1957, Ostrom set out with his ax and a compass to head one mile north and said he'd be back at the end of the day. He didn't return. Harry and Ivan searched nonstop for two weeks but were unable to find the man.

    On June 12 the floatplane arrived to pick up the men, and the pilot was told of the disappearance. The plane returned to South Porcupine and gathered searchers for the return trip. The Royal Canadian Air Force was advised of the disappearance. They looked at topographic maps and said the area was too dangerous and refused to participate.

    Friends and veteran bushmen did go into the area and allegedly found tracks. A June 18, 1957, article in the *Windsor Daily Star* had the following: "Two members of the ground party looking for the missing man reported Tuesday they have been following tracks for three days. Ostrom now is believed to be in a triangle formed by Mile and McKee Rivers, which meet six miles south of Jawbone Lake, and two parties of searchers have been dispatched down each river in canoes." It's fascinating that searchers were following tracks six miles south of the lake, and Ostrom was heading north. He had a compass and knew the area from past trips.

    There was an article published on July 24, 2012, in the *Timmins Times,* which discussed a series of missing people around Timmins. Many of the missing they discussed have been written about in prior

Missing 411 books. The article made a special point that many of the missing were berry pickers that were never found.

There is a cluster of missing people in and around Timmins. Most of the missing are older males.

Jack Ostrom was never found.

Meryl Newcombe
Missing: 10/29/59, Chapleau, ON
Age at disappearance: 50 years

George Weeden
Missing: 10/29/59, Chapleau, ON
Age at disappearance: 63 years
Point of Separation• Disability/ Illness
Hunter[a] Water•

Newcombe and Weeden

George Weeden and Meryl Newcombe were at a hunting camp that was owned and operated by the Newcombe family. They were moose hunting near the lodge when they failed to return from an outing on October 29; they were never seen again. They were last seen between mile marker 106 and 107 of the CPR Line. The men were supposedly last seen at their camp on October 23. Workers on a passing train had seen the guys near the camp. Searchers also located two aboriginal trappers, Clem and Herb Nabigon, who had seen them later that same day in the same area. Meryl's wife reported the pair missing on October 29.

The Newcombe family camp was located on the north shore of Friendly Lake near Broughton Township at the Canadian Pacific mileage marker 107. This is located approximately 111 miles west of Chapleau.

George Weeden was an individual that was never going to walk or hike long distances. In 1941 George had been seriously injured in a train accident, where he sustained a broken back and debilitating injuries to his right leg. It was also stated by family members that he had a bad heart.

One of the largest searches for the 1960s was conducted for these two men. There was a second search in the spring of 1960 after the snowmelt occurred, never finding one clue of what happened to the pair. There were over one hundred searchers scouring the bush and rivers for the men. They placed nets across rivers and dragged lakes. They found nothing. The search was suspended because of a bad storm.

Summary

The case of Weeden and Newcombe is highly unusual, very frustrating, and doesn't make much sense. The men were at a remote hunting camp owned by the Newcombe family. These were seasoned outdoorsmen who were not going to walk far from their vehicle; they were staying close to the truck and railroad tracks because of Weeden's injuries. Both men were undoubtedly armed because they were hunting. The men would not have been attacked by a bear; they were hibernating in late October. Both men were hunting in the Crown Game Preserve, known for its outstanding variety of birds and mammals. The Ojibwe First Nations Tribe lives in the middle of this area and knows the variety of game that it offers. They have the ability to hunt the area at times when others cannot. The weather in this area would've been very cold, snowy, and difficult to walk in; you would never hike long distances at this time of the year in this area.

The law enforcement officials conducted an extensive search in the spring after the pair disappeared and after the snow had melted and still could not locate the men. It may be plausible for one man to disappear in this region in late October. How two men could have disappeared baffles my common-sense approach to search-and-rescue.

Theories about what happened to the hunters vary widely. Family member claim that the men were murdered. They don't have any evidence to support their claims other than the outdoor abilities of each hunter. Canadian police have never made the case a criminal investigation, and it is still classified as a case of missing people. The trappers identified in this story believe Newcombe and Weeden fell into a river and died.

Sander Lingman
Missing: 11/01/60, Gripp Lake, northwest of Nakina, Ontario
Age at disappearance: 35

Gripp Lake is approximately forty-five miles northwest of Nakina and ten miles south of the Sedgman Lake Provincial Nature Reserve. This is a desolate area of Northern Ontario with few roads or people.

Sander was with a group of people who were staking claims in the area. The men left at the beginning of the day and were supposed to return at night. Sander never returned. A search of the area found no evidence of Sander Lingman. A rural detachment of the RCMP in Greenstone is handling the investigation.

Diane Prevost
Missing: 09/17/66, Grundy Lake Provincial Park, Ontario
Age at disappearance: 2
Water•

On Saturday, September 17, 1966, Diane Prevost was camping with her parents, three siblings, and her grandparents. On this day Diane's dad was fishing at the dock, and she was playing on the beach nearby. Her mom was initially with her but decided to go back to the campsite. She notified Diane's dad, Bernard, that she was leaving and to watch Diane. He said he would. Bernard turned to fish and a few minutes later turned back around and Diane was gone.

Diane had expressed sincere fear of the water in the days before the disappearance. While her siblings routinely went in and around the water, Diane would not. The family never believed that Diane went near the water or possibly drown.

Police were notified and a lengthy search of the park took place. As nightfall started to hit, Bernard asked the police to close the gates of the park to ensure that no cars would leave without being searched. The police refused. Bernard insisted that the police search the woods, not the lake, because he feared his daughter had gone into the forest. Police concentrated on the lake. On Sunday, divers were brought in and searched the lake. Diane was not found in the water.

Two years after Diane disappeared, bones were found near a bathroom in the park. It was feared this was Diane. The bones turned out to belong to a dog.

This was the first recorded case of a child's disappearance in the Sudbury Police District. To the compliment of the police, the search for Diane lasted four weeks and covered thousands of acres of forest; but no evidence of Diane was ever found.

In August 2008 Diane's sister, Lise Nastuk, sought the assistance of a psychic to see if Diane could be located. The psychic stated that she would be located, but Diane has not been found.

Adrian McNaughton
Missing 6/12/72-PM, Holmes Lake, Calabogie, ON
Age at Disappearance: 5 years
Water• Weather• Canines

Holmes Lake is a small body of water 225 meters in diameter and sits sixty miles west of Ottawa and approximately one hundred and forty miles northwest of the high peaks of New York. Algonquin Provincial Park is twenty miles north west of the lake. Holmes Lake sits in a very

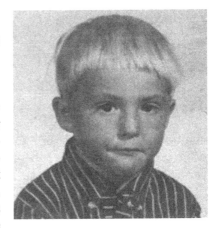

Adrian McNaughton

isolated area with hundreds of small bodies of water within five miles. A small dirt road leads from Calabogie Road into the three small lakes in the immediate area. The entire region is nothing but a very swampy area extremely thick with vegetation.

On June 12, 1972, Murray and Barbara McNaughton were the parents of four small children. Barbara had decided that she needed to stay home with the smallest child (Shontelle, two years) while Murray took the other kids fishing.

Murray left the family home in Arnprior and drove the approximate ten miles west to Holmes Lake. Adrian at five-years old was the youngest McNaughton to go on the fishing trip and was excited to make the journey. It would appear that Adrian's interest in fishing waned as it got into the afternoon hours. In a June 10, 2009, article in the *Ottawa Citizen Newspaper*, Murray described what happened just prior to Adrian vanishing: "I'd just baited the hooks for the kids. Adrian was sitting there with the new bamboo fishing pole I'd bought him. He had that funny look on his face so I knew something was bothering him. I asked him what was the matter and he said he didn't feel like fishing anymore. A few seconds later he was seen wandering off to his favorite spot, a bed of pine needles not far away." It wasn't long after this point that Adrian vanished.

Murray and the other children called Adrian's name and searched for him around the lake until they had searched almost the entire area. The Royal Canadian Mounted Police (RCMP) was notified.

The initial days had the RCMP leading the search and the following days had the Canadian Army, volunteers, fire fighters and others grouping together to look for the boy. The search reached a peak of nine thousand people scouring the lake and surrounding region for the boy. After twelve days of searching, desperation started to hit the searchers and a clairvoyant was consulted, the same Dutch man who assisted in the Boston Strangler case. He advised searchers to look on an adjacent ridgeline. They did and found nothing of value.

There was only one possible piece of evidence that was found in the search of Adrian. Eleven miles from Holmes Lake searchers found small footprints around another lake that they felt could possibly belong to the boy, it was never confirmed.

According to a June 21, 1972, article in the *Mercury-Advance* newspaper, searchers were faced with heavy rain compromising their efforts and this led some to believe that Adrian may have a difficult time surviving the elements. Some of the advanced search teams were under the belief that Adrian may be walking in circles around the lake. If that belief was true, it's unclear why he hadn't been found.

RCMP divers cleared every swamp, creek and lake in the area around the location where Adrian vanished. After twelve long search days involving canines, helicopters and thousands of searchers, Adrian was never found.

Summary

There had been rumors that some people believed that Adrian might have been abducted and picked up by a vehicle, as highly improbable as that was. There was not a lot of traffic in the area and there was only one dirt road to the lake at the time.

Readers should know that news sources that had been using two different renditions of Adrian's first name in the vast majority of articles, Adrian and Adrien. I used Adrian as it is still used by the RCMP.

Elizabeth Ann Kant
Missing: 10/16/72, Adair Township, seventy-three miles east of Cochrane, ON
Age at disappearance: 45 years
Point of Separation• Hunter• Water

Ms. Kant was with a hunting party in a desolate area approximately seventy-three miles east of Cochrane, Ontario. During the hunt, Elizabeth got separated from her party near camp 23 at Abitibi. This is an area near where the Abitibi River enters the lake and very close to Abitibi-De-Troyes Provincial Park. The point where the party got separated was approximately 2.4 miles south of camp 23. This was the last time anyone saw Elizabeth.

She was last seen wearing a brown short-sleeved sweater, green ski slacks, red-and-black hunting coat, and black rubber boots.

A large and lengthy search for Elizabeth failed to find her.

Brian Henry
Missing: 05/05/74, Canadore College, Ontario
Age at disappearance: 21
5'6", 130 lb.

On May 5, 1974, at approximately 3:00 p.m., Brian Henry got a ride from his father to Canadore College in North Bay, Ontario, to walk the nature trails. The area around the college can be quite remote. The college is located in the southwestern portion of the city near several rivers and lakes. Brian's dad arrived to pick the young man up, he never arrived. There were searches of the area, but nothing was ever found of Brian Henry.

Case matches college disappearances in Missing 411: A Sobering Coincidence.

Jane Smith
Missing: 08/09/75, Laurentian University, Sudbury, Ontario
Age at disappearance: 20

In August 1975 Jane Smith was a student at Laurentian University in Sudbury, Ontario. She lived in a rural portion of southern Sudbury on Charlotte Street. Approximately a half mile to the southwest of Jane's residence is the Fielding Bird Sanctuary, and one mile to the southeast is the Lake Laurentian Conservation Area. There are many forests in the area around Charlotte Street.

At 2:00 a.m. on the day she disappeared, she was seen going to bed. At 7:30 a.m. the same morning, Jane was gone. She left behind all of her personal belongings. Police now say they "cannot rule out the possibility that Jane has been a victim of foul play due to the duration of time since she went missing."

Jane's disappearance is hauntingly familiar to three other students missing in the United States, also from rural locations. Ruth Baumgartner disappeared on May 4, 1937, from Wesleyan University in Delaware, Ohio. She was twenty-one when she disappeared in the middle of the night from her dorm room. Ron Tammen was attending Miami University in Oxford, Ohio. On April 19, 1953, he disappeared from his dorm room in the middle of the night. Ron was nineteen years old when he went missing. Richard Cox was a cadet at the U.S. Military Academy at West

Point, New York. On January 14, 1950, Richard disappeared in the middle of the night with no clues as to where he went. Richard was twenty-two years old. There are many other students that match this profile.

Raymond Juranitch
Missing: 10/08/75, Ogoki Reservoir, Timiskaming, Ontario
Age at disappearance: 48

The Ogoki Reservoir is fifty miles northeast of Armstrong, Ontario. It is a large body of fresh water with several small islands. Raymond Juranitch went hunting and fishing in the area and set his camp on one of the small islands.

Something tragic happened and he disappeared. His belongings were found strewn around the island as though someone got upset and destroyed them. It's interesting that his camp was destroyed as this is a very isolated region with few visitors at this time of the year.

Raymond was last seen alone in a fifteen-foot aluminum canoe powered by a 9.8-horsepower outboard motor. Raymond was a rugged outdoorsman who knew the outdoors well. Raymond has never been found.

Foster Bezanson
Missing 10/25/80, Cochrane, ON
Age at Disappearance: 64 years
Hunter

The area surrounding Cochrane gets very desolate very quickly. It is surrounded by wildlife and has significant water sources very close to the city. The townships in this area of Ontario are not close to each other; there are long stretches of roadway without people, commercial services or residences. Small farms do dot the landscape in this area.

Foster left the Abitibi Road 48 area, near Cochrane to spend the day hunting, he was armed. Mr. Bezanson was last seen on Translimit Road 4 east to mileage 60, north 2 one mile on Abitibi Road 48. He was armed with a 30-06. This area of Ontario is fairly flat. When Foster failed to arrive home a search was initiated. Mr. Bezanson was never found.

There are several people missing in the same region as Foster under similar circumstances. No evidence of Foster was ever found.

Toivo Reinikainen
Missing: 09/26/84, Walsh Township, Ontario
Age at disappearance: 36

In September 1984 Toivo Reinikainen was working at a remote timber camp north of Marathon, Ontario. He worked for the Great West Timber Company and stayed at a company facility.

Toivo was last seen at the camp in the early morning hours of September 26. Deadhorse Road is a public-access road that goes to the facility, but it is very rough and remote.

Approximately one hundred miles east from where Toivo disappeared, another individual disappeared from another timber camp. The disappearance of Aju Chukwudiebere Iroaga is chronicled in the Calayca case.

Jessica Azzopardi
Missing 7/24/85–3:30 p.m., Elmstead, ON
Age at Disappearance: 20 months
Water•

This incident occurred at 506 Pearl Street in Lakeshore, Ontario, in an area called Elmstead. This area is just two miles east of Windsor with the residence sitting on Lake Saint Clair. This location is less than two miles from the United States border and the city of Detroit.

On July 24, 1985, Liana Azzopardi was at her residence with her daughter, Jessica, and her mother, Val. Liana had laid down to take a quick nap, and Val was watching Jessica and another friend. The kids were initially in the side yard picking onions and then came indoors. At approximately 3:30 p.m., Val realized that Jessica was no longer in the home and walked out the side door to see if she was in the yard. Val walked out into the backyard that leads to Lake Saint Clair and saw Jessica's diaper lying on the lawn fifty feet from the water. Val knew that Jessica was deathly afraid of the lake and wasn't concerned she would go anywhere near it, so she searched the yard again. After several minutes of searching, Val woke Liana, and they both searched the area again and still could not find the girl. They called law enforcement.

Local RCMP started their search for Jessica. A neighbor across the street from Val, who was mowing his yard, was questioned first. They asked the neighbor if he had seen anyone driving the neighborhood or anything else suspicious; he had not. By the end of the first day, there were hundreds of RCMP, helicopters, Coast Guard, and volunteers swarming the water and the grounds looking for Jessica.

At the end of the first night of searching, there were already rumblings that Jessica may have been abducted. The relatives knew the girl would never go near the water, and they also knew she was nowhere near the home. The only answer in their minds was kidnapping.

At 7:30 a.m. on July 25, Jessica's lifeless body was found floating six miles southwest of the Azzopardi residence. The girl had several small bruises on her body but nothing that was life-threatening. The RCMP publicly stated that they didn't believe the body could travel that distance in only sixteen hours, but they would wait for a ruling from the coroner on a cause of death. The feelings of the RCMP were supported by Coast Guard Petty Officer James McInnis when he was interviewed on August 7, 1985, for the *Windsor Star*: "Still McInnis expressed doubts last week that the body could have drifted that far in 16 hours between the time the girl was reported missing and the time her body was recovered." The report that cut through the heart of this case and set the city of Windsor and Detroit reeling was an article in the *Toronto Star* dated July 31, 1985: "A 20-month-old girl whose body was found floating near Belle Isle last week probably died 90 minutes before the discovery, a Detroit pathologist stated." Drowning was determined to be the cause of death, but this report indicated that Jessica was alive as late as 6 a.m.—how could that be? The coroner also indicated that Jessica had ingested a certain form of algae that was common in the river, meaning she didn't die in a swimming pool or bathtub. The report by the coroner was further bolstered by the fact that Jessica's body was floating, meaning to some that she had been in the water less than ninety minutes.

RCMP, coroners, Coast Guard, and other officials were in the newspaper daily for several weeks after Jessica went missing, all attempting to explain what happened. After nearly three weeks of investigation, the RCMP went public with a ruling that Jessica died of accidental drowning, but her case is classified as an unexplained death.

Summary

A neighbor across the street from the Azzopardis' was mowing his front lawn at the time Jessica disappeared. The man stated he didn't see any cars containing suspicious people on the street. We can reasonably surmise that Jessica did not leave via the front of her residence.

Jessica's diaper was found on her lawn in an area between her residence and the lake. Can we guess that Jessica left her property by going toward the lake? Jessica was not out her side residential door more than minutes when Val came looking for her. If there had been some type of motorized craft waiting on the water, you'd think Val would've heard it leaving the area. It's very hard to believe that a predator would be waiting in the backyard on the rare chance that Jessica just might happen to walk out alone, since that rarely if ever happened. Does this mean that a predator was waiting in the back-yard, and, if so, how did they leave the premises? Does this mean that if there was a predator outside, that this predator had the ability to lure Jessica outside?

If we are to believe science and the coroner, Jessica didn't die until 6 a.m. on July 25. Where was she, and what was she doing between 3:30 p.m. and 6 a.m.? The Coast Guard affirms that a body can't travel in the existing natural flow of currents the distance it did; something else happened. How did she arrive at the location where she was found? The coroner did state that Jessica was not the victim of a sexual assault.

There is an absolute connection between Jessica and the water. Common sense needs to rule in this case. The girl didn't swim for thirteen hours, and she sure wasn't at her residence. There had to be some intervening entity that allowed Jessica to survive out of the water for that period of time and also to transport her to where she was eventually found on the river.

Think about the many cases I have chronicled where children seemingly were not within the search quadrant. We know that Jessica certainly wasn't in the water for the entire time she was missing. Maybe Jessica and other missing people go somewhere during those hours when it is determined they aren't inside the search quadrant. Where do these people go?

This is one of the many cases where science can't answer the toughest of all questions: what happened to Jessica Azzopardi?

Clayton McFaul
Missing 8/15/86, Havelock, Ontario
Age at Disappearance: 59 years

Clayton got an early start the day of his disappearance. He told family that he was going onto the family farm to do his chores and never returned for lunch. The family called local law enforcement.

It was determined that Clayton was extremely punctual about his meal times, he was not the type to be late. He was a small man in stature, 5'3", 141 pounds and balding.

Several searches of the surrounding countryside failed to find any evidence of Clayton.

Michael James McIntyre
Missing: 04/07/94, Round Lake, Ontario
Age at disappearance: 37

In April of 1994, Michael McIntyre was living with his father at Round Lake, approximately six miles northwest of Killaloe. Michael was known as an outdoorsman who regularly walked the woods. He knew the area and was comfortable by himself in the forests of Ontario. On April 7, 1994, Michael disappeared somewhere in the area around his father's residence. Law enforcement officers believe it is highly unlikely that Michael became lost anywhere in the area surrounding his dad's house. There are no clues as to where he is now.

William Reed
Missing: 08/01/95, Redbridge, Ontario
Age at disappearance: 69
Water

William Reed lived in Redbridge, Ontario, and a note found in his residence indicated that he had gone fishing. It was unusual for William to leave unannounced, so this caused concern for his friends and family. The note stated that William was going to Phelps Township. A search of the Phelps area found William's truck, with his wallet and keys inside, on Gibson Mill Road. Nobody knew where William went. His truck was found near a river, an empty lot, and a light industrial area. An extensive search of the area produced no conclusive results.

Frank Szpak
Missing 09/23/96, Kirkland Lake, Ontario
Age at Disappearance: 69 years
Berries

Frank left his residence to go blueberry picking in a local wooded section. When Frank did not return the local RCMP conducted a massive search and could not locate him.

Bernard Champagne
Missing: 7/10/97, Val Cote, ONT
Age at Disappearance: 80 years
Canines• Water

Bernard was an elderly gentleman living in a rear building at a rustic cabin on the outskirts of Val Cote. The owner of the cabin kept close tabs on Mr. Champagne and quickly realized he was missing.

There was a massive search of the area that included canines, helicopters, airplanes and a ground search without finding any trace of Bernard.

Case Summary

This is another case where readers need to take a breath and not be numb to these disappearances. Think clearly, how far could an elderly eighty-year old man get in the bush of Ontario? How is it possible that Mr. Champagne was not found? Why would Mr.

Champagne ever want to walk out into the bush? Even if the man was senile, how far could he really get when others are trying to keep track of them? Why didn't the canines track his scent?

Raymond Tunnicliffe
Missing 8/26/02, Tracy Lake, ON
Age at Disappearance: 79 years
Berries• Canines• No Tracks
Raymond was from Saskatoon and left his residence for Tracy Lake to go berry picking. One of the last stops he made was at the general store in Weyakwin and advised the owner he was hiking to Tracy Lake. Tunnicliffe told the storeowner if she didn't hear from him in 3 days to notify authorities, well, she did.

The owner reported Raymond missing and this started a two-week search. The RCMP utilized planes, canines, ground teams, everything imaginable to find Raymond. This quote in the 8/26/02 *Lethbridge Herald* by a family member regarding RCMP search efforts follows and describes their feelings and frustration;

"There's absolutely nothing. We've almost narrowed it down to alien abduction because it's so clean."

Case Summary
The quote in the *Lethbridge Herald* perfectly summarizes the feelings of many SAR teams when their efforts produce no results. It's understandable law enforcement may not always be able to bring back a live body, but when they don't find footprints, clothing, blood, campsites, etc, it is truly mind-boggling what might have happened. I think it's also notable that Raymond went to the extraordinary measure of telling the storeowner about his trip and advising her to call authorities of he doesn't return, it makes me wonder if he was expecting trouble.

Joseph Grozelle
Missing: 10/22/2003-1:00 a.m., Kingston, Ontario, Canada
Age at disappearance: 21 years
Water• Intellect• Unknown Cause of Death
There is only one case in this book like this one. This incident has more twists and turns than anything my imagination could even

make up. If we made a movie about this, people would say it's too fabricated.

This case happened at the Royal Canadian Military Academy in Kingston, Ontario, Canada. Kingston sits at the far northeastern end of Lake Ontario, approximately 160 miles southwest of Montreal. The Royal Military Academy is the only military college for the Canadian armed forces. It is the premier location to go to college if you want to be in the upper echelon of the Canadian military.

Joseph Grozelle

Joseph Grozelle was in his junior year at the academy and doing very, very well. It was October 2003, and he had just recently been elected his squadron leader, a huge position for any cadet. He also played on the academy's basketball team and was doing very well academically. He was a well-rounded, mature, and smart person. From everything I read, he exemplified the profile of a person you'd want in your military.

On October 22, 2003, Joe was in his dormitory room working on a school paper for his law class. His longtime girlfriend, Melissa Haggert, was also studying on his bed. At 1:00 a.m., Melissa stated that Joe was still working on his computer and she fell asleep. She woke at 5:30 a.m. to find Joe missing and his cell phone, watch, and wallet still at his desk. She got her items together, and at 6:00 a.m. she left the room and headed for her classes. She periodically checked Joe's room through the day and headed to his basketball practice at 4:30 p.m. When he didn't arrive at the gym, she notified the squadron officer, and a formal missing person case was filed.

When an incident happens on military property, it's a military investigation. They searched the grounds, water areas, and building very thoroughly. The military went through his computer and worked with the Ontario police and Kingston police. The police investigation was headed by the National Investigative Services branch of the military.

The military college sits on a peninsula with the Cataraqui River on the west side and Lake Ontario the other. The river enters the lake at the point of the academy. On November 13, 2003, Joseph's body was found in the river. It went for autopsy, and the coroner could not determine the cause of death. The body suffered from decomposition, but few specific details of the body's condition were released. There were strong rumors that the military believed that Joseph had committed suicide, but they couldn't prove it. Joseph's mother and father were adamant that their son was happy and successful and would never commit suicide.

During the coroner's inquest, Joseph's girlfriend testified that he had once told her in great confidence that when he was in high school, he had tried to kill himself. She stated that he had been depressed over a girl. He went home, took a bunch of pills and alcohol, and then threw up.

During the time that Joe was missing, there were over two hundred reports of supposed sightings. None were ever confirmed and each was probably misidentification, typical in cases like these.

In November 2004, the military exhumed the body with witnesses and did a second autopsy with an independent medical examiner and a public examiner in attendance. They were looking for broken bones and obtaining tissue for testing. In the first autopsy, the coroner stated that he wasn't looking for broken bones. X-rays were taken and testing was completed. Joseph had no drugs or alcohol in his system. On October 18, 2006, an inquest started. On October 26, the inquest ended. There was a second inquest in April 2007. All the coroner's inquests came to the same conclusion: cause of death was undetermined.

If you look inside this book at the number of unusual deaths associated with water along the northern shores of Lake Ontario, you will be surprised.

After two autopsies, two inquests, toxicology tests, and inquiries by three different law enforcement agencies, nobody can determine what killed Joseph. The *QMI Agency* posted an article on February 11, 2010, about this incident and had a statement from

Joseph's family: "The Grozelles have always maintained that their son's death was neither an accident nor a suicide."

Approximately forty miles west from the academy is the Canadian Forces Base at Trenton, Ontario. Colonel Russell Williams was the 8 Wing Commander at the base from August 2003 to June 2004. In the same article quoted above was this: "Ron Grozelle says murder charges against the base commander at CFB Trenton should prompt a new police investigation into the death of his son, Joe, the Royal Military College cadet who mysteriously disappeared in 2003." Later in the same article is this: "Williams is charged with murdering 27-year-old Jessica Lloyd, who went missing two weeks ago, and 37-year-old Marie Comeau, a corporal who worked at the airbase. Comeau was found dead in nearby Brighton in November." What an absolute bizarre set of circumstances.

No, I don't believe that Colonel Williams had any part in Joseph's disappearance, but I would call it coincidental.

I find it surprising that Joseph's body was found in the river and not in the lake. The only way that should've happened is if his body had entered higher upstream. Joseph was an absolutely stellar individual. I put zero importance on the fact that he took pills and drank alcohol when he was in high school. Everything in his life was going perfectly.

His behavior does mimic others who have disappeared. They somehow do something out of character and go somewhere that makes no sense. Why would he leave his room at 1:00 a.m.? I don't think it was to buy drugs; he got tested at irregular intervals and he had left his wallet and cash in his room. Finding drugs in his system would be the end of a career. What pulled him out of the room without his cell phone and wallet or keys? In this day and age, how many twenty-one-year-olds go anywhere without their phone? I would like to know what he was wearing when he was found. Did he have all of his clothes and shoes on? I did read one report indicating the decision of the coroner's final inquest in 2007: "unascertained, non-natural." I would guess this means that it wasn't a natural death of unknown means. I can tell you that the word "drowning" was used in many articles, but I never found it in a coroner's ruling. One last point that mimics many of the disappearances in this section of the book appeared in a *Sun Media* article dated March 29, 2007: "While Grozelle was missing for three weeks before his body was found, a pathologist has testified the body's condition was consistent with being in the water one or two weeks." Read that sentence again. He was missing for three weeks but only in the water for one or two weeks. These facts cannot be ignored and pushed to the side.

How many times are you going to read that a young man disappears and is found in water deceased, but hadn't been in the water the entire time of his disappearance? Who is holding these men? What are they doing with them?

This should be the lead story in every news agency throughout the world.

Why isn't the press talking about this?

Refer to Missing 411-A Sobering Coincidence for a book filled with cases identical to Joseph's.

Christina Calayca
Missing: 08/06/07, Terrace Bay, Ontario
Age at disappearance: 20
5'2", 125 lb.
Water• Jogger• Park

Christina Calayca

In August 2007 Christina Calayca was camping with a church group, her cousin, and two of his friends at Rainbow Falls Provincial Park. The park is on the Trans-Canada Highway (Hwy. 17) between Schreiber and Rossport and occupies a remote area of the coast.

Christina was a Toronto teacher and not someone who camps or visits the woods regularly. On the day of her disappearance, Christina went jogging with one of her cousin's friends. Somewhere during the run, the two went different directions and Christina was never seen again. She has not contacted family or friends since.

Thunder Bay police conducted a massive search consisting of eighty police officers, volunteers, helicopters, canines, and airplanes. The seventeen days of searching didn't produce one clue.

Law enforcement officials stated that there were no aggressive bears in the area, and they believed Christine could have survived in the wild because of the relatively warm nights and the abundance of fresh water. They have ruled out any involvement of her cousin or his friends, and they have stated that they do not believe she was abducted.

It is hard to believe that Christina was disoriented or lost while running in the park. The trails are well defined and many of the roads are paved and easy to follow.

Approximately 120 miles east of where Christine disappeared, another individual went missing on May 16, 2006. Aju Chukwudiebere Iroaga was a forestry worker planting saplings in a remote region fifty miles north of White River, Ontario. This is a desolate area along the White River. The twenty-six-year-old tree planter had quit his job and was assigned to meet a helicopter to be lifted out of the area. He never arrived for the trip. There are hundreds of lakes, streams, and creeks in this area and an abundance of wildlife. Aju was described to be in very good shape and able to survive in the wild. Police conducted an extensive weeklong air and ground search but found nothing. Aju's case and Christina's case are similar, as they were both alone in the wild and in relative proximity when they disappeared.

Lachlan Cranswick
Missing: 01/23/2010, Deep River, Ontario, Canada
Age at disappearance: 41 years
Intellect• Water• Physicist

The disappearance of Lachlan Cranswick could fit under a multitude of categories I've documented in the past. I have written two different chapters in two books about disappearances in Australia that mimic disappearances in North America. As it happens, Lachlan is a native of Melbourne, Australia. I have also written chapters about intellects that vanished and specifically about physicists who have disappeared under very unusual circumstances. Lachland was a nuclear physicist. He was a research scientist employed by Atomic Energy of Canada assigned to their Chalk River Labs at Deep River.

On January 18, 2010, at approximately 4:30 p.m., Lachlan was observed boarding a bus at the labs. This was the last confirmed sighting police had of the scientist. Lachlan was known to enjoy hiking, curling, and skiing and snowshoeing. He was an avid outdoorsman, according to his friends.

On January 23, Lachlan was expected to be at a curling championship at the Deep River Curling and Squash club, in which he served as vice president. He never arrived for the games, and he was reported missing.

Lachlan was known to be doing research on radioisotopes. He was also the chairman of the IUCR Computing Commission and was considered an expert on powder diffraction. According to Wikipedia, powder diffraction "is a scientific technique using X-ray, neutron or electron diffraction on powder or microstalline samples for structural characterization of materials."

The police responded to Lachlan's home on Summit Street in Deep River. They found an unusual homestead. The residence sits in a typical housing tract that is approximately one thousand feet southwest of the Ottawa River. The city of Deep River is just northeast of Algonquin Provincial Park and an area where I've written about several disappearances. A February 5, 2010, article in the *Toronto Sun* had the following information on what officers found at the residence: "Officers checked his residence on Summit Street and found the door was unlocked but Cranswick was not home. Police say his car was parked in the garage and a collection of personal items, including a Global Positioning System (GPS) and wallet, were found in the house." Other articles stated that they also found his personal computer in the house and the garbage cans outside, placed outside the night of January 18.

A search for Lachlan was started immediately once law enforcement realized he wasn't at the residence. A local ski club checked nearby trails, and law enforcement utilized dogs and locals to check streets, harbors, and a nearby river. Nothing was found. A June 21, 2010, article in the *IF Press* had this statement: "Searchers found no tracks leading to the river." Police indicated that the river was frozen solid with the only open patches found near the marina, which were visible only by helicopter. At the time the scientist vanished, the river had ice that was four feet thick. Rupert Cranswick, Lachlan's brother, flew to Deep Water from Melbourne to assist in the search. A March 1, 2010, article on stuff.co.nz had the following statement from Robert: "The circumstances of the disappearance are just bizarre, said the man's brother, Rupert Cranswick." Later in the same article was this statement: "I talked to lots of locals there and they think something extraordinary happened to him, Rupert said."

The disappearance of Lachlan Cranswick sparked worldwide talk about various conspiracy theories. Some people felt he knew something special and he was kidnapped, while others thought he was murdered.

On June 11, 2010, two canoeists were in Welsh's Bay east of Deep River Marina and found a floating body in two and a half feet of water. The coroner ruled that it was Lachlan. He was wearing his work coat and his lab's identification.

The puzzling part of this story is that we couldn't find anything indicating Lachlan's cause of death, as determined by the coroner. Police theorize that based on his phone and computer logs, Lachlan placed his garbage cans outside at 11:30 p.m. and then took a late-night walk. Yes, a late-night walk in northern Ontario in early January. A June 16, 2010, article in Australia on ABC News had the following statement from Lachlan's brother, Robert: "I still find it hard to believe he was going for a walk at 11:30 at night when he had work the next morning." Robert also stated that he was told by the police that they still have no idea what happened.

I could not determine if Rupert and Robert Cranswick were the same individual or misspellings by various news agencies. There was also conflicting information about the conditions present when Lachlan vanished. Some articles stated that there were open areas of water far out into the bay outside of Deep River. Other articles stated the ice was four feet thick. It is a fact that searchers did not find any tracks leading through the snow out to the river. Canines never picked up his scent.

Lachlan's brother indicated that authorities have no clue what happened to his brother.

The idea that a nuclear scientist is going to go for a midnight walk on a January night in northern Ontario when he has to go to work the next day seems extremely odd. He doesn't lock his door, doesn't secure his computer, wallet, or watch, and wanders off. If you gauge the unusual stories of how other physicists have disappeared, this ranks near the top in strangeness. I'd still like to read the autopsy result and understand what the body tells us. I'd also like to see the toxicology report.

Daniel Trask
Missing 11/03/11, Diamond Lake, Temagami, ON
Age at Disappearance: 28 years
Water• Missing Clothing

It seems that in every book I write there is always one person that vanished that really shouldn't have. My nomination for the person in this book who should still be here is Daniel Trask.

Daniel spent his free time exploring the far corners of the Temagami region of Northern Ontario. Daniel enjoyed being alone in an area rich with Native American/First Nation history. The Iroquois Indians used to call this region home. Hundreds of years after they left the region, their pictographs are still visible on large rocks on Diamond Lake. The area that Daniel enjoyed visiting was almost as far in the middle of nowhere as someone could get without being seen on a regular basis.

The trips he made started from where he called home, Waterloo. In the summer of 2011, he made the approximate 270-mile trip north to the Temagami area. The closest large town in the area was Sudbury, seventy miles to the east.

Daniel spent the majority of his summer canoeing the Temagami lakes and rivers. The region has almost as much water as land, and the land that does exist can be very swampy and wet. Daniel must've learned something while he was in the bush. He came home and showed family and friends interesting rock formations that he would place on the ground. Some of the designs were obviously arrows and such, showing direction, but others were more complex and different, such as rock stacks. He would also make unusual stick structures. He also had pictures of these that he showed to friends.

Daniel's dad is a retired Kitchener firefighter, and his brother, Adam, is a fulltime firefighter and outdoorsman. After Daniel returned from his summer trip he told others that he missed visiting the Temagami and was going to go back.

On November 3, 2011, Daniel left his Waterloo home and drove to a location on Red Squirrel Road and Camp Wanapitei. He parked his car, took out his snowshoes and supplies, and headed into the bush. The location where he stopped was a gorgeous spot adjacent to Lake Temagami. Daniel made the trek to this location for a First Nations tradition called "Changing of the Seasons." Daniel understood the woods very well and also understood the history of the area and what that meant to the local Native Americans and First Nations People.

It's unclear exactly how long Daniel was gone before the red flag was waved, asking for assistance. His parents and friends went to the area and searched for him. Eventually Daniel's car was found, but the area is vast, and nobody was quite sure where he had hiked. Law enforcement services responded with helicopters, canines, and many ground searchers on snowmobiles and on foot; they found nothing. Eventually searchers had to terminate the effort and hope that after the snow melted, vacationers would find Daniel's body.

On May 20, 2012, paddlers were on the northeastern fork of Diamond Lake when they saw something unusual on the eastern bank. Almost exactly across from the pictographs on the lake, they found Daniel's snow pants and coat. Searchers went back into the area and searched the eastern bank of the lake and found what they believed to be his campsite, just north of his clothing. They found his sleeping bag even further north of the campsite, an unusual find. After several weeks of additional ground and air searches, Daniel could not be found. Just in case you didn't know, this region of northern Ontario in November is freezing cold; you absolutely need cold-weather gear.

Posters and flyers distributed about Daniel stated the following information about the clothing he was wearing or had in his possession:

- Gray/white Atlas snowshoes
- White zippered hoodie sweatshirt
- Gray sweat pants

- Orange T-shirt
- Black T-shirt
- Black backpack
- Black gloves

**Look for creative rock structures

Summary

Searchers neither found Daniel's backpack nor a majority of the clothing he had with him. They did find the most important two pieces of clothing that would've kept Daniel alive in the harsh winter: his coat and snow pants.

Daniel knew this area better than most. He wanted to view the region during the changing of the seasons, and from all indications he was dressed for the event. Daniel would've taken his snow pants and coat off only during one time, when sleeping. There appears to be only a few options to explain how his pants and coat were found, and Daniel wasn't. He was either awakened during the night, and something extreme happened to him, or somehow, someone or something took Daniel and somehow took his clothes off of him. I know that this statement seems odd, especially for such a thing to happen deep in the woods. In my past books I have written stories about people who disappeared and were subsequently found in small pieces, yet their pants were found fully intact with no bite marks.

Update: Daniel's body was located under conditions that did not explain what happened. His remains were located near Lady Evelyn Lake near Temiskaming Shores on May 25 2015. There were no details on the condition of the remains or the cause of death.

Jeffery Boucher
Missing: 01/13/2014-7:00 a.m., Whitby, Ontario, Canada
Age at disappearance: 52 years
Water• Unknown Cause of Death• Jogger

On March 29, 2014, Detective Jeff Kennedy from the Durham Regional Police in Whitby, Ontario, Canada, held a press conference on the Jeffery Boucher case. One statement made by the detective fully encompasses my beliefs about this event: "This is a very curious case."

Jeffery was a fifty-two-year-old teacher at Bowmanville High School in Whitby. He taught business and geography, but his interests were wide and athletic. He met his wife, Kirsten, while doing an outdoor event. He loved to ski, he ran every morning, and he had an affinity for teaching. Each morning Jeff would rise at near 5:00 a.m., go downstairs into a room where he wouldn't wake his wife, and change into running gear. It didn't matter if it was the middle of the frigid Ontario winter; Jeff ran daily. He enjoyed putting on his music and headphones and running in one of several open space areas near his home. His favorite area was the Heber Down Conservation area just north of his home.

The Boucher residence was located on Gilchrist Court in Whitby. Just to the west of the residence was a creek that ran from the conservation area to the north to Lynde Shores Conservation Area and to the south onto Lake Ontario.

Jeff would usually run for an hour and then shower and get ready for work. He had a relatively short commute to his high school in town. On January 13, 2014, Kirsten stated that she had slept very soundly and awoke to find Jeff gone. By 8:30 a.m. he hadn't returned. He had left behind his car, wallet, passport, and keys.

Jeff and Kirsten had two daughters. Katja was twenty years old and a student at Waterloo University. Bettina was eighteen and a senior in high school. Both girls stayed home and went to the conservation area north of their home to look for their dad. The trails running through the wildlife area were snow laden and frozen. Once the police were notified, an immediate search was started. Over the course of the following seven days, the Durham Regional Police utilized helicopters, tracking dogs, all-terrain vehicles, and people on foot. Local search and rescue organizations and the public assisted.

After nearly a week of searching, law enforcement called off the effort and stated that they had no clue what happened to the runner; they didn't have any leads or evidence. The held a press meeting and said that they had intensively covered an area out to a five-kilometer radius.

In February 2014, the Durham Regional Police requested assistance from the Toronto police for the use of their underwater robotic side-scanning camera. The unit was utilized near the pier and wharf in Lake Ontario. After an extensive search effort, they found nothing.

Kirsten Boucher is a very smart professional lady. She taught mathematics at a nearby school and immediately went to the Internet to develop information and assistance in finding her husband. The ladies developed a Facebook page and she found amateur investigators that fed her information. Nothing that she pursued amounted to anything, but she stated that the groups were very supportive.

There were few details about Jeffery until March 11, 2014. A private citizen walking in the area of Heydenshore Pavilion found a tennis shoe near the water line. The item was turned over to law enforcement, who confirmed it was Jeffery's. This find caused law enforcement to start helicopter flyovers along the coast. There was again a segment of time where there were no other leads. On March 29, 2014, at 11:00 a.m., a citizen found Jeffery's second shoe in an area west of Crystal Beach. The find of the second shoe caused another search of the area. At 2:30 p.m. a man was walking his dog along Lake Ontario near Thickson Road South and Crystal Beach Boulevard when his dog walked up to something at the shoreline. The dog had found the body of Jeffery Boucher. As if the discovery wasn't odd enough, Jeffery was naked and encased in ice. The police recovered the body and turned it over for autopsy on March 31, 2014.

Readers of my past books know that the cases we investigate are unusual. The Boucher case was unusual from the start and the reports coming from the coroner only supported that. Days after the autopsy, the police stated that the cause of death couldn't be determined until the toxicology was completed. Many, many months after the initial autopsy, the ruling from the coroner was vague. A January 7, 2015, article in the *North Umberland News* had an interview with Kirsten Boucher about one year after the disappearance. Here is what Kirsten stated about the autopsy: "'They can't determine a thing. They could determine that there are no traces of cocaine, but we knew that,' said Ms. Boucher, with a laugh, recalling her husband's wholesome nature and passion for fitness. 'It's nonsense. Nothing makes sense.'" The coroner could not determine the cause of death. The police made statements that they believed he fell off the pier and died in the cold water. There was no evidence he was ever on the pier, yet that was their theory.

I think it's important to look at the physical evidence the police had. The coroner never released the autopsy report. The police do know that Jeffery was naked and was missing his shoes. As someone who has run daily for twenty years, I can tell you that Jeffery's shoes were tight on his feet. As a runner, if your shoes are loose, you get blisters. He ran for an hour daily; those shoes were tight on his feet. He was also wearing long running pants, a shirt, and a jacket. Everything was stripped from his body.

I have written about several cases in the past where bodies were found without shoes and/or naked. If people survived, they never remembered how they got into that position. I do not believe that Jeffery Boucher ran out onto the pier. If he did go onto the pier and slipped and fell, there would be injuries to his body or head. No injuries were found. If he fell into the water, he probably could've swum to a ladder or beach to save himself. He was a mature man of habit. He was stable, with good judgment and a rational thinker. He was in outstanding physical condition and probably could've survived incidents that would've killed the majority of us. An important point is that Jeffery was a runner. I have highlighted runners in past books and how they are susceptible to unusual disappearances.

Once Jeffery's body was recovered, the Durham police held a press conference that night. Detective Jeff Kennedy made the statement several times that there was no evidence of foul play. How the detective can overlook the lack of shoes or clothing on the body is beyond my rational thinking. Why didn't canines pick up Jeffery's scent on nearby trails? Bad weather did inundate the Whitby region immediately after Jeffery disappeared, a common element I cite in my books on these disappearances.

Remember a key element to the disappearances around the Great Lakes, these disappearances have been happening for centuries. I would like to have the Whitby medical examiner do an expanded toxicology panel on Jeffery and understand what they found, not what they didn't find. Was there GHB in his system?

When medical examiners and law enforcement can't answer why or how, they want these cases to go away and they'll attempt to make everything seem normal.

Douglas Queen
Missing: 03/17/2014-Noon, Humber Bay Park, Toronto, ON, Canada
Age at disappearance: 48 years
Water

It's amazing the number of odd coincidences I bump up against while researching missing people. I was deep into the research of Jeffery Boucher when another teacher thirty-three miles west of Whitby, Ontario, went missing, Douglas Queen.

Let's first look at the similarities:

Jeffery Boucher	Douglas Queen
Age: 52	Age: 48
Occupation: Teacher	Occupation: Teacher
Two Children	Two Children
Found: 3/31/14	Found: 03/20/14
Location: Lake Ontario	Location: Lake Ontario
Cause of Death: Unknown	Cause of Death: Accidental Drowning

Distance between incidents: 33 miles

I did an extensive archive search and could not find another teacher in the greater Ontario area that drowned in Lake Ontario under circumstances anything close to what I have described in both stories. To have two teachers, four years apart in age, disappear within months of each other is extremely unusual.

Douglas was a twin; his brother was Andrew, and they were very close. They were raised in Richmond Hill, Ontario. Douglas and Andrew went to the University of Toronto and later in life played in the same folk band, Jughead, where Doug was an accomplished piano player. Douglas was married to Trish, and they had two children, Dylan and Jack. The couple had been married for eleven years and had lived in the Humber River area of Toronto for the last several years.

Douglas loved children and had been a music teacher at Brock Public School in Toronto for the last eighteen years. On March 17, 2014, it was a normal morning at the Queen household. Douglas assisted the kids in getting ready for school, kissed Trish good-bye, and headed for work. When Douglas arrived at Brock School, he was called into the principal's office and advised of a fourth-hand complaint against him. The policy of the school board was to suspend a teacher based on an allegation while it is investigated. Douglas left the school at approximately 10:30 a.m. and traveled to Humber Bay Park. An October 10, 2014, article in the *Globe and Mail* had the following information about what Douglas did after entering the park: "Phone records show Mr. Queen made three calls to his union at 11:40 a.m., 11:49 a.m., and 11:58 a.m. At some point he walked to the lake and climbed the rocks, perhaps to wait for news." The last sentence is a guess. Nobody knows what Douglas did after the last call to his union. Trish did try to call him at noon to remind him of a dental appointment; he didn't answer. When Douglas didn't arrive home at the end of his day, Trish called police.

Law enforcement pinged Douglas's cell phone and found he was last at Humber Bay Park. This is located on Lake Ontario, approximately thirty-three miles west of Whitby in the greater Toronto area. There was a massive three-day search including boats, dogs, and foot patrols. They found nothing.

On March 20, 2014, Trish decided to go to the park and walk the shoreline. Unbelievably, she saw Douglas's coat in the water and found the body of her husband. In the same article quoted earlier was this: "I just started screaming," she recalls. "The police had been thorough. How could I be the one who found him?"

The body went to the medical examiner, who ruled that Douglas had trauma on his forehead. He was found in a few feet of water. The ruling was that he accidentally drowned. The theory put forth was that he was walking on the rocks, fell, hit his head, rolled into the water, and drowned. The death was not a suicide, ruled the coroner.

The complaint against Douglas made at the school was later ruled to be unfounded. There were rumors in the community that

Douglas may have committed suicide because of the allegation. He was a smart man. He knew the allegation was baseless. I stand by the ruling of the coroner.

I do find it very odd that Douglas had an injury on his forehead. People walking and slipping usually get their arms in front of them to protect their head. It would seem more likely to sustain a serious injury by falling backward on the rocks. The injury would've had to have been so debilitating that it rendered Douglas unconscious for him to drown in a few feet of water.

The timing and location of Jeffery and Douglas's deaths seem very coincidental. There were no witnesses to either event.

Ethan Stokes
Missing: 01/25/2015-1:45 a.m., Lindsay, Ontario
Age at disappearance: 20 years
Water

This incident occurred in the small Ontario town of Lindsay. It's located thirty-five miles north of Lake Ontario in an area with many bodies of water. The Scugog River bisects the town. One of the centerpieces of Lindsay is Sir Sandford Fleming College. The Lindsay campus focuses on outdoor adventure skills, advanced water operations, and conservation and environmental law enforcement.

Ethan Stokes was originally from Holland Landing, Ontario, and had moved to Lindsay to attend Fleming College. He was majoring in drilling and blasting. On January 24, 2015, Ethan went with friends to the York Tavern in downtown Lindsay to celebrate his birthday. Friends described him as in control and having fun. At 1:45 a.m., the bar started to close and Ethan's friends went in different directions. He told people he was walking home. A few close friends of the Fleming student called him at 6:30 a.m. the same morning and didn't get an answer. They checked his Facebook page and found it wasn't updated. A missing person report was filed with the Kawartha Lakes OPP (police).

A group of students from the college formed groups and decided to search the area between the tavern and Ethan's home. They divided the areas into quadrants and eventually came to the conclusion that nothing was unusual.

A Lindsay resident residing near Durham Street saw a hole in the ice on the Scugog River. The police were called and on January 27 put divers in the water. Approximately forty minutes after the police entered the river, they found Ethan's body approximately one hundred feet from the hole. There were no reports indicating the condition of the body or what he was or wasn't wearing. The body was transported to the Center for Forensic Sciences in Toronto. No other reports have been released.

Paul Yelland
Missing: 10/23/17- 12:30 p.m., Wa-
taBeag Lake, On
Age at disappearance: 66 years
Water• Hunter• Canines

Paul Yelland

The region around Timmins has always had many disappearances that are unusual and never solved; here is another.

Forty air miles southeast of Tim-mins is a cluster of lakes, easily over one hundred. One of the more mam-moth lakes in the region is Watabeag, ten miles south of this lake is Beaver Lake and this is the location where this person vanished.

Paul Yelland was a sixty-six-year-old hunter from the small town of Midland, Ontario approximately sixty miles north of Toron-to. He made the three hundred mile trip north to hunt an extremely remote area. He was last seen on October 23, 2017, just outside of Beaver Lake riding his Honda TRX four-wheeler wearing an orange helmet and an orange hunting vest.

The Ontario Provincial Police got a report that Paul hadn't been heard of or seen and sent a search team to scour the area. The initial effort included a helicopter and twelve ground teams, and they found nothing. An October 31 Press Release by the Provincial Police stat-ed this, "The Kirkland Lake Detachment of the Ontario Provincial Police (OPP), the OPP Emergency Response Team (ERT), the OPP

Canine Unit and the OPP Aviation Services are using four-wheelers and a helicopter today to continue their search in the area of Beaver Lake near Watabeag Lake." This statement confirmed that the search was ongoing and using canine resources.

There was a two-week search for Paul that didn't locate his ATV or any items belonging to him. This is an odd case in that he was wearing very bright clothing and helmet, people had seen him in the area, but nothing was located. I have documented hundreds of cases where people vanish and are never found in areas where there are many small bodies of water.

Paul Yelland has never been found.

Quebec

Population: 8,500,000
Capital City: Quebec

When I was working in business development for the diamond industry technology group, the manufacturing facility we were using was in Laval, Quebec. We frequently had business meetings at various points in the province. The most memorable time I ever had at a meeting was sitting in the lobby of the Fairmont Hotel in the old Quebec City. You can sit in the hotel, look out over the St. Lawrence River in an old and memorable resort. After dinner, we walked the streets of old Quebec talking business. The brick roads are narrow, the majority of the buildings are ancient, and the area would remind you of a European city. It was a memorable and enchanting city.

The province of Quebec is the largest in area of the ten provinces, 595,000 square miles. Quebec is second in population to only Ontario. Nearly half the population lives in greater Montreal where the predominant language is French with 40% of the residents bi-lingual to English. The legal drinking age in this province is 18 years old.

Here is a list of the largest cities in Quebec by population:

Montreal: 1,800,000
Quebec: 535,000
Sherbrooke: 165,000

There is a broad political divide between eastern Canada and the west. The east is known as a politically liberal haven and the west as a more conservative region. When I was in Canada years ago, I remember that some of the westerners I was working with were concerned that the Canadian government made British Columbia schools teach their kids learn French, this irritated them greatly!

Quebec list of missing people by date.

Name	Date/ Time Missing • Age • Sex
Daughter of Belliveau	1865 • 5 • F
Grace Cooper	08/08/13-1:00 p.m. • 5 •F
Emile Erazola	05/25/27•4•M
Dominique Danis	11/23/47, 12:30 p.m.• 52•M
Glen Moquin	08/09/93-Noon• 22• M
Chris Brown	11/11/95- 2:00 P.M.• 26• M
Guy Ouellet	07/18/98-2:00 P.M.• 42• M
Jimmy Rambone Jr.	09/03/03–3 p.m. • 51 • M
Mark Kraynak	08/22/05-3:32 a.m.•23•M
Steven Wright	08/22/05-3:32 a.m.•20•M

Daughter of Belliveau
Missing 1865, Anticosti Island, QC
Age at Disappearance: 5 years
Water• Point of Separation

Anticosti Island is located in the Gulf of Saint Lawrence, approximately two hundred miles northeast of Quebec. It is the ninetieth-largest island in the world and approximately 3,047 square miles in size. The water around the island is noted as being treacherous to ships in bad weather and has the nickname "Cemetery of the Gulf" because of the four hundred shipwrecks that surround the island.

The island has traded hands many times in the last five hundred years. In 1974, the Province of Quebec purchased the island for twenty-four million dollars. It is now managed by the Ministry of Recreation of Quebec and known for its outstanding deer hunting and fishing for trout and salmon. There are twenty-four rivers with many cutting deep gorges through the island.

The First Nation Innu Tribe initially claimed Anticosti, and they occupied the island for hundreds of years. The tribe named the island "Notiskuan," meaning, "where bears are hunted."

In 1979, Donald McKay wrote the book, *Anticosti, The Untamed Island*. Donald wrote that the island changed hands many times early in the 1800s and had many visitors. Early inhabitants in the 1850s found trees that appeared to be gnawed down by beavers, but there were no beavers on the island. Other animals that were known to be on the nearby mainland (moose, beaver, caribou, snakes, wolves, and muskrats) were not found on the island. Settlers found the main inhabitants of Anticosti to be bear, foxes and otters.

In the 1860s, settlers from Newfoundland started to arrive on the island with the idea of fishing its waters. There were three main families that arrived in 1865: the Wrights, the Belliveaus, and the Lejeunes. The families lived in a small settlement together. It wasn't long after the Belliveau family arrived that their five-year-old daughter wandered a short distance into the woods to pick wildflowers and didn't come back. All of the families joined forces and searched for days for the girl.

There are very few details on the disappearance, and none listed the girl's first name, but all indicated that she was never found.

Summary

The one part of this story that resonated with me was the reason the girl went to the woods. There are many stories I've written where a very young girl walks a short distance to pick wildflowers and then vanishes.

Some may believe that a First Nations tribe took the girl. I could not find any information that any settler on the island was ever attacked or molested in any way by the Innu people.

It does seem a little unusual that at one point, before settlers arrived, the island appeared to have an abundance of many different mammals in the 1850s to 1860's, and they then vanished. What happened to the mammals? What happened to Ms. Belliveau? Why would mammals suddenly vanish from a huge island, fairly near the time that this young girl disappeared?

Grace Cooper
Missing: 08/08/1913-1:00 p.m., Burnt Island, Lake Timiskaming, Quebec
Age at disappearance: 5 years
Water• Weather• Point of Separation

When I explain water-related disappearances and their relationship to missing people, this incident would exemplify my point. Burnt Island is in the middle of Lake Timiskaming on the border of Ontario and Quebec. It is approximately seventy miles southeast of Timmins, a location where there are several missing people. The island is approximately two miles across at its widest. It can be very thick and lush and has cliffs on the east side.

The details of exactly how Grace Cooper managed to get away from her family are vague. On August 8, 1913, at 1:00 p.m. she was missing. Over eighty searchers joined her family in a comprehensive search of the south shore of the island, the location everyone believed she would travel. Several days were spent searching every inch of this area without finding a clue.

On the fifth day of the search effort, C. H. Burton and John McLennan decided to move away from other teams and head east. The east side is extremely rough as is described in the August 14, 1913, article in the *Toronto World*: "The bush in many places in almost impenetrable to a strong man, and a want for food and wet and cold weather might have caused the death of many a seasoned bushman lost for such a period." During this time a large storm hit the island and made travel and searching difficult. Rain and cold temperatures lingered in the area for two days.

Just as Burton and McLennan were at their farthest point from the Cooper family camp, they located Grace, on the fifth day. Where they found the girl is very peculiar as is described in the same *Toronto World* article: "Her head was resting on one log and her feet on another and caught in this position, she had been evidently unable to free herself." Readers of my past books have been told of other children who went missing who were found trapped and unable to move in dangerous locations. Grace was two feet from a one-thousand-foot cliff and water. It seems timely that she was caught and pinned in that exact location.

The same *Toronto World* article had an interesting statement near its end: "How the child reached the other side of the island and was found alive is a mystery."

Summary

Grace Cooper disappears on an island that is essentially two miles by two miles—four square miles. The eastern end of the island is the most difficult to travel, and many have died in that area. Searchers go to this region and find her pinned and unable to move.

She lived five days through a major storm. Searchers are mystified she got to the location where she was found and equally amazed she was alive. Did she pin herself, or was she placed in that location?

Emile Erazola
Missing: 05/25/27-PM, Montreal, Canada
Age at disappearance: 4 years
Weather• Lack of Memory• Lack of Tracks• Missing Clothing• Water

It's rare to find a story about a missing person that reveals valuable clues and insight as to what may be happening to these people. In this disappearance, there are several elements that can only lead you down one road, something very strange happened to this young boy.

The Erazola family lived at 2305 Messier Street in Montreal. The May 30, 1927 edition of the *Edmonton Journal* explained what happened, "The boy disappeared late Wednesday evening when he, his five-year-old brother Francois and their aunt, Lucienne Erazola became lost during a rainstorm. The party was on their way to visit a relative (Located at 4441 Chambord St.) when the storm broke, but they never reached their destination." When the boys and the aunt didn't come home, the family called the police.

The morning of May 26 had a family on Cadillac Street in Longue Pointe calling police about an older woman and a young boy. The police responded and found Lucienne and Francois. The May 28, 1927 *Gazette* newspaper had these details, "They never reached their destination. Miss Erazola lost her memory and on Early Thursday was found on Cadillac Street, Longue Pointe with her nephew, Francis. She and the boy were seeking shelter from residents on the street when a citizen reported their plight to the police. Miss Erazola could not say where she had been during the night, nor did she remember losing sight of Emile. Francis told the detectives his brother disappeared after crossing a stream with water up to his neck. Emile, according to Francis, then lay down on the bank, as he was too weary to continue." The police added that the story didn't totally make sense since Francis was only wet up to his knees and Lucienne shoes were the only item that was wet.

On Saturday morning, May 28, police assembled over one hundred officers, special constables and volunteers and covered every inch of fields and barren regions looking for Emile. They started on the far east end of Rosemount Boulevard and started covering ground. Articles stated that the police personal clothes were tearing in the bush when they first came about a lone sandal that matched Emile's. Later in the afternoon they found this, documented in the May 30, 1927 edition of the *Gazette*, "A little further away they found a pair of knickerbockers (Later found to be Emile's). These were turned inside out and were torn to shreds. It was evident to the policemen that the boy had removed these articles of clothing because it hampered him in walking." The police thought they were on the trail of the boy and had several ponds in the area emptied. They found nothing.

The May 30, 1927 edition of *The Gazette* had these surprising details, "Lying in a field below Rosemount Boulevard, three quarters of a mile west of the Franciscan Fathers Monastery, far from his home, dead of exposure, four-year-old Emile Erazola of 2305 Messier Street was found yesterday afternoon by a young girl walking through a field, after 75 policemen and detectives had searched vainly for three days in an effort to discover the boy. The police had neglected nothing in their efforts and had even called into use two water department groups to empty a pool of water into which the boy might have fallen. The body was found at 4:00 p.m., less than a 1/2 mile from the spot police searched." The coroner stated he believed the boy had been dead 2-3 days and was only wearing one stocking, one sandal and under clothes. Later in the same article quoted above was this, "When the body was found yesterday afternoon examination of the bushes surrounding the vacant field failed to show how the boy managed to get into the field. The body bore no marks of violence beyond a few cuts and bruises about the legs, probably occurring when he fell through the bushes." The police stated if the boy had stood up, he would've been seen from Rosemount Boulevard.

Let's review the facts. Emile disappears the night of May 25. He is found on May 28. The morgue estimated the boy had been dead 2-3 days.

The May 30, 1927 edition of the Leader-Post had these details, "The search for four-year-old Emile Erazola who has been missing for four days, ended today with the discovery of the youngster starved to death in a field in the north end of the city." Which rendition should we believe? I do not believe that a four-year-old boy can starve to death in 24 hours, which is how long he was missing before he supposedly died. There was one additional report in the May 31, 1927 *Gazette*, "Coroner McMahon gave a verdict of accidental death in the case of Emile Erazola four years of age." There were no other details about the opinion, just accidental death. That opinion doesn't say what the cause of death was, which indicates to me, he didn't know. If it was hypothermia, drowning or starvation, the coroner would've indicated this as the cause, he didn't.

One article stated that Emile's aunt had memory lapses, ok, what about Francois, why couldn't he remember everything that happened during the night? Something happened to this group in the middle of a major storm. It was never clear where the trio was during the night. It's a fact that one of the three lost a shoe and clothing, Emile. The million-dollar question that concerned police, how did Emile get into the field? I applaud the police officers on scene for actually being concerned about how Emile got into the position he was found.

If there were no tracks of Emile's going into the field, and no footsteps of others as though they put him down, then this only leaves one option that has been consistently told to me by readers, he was dropped or placed from above.

The important facts of this story:

- No tracks leading to the body
- Loss of memory of witnesses
- A weather event happens as the person goes missing
- One witness states that the victim was in water just prior to disappearing
- The victim is located with clothing missing
- Unknown cause of death

Dominique Danis
Missing: 11/23/47, 12:30 p.m., Serpent Lake, QC
Age at disappearance: 52 years
Point of Separation• Water• Weather

According to articles, Serpent Lake is located approximately one hundred miles north of Hull, Quebec. Hull is located across the Ottawa River from Ottawa.

On November 23, 1947, at approximately 11:30 p.m., Dominique Danis was hunting the Serpent Lake area with his son Bruno. Bruno was a veteran of the Royal Canadian Air Force and had participated in World War II as an air gunner. The men decided to split up in the morning hours and meet again at 12:30 p.m., have lunch, and map plans for the afternoon.

At twelve thirty Bruno was the first to their car, and Dominique followed soon after. He told his son that he had spotted a large buck and wanted to go back immediately to track it. Bruno understood, and his dad went back into the forest.

Late in the afternoon, Bruno again came back to the car and waited for his dad. Dominique never arrived. Bruno waited for a few hours and then left to summon assistance.

The local RCMP got additional assistance from local villagers, who came to the search area and volunteered their time.

Searchers reported few leads. This *Ottawa Journal* article of November 27, 1947, had these details: "Tracks had been discovered in the snow Wednesday [November 26] leading to a huge swamp near Yellow Lake about 100 miles northeast of Ottawa. In that areas there were no logging camps and only a few isolated shacks where Danis might take refuge." There were no fires found in the area and nothing to show he may have camped. There was nothing else found in the region.

On November 26, Bruno Danis was desperate to find his dad. It had been snowing lightly the last few days, and it appeared that the weather might be deteriorating. Bruno rented a private plane for two days and hoped to see either his dad or a fire from the sky. It was a valiant attempt by a son to find his father.

After five days of intensive searches, local game wardens and law enforcement officials terminated the effort to locate Dominique.

If you look at this area on Google Maps, you can see that the forest is extremely thick with foliage and swamps, creeks and ponds. At the time that the search for Dominique was terminated, local authorities believed that they would return the following spring and easily find his body. On May 6, 1948, officials did return for two days and searched the area around Serpent Lake. Officials did not find anything of value.

I truly admire the way that Bruno handled the loss of his dad. He kept a level head, made the right choice in renting a plane and searching for his dad.

Glen Moquin
Missing: 08/09/93- Noon, Camp Joli-B, Quebec
Age at disappearance: 22 years
Water• Missing clothes/shoes• Disability/Illness

Glen Moquin

Camp Joli-B is a youth camp on a body of water fifteen miles southwest from Rouyn Noranda, Quebec and just three miles west of the Ottawa River. The victim in this incident lived two hundred miles south of the camp in a city named Bristol, just on the other side of the border from Ontario. In a very, very odd coincidence, his home was also only three miles from the Ottawa River even though it was two hundred miles from the location of the disappearance.

Glen Moquin was from Bristol, Quebec. In late September of 1993, he got a job in the kitchen at Camp Joli-B. By every account I could find, everything was going fine at the camp for Glen until August 7, 1993. Various articles state that in the days preceding his disappearance, Moquin had complained to staff about severe headaches. The kitchen assistant was last seen on noon on August 9. The staff became concerned about his absence, and a search was started and is described in this August 21, 1993 edition of the Ottawa Citizen, "The following day a search party found his clothes-underwear and shoes included-in a pile about one kilometer from the camp. His wallet was found further away with no cash in it. His identification cards were scattered about."

The police continued to search for four days and could not locate the young man. There were various reports that a man resembling Moquin was seen in Northern Ontario. There were even more sightings in multiple areas, all unconfirmed.

Mr. Moquin described his son as a good athlete, great swimmer, and very comfortable in the outdoors.

For readers new to my books, this story is almost a cookie-cutter edition for many disappearances I have documented. A man stripping all of his clothing off in the woods and never being seen again makes zero sense. Most readers would immediately think that some mental illness was involved, except that Glen was a very stable person with no history of psychological issues.

The headaches that Glen was experiencing is something I went to great lengths to explain in Missing 411: Hunters. There were dozens of examples in the book of hunters telling their partners that they were not feeling well and were going back to their vehicle only never to be seen again. The hunters did not feel right, left the presence of others and vanished, very similar to Moquin.

It is an extremely unusual coincidence that Glen lived a couple of miles from the Ottawa River. He travels two hundred miles north into a wilderness zone and gets a job within a few miles of the Ottawa River and vanishes never to be found.

Glen's father made statements to the press that he believed the headaches his son was experiencing played some role in him vanishing. I think his dad was right. My issue is, where did Glen go naked?

Guy Ouellet
Missing: 07/18/98- 2:00 P.M., Oka National Park, Quebec
Age at disappearance: 42 years
Point of Separation• Water• Unknown Cause of Death

Oka National Park sits on the northern banks of the Lake of Two Mountains, and this is located directly west of Montreal. The lake flows into the Saint Lawrence River. The park is surrounded by a suburb of Montreal and is a highly urban area.

In July of 1998, Guy Ouellet was a married forty-two-year-old father of three. He had twins, a boy and girl thirteen years old and another fifteen-year-old daughter. On Saturday morning July 18, Guy was on vacation till July 28 from his work managing a kitchen at the St. Laurent Convent. At 8:00 A.M., Guy and his wife went to a local donut shop near their residence in Deux-Montagnes. The couple had a few cups of coffee. Marjolaine gave her husband five dollars, and they finalized plans to meet at 2:00 P.M. for a Saturday night together going out for dinner. Marjolaine left for her job in Lavalle as a nurse's aide for the mentally disabled and Guy rode off on his bike for a day riding around Oka National park.

Guy was described as a man that knew the outdoors well. He was an avid hunter and routinely discussed survival tactics with kids and friends. He had recently lost weight and was feeling healthy and happy and was going to enjoy a Saturday in the park near his residence.

Family and friends had confirmed that they had contacted Guy during the day on his cell phone up until noon when nobody could reach him. At 2:00 P.M., when he agreed to meet his family at their home, he never arrived.

Guy was a very family-oriented man who was never late, kept his family informed on where he was and what he was doing. Almost from the onset of him not arriving on time, the family knew something was very wrong. As the hours passed, the family decided to call the local police and report their clan leader as a missing person.

The Deux Montagnes Police were the first to handle Guy's disappearance. They put one hundred police officers into the park along with a helicopter to cover the rural acreage. Even though the park is on the perimeter of the city, Oka National Park gets very thick and rural. The parks 9.2 square miles sits adjacent to the north shore of Lake of Two Mountains. The first indicator as to Guy's location was made public in the July 21 edition of *The Gazette*, "Yesterday afternoon, they intensified their search around the beach at Oka Provincial Park after confirmation that a transmission tower at Vendreuil tracked the signal from his cellular phone there shortly after 5 a.m. Sunday, July 19." The triangulation of a cell phone signal in an urban area can be very accurate. The fact they had a signal near the beach is an interesting note because I believe that many of the disappearances are connected to water. When the police obtained this response, they probably were reasonably sure that Guy would eventually be located in the lake. At 5 a.m. on Sunday, Guy would've been missing for 15 hours. If he was near the beach at that time, he could've easily found his way out because the primary paths around the lake pass right by this location.

One day after the cell phone article was this update in the July 22, 1998 edition of *The Gazette* had these details of the search from the SAR commander, "We've done the bike path three times," Beauchemin said. "We started with 10 feet around the path, then 20 feet, then 50 feet. If he were hit by a vehicle, you'd think by 50 feet we'd find something." The police also put divers in the lake and then dragged the water multiple times, not finding anything.

The primary detective on the Ouellet disappearance was Detective Bouchard from the Deux Montagnes Police. He made this statement in the July 24, 1998 edition of the *Gazette*, "In the Ouellet case, which is being investigated by police in Deux Montagnes, "It is very mysterious," Bouchard said. "You're near a body of water. He's never done this before. He's a good family man, apparently. He just disappeared off the face of the Earth." In the hundreds of search hours by family friends and police, nothing was found that belonged to Guy. The police were even mystified that they could not locate a large object like his bicycle.

One month after the disappearance, police decided to search two ponds with divers that were fenced. The police spent the day in the water and located nothing. The law enforcement regrouped, had meetings, and walked the park multiple times trying to understand how they could've missed the man.

In 2000, *The Gazette* newspaper in Quebec went back and interviewed Guy's wife and family. The group explained that times had been tough on them. The family had to move from their home, they didn't have any closure on what had happened, and there had not been anything new on the case in 17 months. Marjolaine was so committed to finding answers; she posted a $30,000 reward for anyone locating her husband, hoping this would attract interest in the case from others.

The police case file on the disappearance of Guy Ouellet would gather dust until it was four years, eleven months, and seven days old. On June 25, 2003, a man that was in the park and lost stumbled across remains deep in the park that would later be identified as Guy. The June 28, 2003 edition of the Gazette had this statement from police, "Constable Gilles Mitchell of Surete Du Quebec would say the remains, found 500 meters off a main road in Oka." They were not positive the body was Guy, but all indicators showed it was him. Months after the discovery of the body, the police confirmed it was Guy. The medical examiner withheld a cause of death until all forensic testing was completed.

The last public statement about Mr. Ouellet's cause of death was noted in the March 10, 2004 edition of *The Gazette*, "An autopsy performed on the body of a man who had been missing for five years before his remains were recovered in Oka Park last summer has proved inconclusive. The autopsy shows that Guy Ouellet did not die of foul play, but the exact cause of death remained undetermined. " The police stated that they consider the case closed.

One major issue that still bothers me on this incident, how did Guy's phone triangulate to a position near the beach and water when he was later found deep in the woods? How in the heck did he end up deep in the woods with a bicycle? What would he had been doing in the woods on a bike?

As I have stated in other books, I have had coroners contact me and state that I was onto something big. They independently said that their groups had discussed bodies where they could not determine the cause of death, and this had bothered them. Many of the facts surrounding these cases were very similar. Each of them had explained that they had the most excellent equipment, facilities, and experts; they should've been able to point to a cause. One coroner asked if I would speak at a convention of coroners and explain my findings; I never did because I never received the invitation.

It's always peculiar to me when police and coroners reach a dead end on a case and then immediately wash their hands of it. The majority of law enforcement never wants to admit when they can't solve something or when they reach a blank wall. If all homicide detectives got together and openly discussed cases where there was not a cause of death identified, the cumulative effect of that discussion would bring enlightenment to the next detective that faces a similar incident.

I can only hope that the finding of Guy brought some comfort to his kids and wife.

Chris Brown
Missing: 11/11/95- 2: 00 P.M., 24 Miles North of Otter Lake, Quebec
Age at disappearance: 26 years
Water• Weather• Canines• Point of Separation• Hunter

Most of the hunters I have chronicled in the past were experienced outdoorsmen who understood what to do when they were lost, and most knew the area they were hunting. Hunters carry one huge loudspeaker that most hikers do not have, a firearm. If you are lost, fire three rapid shots in succession to let others know you are lost. In this incident, there were no shots heard.

Chris Brown

In November of 1995, Chris Brown was a married father of two living in Low, Quebec. Chris and four friends planned a trip to hunt twenty-four miles north of Otter Lake or approximately twenty miles west of Low.

On November 11, 1995, The five buddies grouped and discussed how they wanted to hunt. This November 15, 1995 edition of the *Ottawa Citizen* explained how the disappearance evolved, "The last person to see the man (Chris Brown) was a trapper, who sent him on a trail which should have led him to aa spot where his four hunting buddies were waiting for him. That was just after 2 p.m. Saturday, around the time he was supposed to meet his friends. The group of five hunters had decided to separate for a few hours early that morning. Point of Separation.

The group of five hunters had established their camp at a remote village that did not have electricity or phones. They yelled and called for Chris throughout that first night, and one then headed for the city to ask for help. Once Quebec provincial police arrived and took command of the SAR, things started to happen as is described in the same article described earlier, "On Monday, the rescue team grew as Otter Lake Firefighters, two police dogs and more volunteers joined the search. The group began searching Tuesday with 20-30 police officers and 30-40 volunteers. But last light, more than 100 volunteers had joined the search.

The weather in the search area had deteriorated since Chris disappeared and is described in the November 18, 1995 edition of the *Ottawa Citizen*, On Wednesday, a record snowstorm that covered the forest with a deep carpet of snow slowed the search for the married father of two young children including an 18-day old daughter."

The search official government SAR for Chris lasted seven days. The police stated that the weather became so severe that they had to terminate their efforts. Family and friends did continue to search for a short period of time and then came back in the spring of 1996. Nothing related to Chris Brown was ever found.

In late November of 1995, after the official search was terminated, Chris' family blasted the search efforts to locate the hunter. In the Ottawa Citizen on November 23, 1995, the family said that searchers showed up late for work; others didn't know how to read a compass, and others walked across tracks in the snow. There were other allegations that the family did not believe that some government personnel took the search seriously.

As someone who has interviewed many victim families about the search and rescue effort for their family members, few are truly happy with the effort. When you understand the search dynamic, if it was your family member that was missing, is there any effort that would indeed be enough? Maybe the SAR that quickly located your family member would be enough? In the cases I am involved in, the efforts are never enough; I understand that mindset. If it were my family member missing, I would be on scene 24/7, advocating for the missing.

There was never a mention of the police or family coming back in the spring with cadaver dogs. These trained canines can smell decomposing flesh from miles away, regardless of the foliage or terrain. Snow may have covered Chris' remains in the winter, but the spring brings with it sun, warmer temperatures, and a different dynamic.

I can't imagine how Chris' wife lived a life raising two infants without their dad and the daily reminder he wasn't coming back.

Jimmy Rambone Jr.
Missing 9/03/03–3 p.m., Nunavik, QC
Age at Disappearance: 51 years
**Disabled• Epileptic• Hunter

Jimmy Rambone lived with his girlfriend, Pam Ruzzo, on his farm in Foster, Rhode Island. Jimmy had a variety of small animals that he cared for daily. Jimmy loved the outdoors and was a lifetime hunter. His wish was to travel to the far reaches of northern Canada and pursue the hunt of a lifetime for caribou.

In early September 2003, Jimmy booked a trip with Canadadventures to travel to Kuujjuaq, east of Kuujjuarapik in Nunavik, for an unguided caribou hunt. He was staying at a location called Camp Sardine near the Caniapiscau River and was transported to the site in a Beaver aircraft. There were a total of four hunters in the group at the camp. Jimmy was one of 3,500 hunters that annually come to Nunavik to hunt; this specific eight-day hunt cost Jimmy $2,900. Pam was going to stay at the farm and ensure the animals stayed healthy while Jimmy took the once-in-a-lifetime trip.

Jimmy wanted to hunt alone, and this wasn't unusual. He had decades of hunting experience, he knew what he was doing, and he was highly proficient with his rifle. Jimmy was also an epileptic.

On September 3, 2003, the hunters rose early and departed their camp. It wasn't long after they left that they heard two shots that could have only come from Jimmy. The group felt that Jimmy must've quickly got a caribou. The hunters came back to their cabin near lunchtime, and Jimmy didn't arrive. The group waited till near 2 p.m. and then started to search for the fifty-one-year-old hunter. At approximately 3 p.m., the sense of urgency started to rise as they found the location where Jimmy had apparently killed a caribou. The scene of the shooting was almost surreal. Jimmy's bright-orange hunting vest was hanging thirty feet from the carcass along with his camera. Jimmy and his rifle were gone.

On September 4, more personnel arrived at the cabin and started to formulate a plan for the search for Jimmy. The Beaver aircraft went into the air and started to look for the missing hunter. It wouldn't be easy. Jimmy had been wearing a camouflage coat under his orange vest; it would make finding him difficult.

Searchers went back to the scene where the vest had been found and started to search the area for clues. There was snow on the ground, but rescuers could not find footprints leaving the area, very unusual. Jean-Pierre Bardou was the manager for Canadadventures and was on the scene soon after the report came in. A September 19, 2003, article in the *Nunatsiaq News* had the following update on the search for Jimmy: "Soon the KPRF and the SQ and a specifically trained dog became involved in the search for the missing hunter. They scouted the terrain with the dog and surveyed low-lying trees, rocks and lakes by helicopter. 'There was no scent. The dog almost got lost,' said Bardou." Later in the same article, "'I fear something tragic happened to him the first day,' said Bardou."

A September 2007 article in *Outdoor Life Magazine* chronicled the disappearance of Jimmy. One portion of the article stated: "He simply disappeared from the face of the earth, or so it seems." The article included the following statement by Pam Ruzzo: "Something's just not right. You don't just vanish."

I did speak with Pam by phone. She explained that she received donations and hired a private investigator to attempt to determine what happened to Jimmy. It is quite a different life this far north. Weather changes quickly, and the Royal Canadian Mounted Police do not have the resources in this region that they would have in a more populated province.

The manager of Camp Sardine, Mr. Bardou, stated that they have only had one other incident where a group was lost for twenty-four hours. Once they put the Beaver aircraft into the sky, the hunters came into a clearing, and they were rescued. The camp had never had an incident like Jimmy's.

Rescuers did tell Pam that there were predators in this region occasionally. The most vicious and dangerous animals are polar bears and wolves. They explained that these animals might possibly attack a human, but they'd also eat the carcass of the caribou and they wouldn't take the rifle, which was never found. There was never a location found that could be attributed to an attack on a human.

Summary

Several elements of Jimmy's disappearance meet the criteria for missing people we would study. Jimmy was an epileptic. Some rescuers believed that it was possible that Jimmy had a seizure, became disoriented, and subsequently got lost and died. Pam did state that Jimmy was sometimes disoriented after a seizure, but only for ten or fifteen minutes.

He was wearing very bright clothing, which was left behind. Leaving the camera at the scene seems like a very odd element. I have stated in other books that there does seem to be an inordinate amount of photographers that vanish.

Bloodhounds brought to the scene seemed disoriented or unable to work, a very consistent element in many disappearances.

The area where Jimmy disappeared is one of the marshiest areas you can find in North America. The region is probably 35 percent water and 65 percent land. Jimmy was very close to a river and a lake when the incident occurred.

Many people who are chronicled in the "Missing 411" books seem to shed clothing for some reason. The idea that Jimmy's vest was hanging in a tree when he knew there were hunters in the area seems contrary to his hunter-safety training.

The most important aspect of this case was the remote nature of this disappearance. Jimmy had no place to walk for safety; Camp Sardine was the lone safe location within hiking distance.

Searchers never did find a location where there were indications of an animal attack. They never found any confirmed tracks of Jimmy's. It's hard to reconcile in my mind how rescuers couldn't find tracks when there was snow on the ground. In a region where there is limited wildlife and virtually no human traffic, it's very hard to understand how a search-trained canine cannot find a scent. This is a very baffling case that may never be resolved.

Jimmy has never been found.

Mark Kraynak, Age at disappearance: 23 years
Steven Wright, Age at disappearance: 20 years
Missing: 08/22/2005-3:32 a.m., Laval, Quebec

Mark Kraynak had already lived a big life by the time he reached his twenty-third birthday. The young man grew up in Pennsylvania and graduated from Laurel Highlands Senior High School in 2000. He served three years as an army specialist with the 82nd Airborne Division based in Fort Bragg, North Carolina. He was awarded a purple heart when he was wounded by a grenade in Baghdad. He had enrolled at Penn State as a sophomore in their business management program at the Fayette Eberly campus.

There is very little information available about Steven Wright other than he was from Guerneville, California.

The background on this story differs significantly from others you'll read in this book, but the facts support inclusion. According to numerous articles, both men were working for Stephen Sirard, CEO of FCF Agency, and were hired to work at a strip club in Toronto. FCF is a California-based company with offices in Toronto, Atlanta, and Santa Rosa, California. Sirard has made statements that Wright enjoyed the work as he could make $1,000 a night. A contrary statement was later made that Kraynak was uncomfortable with dancing and asked to quit after two weeks. He later got a job as a construction worker in Toronto. One article stated that Sirard has been associated with the adult film industry in Canada.

Mark and Steven were good friends and hung out together regularly. On the night of August 21, the men were drinking and partying at Club Vatican in Montreal. The guys decided to take a cab for the thirty-minute ride to Laval, Quebec, to a club called Red Lite. There is surveillance video showing the two arriving near the club and running from the vehicle that gave them a ride. Mark's mom stated that it appeared to her when she viewed the footage that it looked like Mark was running for his life. The police theorized they stiffed the cab driver even though they never identified the cab or the driver. It was 3:32 a.m. on August 22 when the footage was recorded. Friends tried to contact the men later that morning and were unsuccessful. A missing person report was filed by Sirard on Monday.

The police started their search immediately and focused on a large quarry four hundred feet from the club where they were headed. They searched the area around the quarry numerous times and could see nothing down its steep sides. Eleven days after the men vanished, a police helicopter was flying over the quarry and found the two bodies fifty feet from the top of the quarry on a small ledge. They had each suffered many fractures. An autopsy was completed, and the police stated that the bodies were too decomposed for toxicology results. They stated that there were no unusual marks or scratches from violence. Guy Lajeunesse, the spokesperson for the Laval police, made the following statement in the September 8, 2005, edition of *Triblive.com*: "Lajeunesse said the rave club is within 400 feet of the quarry. Although a six-foot high fence with barbed wire surrounds the quarry, he said it's impossible the men could have bent the fencing to try to pass through if they figured it might be a shortcut to the Red Lite. We've got no reason why they fell from that place. That's very bizarre." Remember the coroner's earlier ruling—there were no scratches or bruising on the body from violence, meaning, they weren't in a fight and there was no evidence they crawled over the top of the barbed wire. They were wearing nice clothes like you'd wear to a club. The idea they were trying to take a shortcut through a quarry is ridiculous. The spokesperson for the police later stated that the FBI and Canadian Police were assisting with the investigation. Yes, Laval is stumped about how the men got over the fence and onto a ledge. I'm sure they are also interested about where the bodies were for eleven days.

While this is not a case where drinking men ended up in the water, it matches cases we have outlined in prior books. Unusual falls that cannot be explained fit the profile. When the police are stumped, you should be stumped. You will read about other cases were bodies mysteriously have ended up in a quarry.

In the same Triblive.com article noted earlier was this statement by Mark Kraynak's mom: "Kraynak's mother, Janice, of New Jersey, has told Canadian Media she doesn't believe her son's death was an accident."

Saskatchewan

Population: 1,169,000
Capital City: Saskatoon
    The majority of Saskatchewan sits above Montana, and one third lies north of North Dakota. Regina is the capital of the province and is located approximately eighty miles north of the United States border. The southern area of the province is generally flat and has a prairie environment.
    The highest point east of the Rocky Mountains in Canada is Cypress Hills Provincial Park in the southwest sector of the province. This is a gorgeous recreation area with lakes, camping, and general recreation. The elevation gets to 4,567', not high by Rocky Mountain standards, but it is to residents.
    This region of Canada only has 80-100 frost-free days during the year. This weather gives its 90,000 farms a shortened growing season. Forty percent of the province is covered by forest, and ten percent is covered by freshwater.
    The second most common language in this part of Canada is Cree. The province bird is the Sharp Tailed Grouse, and the provincial animal is the White-Tailed Deer.
    Here is a list of the largest cities in Saskatchewan:

Saskatoon: 246,000
Regina: 215,000
Prince Albert: 36,000
Moose Jaw: 34,000
Swift Current: 17,000
    Saskatchewan is one of only two provinces in Canada that does not have a saltwater coast. It is also slightly unusual as they do not have a major metropolitan.
    One interesting fact I learned from one source while researching this section, the word "hoser" is a term that came from Saskatchewan and is derived from someone who stole gas using a siphon hose.

Saskatchewan Missing Person List by Date

Missing Person	Date Missing• Age• Sex
Allen Anderson	06/24/27-10:00 a.m.•2•M
Eddie Hamilton	07/06/28• 2• M
Freddie Mollenbeck	05/22/37-p.m.•2•M
Hazel Scraba	05/23/37-Unk •11•F
Ludvina Machishyn	05/23/37-Unk •10•F
Irene Rempel	10/10/50–2 p.m.•3•F
Richard Spyglass	08/05/64•5•M
Ashley Krestianson	07/14/94•8•F

Allen Anderson
Missing:06/24/27- 10:00 a.m.- Kipling, Saskatchewan
Age at disappearance: 2 1/2 years
Weather• Canines

I have documented a series of missing people in the region just north of the United States border starting in British Columbia extending east to the Atlantic. This incident happened ten miles outside of Kipling, Saskatchewan, seventy miles north of the United States border and ninety miles east of Regina. The area is sprinkled with farms, ranches and small bodies of water. This June 25, 1927 edition of *The Province* had details of this case, "More than 100 men are searching for the 2 1/2-year-old son of Henry Anderson, a farmer living ten miles from Kipling, Saskatchewan. The child wandered away from his home at 10:00 a.m. Friday morning and at 11:00 a.m. at night no trace of him had been found. An electric storm accompanied by rain this afternoon has made the search more difficult." There were very few additional details of what precipitated the disappearance.

From the beginning of this search, hundreds of volunteers in the community inundated the Anderson farm and covered every inch of the property. At one point it was believed that small tracks may have been made by Allen were found in a nearby plowed field and canines were called from Winnipeg. In the days it took to call and get the dogs to the property, it rained four more times. The extent of the weather issues is explained in the June 30 edition of the *Leader-Post*, "Wednesday afternoon from 3 to 5 o'clock one of the heaviest storms of the past 15 years put a stop to the hunt. Until after six o'clock, men trailed into town wet to the skin, but cheerful, and announced they would resume the intensive search Thursday. Some of them say they will remain on the job until some clue of the missing boy is found."

The police detective running the search for Allen called in the local First Nations reservation to help with the SAR. The trackers looked at the marks left in the field and determined it was a dog, not human tracks. This July 2, 1927 article in the *Leader-Post* had more details of the search, " After a week of intensive searching, during which every inch of ground for a radius of three miles from the Anderson home has been thoroughly covered, no clue has been found to lead to the whereabouts of Allen Anderson, two and a half years old who disappeared Friday of last week. Indians who have been tracking for three days and assisting in the search for the boy, gave grunts of disgust tonight when they returned to the Anderson home and in broken English announced they were unable to find anything that would lead them even to suspect the child had ever traveled any part of the district on foot."

The First Nations people searched until July 7 and terminated their effort. The canine manager from Winnipeg announced that the dogs did not pick up a scent, probably due to the amount of rain they had in the area since the child vanished.

The Anderson's and their neighbors searched for weeks after the formal effort stopped. The detective handling the case was on site for the entire two weeks and stated that he didn't think foul play was involved. He did make a statement early in the search that the boy probably drowned in one of the sloughs or creeks; they were either all drained and hand searched without finding anything. A July 2, 1927 copy of the *Leader-Post* had these statements from police, "Police, tonight, after exhausting every theory, state it is the most baffling case that has come to their notice."

Allen Anderson was never found.

Eddie Hamilton
Missing 7/6/28, Elrose, Sask
Age at Disappearance, 2 years
Berries• Water• Point of Separation

Mr. and Mrs. Freeman Hamilton from Elrose took their two-year-old son (Eddie) with them as they went berry picking just south of their hometown. They exited their car in the thick berry infested area and Eddie immediately walked off in one direction. The Hamilton's momentarily lost sight of the boy and never saw him again.

The area that the Hamilton's were in was flat ground for three miles to the south until you reach the White Bear Hills that surround White Bear Lake. There are three small lakes all approximately one half mile long and narrow. There are sets of hills on each side of the lakes and the bodies of water sit inside a small valley. These are the only hills anywhere in the vicinity where Eddie disappeared.

Once Eddie was out of sight, the Hamilton's immediately started to call his name and search for him; they did not receive an answer. The parents searched the area multiple times and couldn't find the boy. The husband now stayed in the area searching and the wife went for help. The RCMP quickly arrived and before dusk a large search had started. The SAR had over 250 participants inside of 24 hours with searchers working around the clock. Planes had been utilized for low flight passes in an effort to see ground movement, none was seen.

A July 13, 1928 article in the *Saskatoon Phoenix* noted that searchers had found "boot prints" and "heel prints" in one area and the following:

"There are footprints however in the vicinity but though the wheat fields and undergrowth for miles around have been thoroughly combed no further clue has been found."

This is an interesting article because the writer made a definite distinction between the boot, heel and footprint that was found.

Several articles stated that this was the largest search in the history of the province. It lasted for over three months and nothing was found. No clothing in the brush, no other footprints, no witnesses, nothing. Almost 2000 people participated in the three-month effort.

On October 25, 1928 a traveling salesman was duck hunting 3 ½ miles from where little Eddie Hamilton disappeared. The hunter was on White Bear Lake when he looked in the water and saw a small figure floating, it was Eddie. The body was retrieved and the parents made a positive identification that it was Eddie Hamilton. The article in the *Winnipeg Free Press* made no mention of the condition of the body or the oddity of the find.

Case Summary

If Eddie Hamilton were found in White Bear Lake, that little boy would've climbed over 1800' of mountains, walked down into a valley and then into the water. There were many, many other small bodies of water in the area of the disappearance that he could've fallen into, but he didn't. The idea that a two year old boy could walk over three miles through thickets, brush, over a mountain without ever hearing the frantic please of his parents is hard to believe, very hard to believe. The fact that he had to climb over mountains to reach the lake is something quite unbelievable for a two year old. You will find several notes in this book that describe small children supposedly hiking uphill when lost and later found at an elevation higher then where they went missing. It is the general belief amongst SAR leaders that children walk downhill when lost, not usually uphill, especially a two-year old going 1800 feet uphill. A guide written to assist SAR commanders states that a 1-3 year old child will be found 95% of the time on flat ground in less than a two mile radius.

Freddie Mollenbeck
Missing: 05/22/37—p.m.—St. Gregor, Sask
Age at Disappearance: 2 years
• Loss of Shoes• Distance• Weather• Cluster Zone

On very rare occasions, multiple disappearances happen in a short period of time and close in geographical proximity. Pay close attention to this case and the following incident. The disappearances happened on back-to-back days in the same general area, with their children missing for multiple days.

Freddie Mollenbeck was a two-year-old living in St. Gregor, Saskatchewan, approximately seventy miles east of Saskatoon. The village of St. Gregor has a population of only one hundred today. This is predominantly a ranching and farming area with many swamps, sloughs, and waterways.

Freddie disappeared on Saturday, May 22, 1937, in the afternoon from his home. The Royal Canadian Mounted Police and local residents from the surrounding area all joined in the search effort. Here is what the May 26, 1937, edition of the *Winnipeg Free Press* stated about the incident: "He was found unconscious in bush lining a slough several miles distance by searchers at 4:00 p.m. Monday. The child was taken to Humboldt Hospital where he is making a recovery. Some 450 men and boys, 80 of them mounted on horses, searched 48 hours under leadership of the Royal Canadian Mounted Police. Barefoot and clad in light summer clothes only, the child was exposed to heavy rain storm Saturday night."

I did an extensive search on this incident, attempting to determine how far Freddie traveled. I could not find anything indicating the distance the young boy was found from his home, other than "several miles." Finding a two-year-old several miles from his home is unusual.

This disappearance may seem mundane at first glance; be patient. The next two disappearances happened the following day one hundred miles almost exactly east of St. Gregor.

Hazel Scraba   Age at disappearance: 11 years
Ludvina Machishyn   Age at disappearance: 10 years
Missing: 05/23/37, Pelly, Saskatchewan, Canada
Distance Traveled• Point of Separation• Unusual Statement• Berries

Pelly is ten miles west of the Manitoba border in an area with hundreds of small bodies of water. The region is known for its farming and wildlife. The area of this incident can get very wild in the areas surrounding the farms and is a mecca for fisherman and hunters.

On May 23, 1937, best friends Hazel and Ludvina were at the Machishyn ranch and were asked to go into the fields and look for lost cattle. The children knew that many of the areas around the property were swampy and wet. The girls went into the fields and apparently got lost. Ludvina's father called upon the residents of Pelly for assistance. The Royal Canadian Mounted Police (RCMP) also responded in force.

Two days and seven miles from the ranch, searchers found small footprints that they believed may be the girls but weren't sure. The rescue teams were challenged in their efforts by severe rain, which had been in the area since the girls disappeared.

According to Robert Koester's book, *Lost Person Behavior*, children ten to twelve years of age, if traveling on flat ground, should be located 95 percent of the time within 6.2 miles or less. A May 27 article in the *Calgary Daily Herald* had this statement about what searchers found: "Ludvina was found yesterday afternoon by a roving band of Indians 20 miles northwest of her home." This means that Ludvina traveled twenty miles in less than three days across fields and swamps while passing many farms, ranches, and roadways. This is an unbelievable distance for anyone to travel in that time frame.

After Ludvina was found, the girl was questioned extensively about what had happened to her friend. She stated that they separated on Monday after they argued about what they wanted to do. RCMP now went back to the location where Ludvina was found in hopes that Hazel was in that same area.

On May 27, 1937, Joe Malonowich was driving a wagonload of food from Pelly to the search teams up north. A May 29, 1937, article in the *Montreal Gazette* explained what Joe found: "Malonowich heard Hazel's shrill cries near the Swan River. Jumping off his wagon, he plunged into the bush and found her sitting under a fir tree on a high piece of ground that had been cut off from the mainland and transformed into an island by the rising river." Hazel was taken to a local farmhouse where she was given food and shelter. In the same article, the girl explained her travels: "At another time, 12 small brown bears passed near her but, 'they didn't even growl,' Hazel said." She said that she drank water and ate berries.

Summary

When you read all of the stories in the four Missing 411 books, children seem to see bears in an inordinate amount of occasions.

Many claim to see the animals sleeping and under other unusual conditions, and they never have a negative encounter. The opportunity to see twelve bears at any one time seems highly unusual.

It seems odd that both girls weren't found by the hundreds of searchers, planes, and RCMP that were looking for them. When Malonowich located Hazel, she was found completely surrounded by water, a very unusual location. She obviously didn't see Joe, because he hadn't seen her from the roadway. Was that Hazel's loud scream that had alerted Joe?

Many lost people are found in, near, or adjacent to creeks and rivers, exactly as Hazel was found.

If I wrote a movie script where one girl disappears and is found on an island in a river, while the other is found twenty miles from where she was last seen, would that be believable?

Irene Rempel
Missing 10/10/50–2 p.m., Regina, SK
Age at Disappearance: 3 years
German• Water• Point of Separation• Canine• Missing Clothing

Regina is located approximately eighty miles north of the Montana and North Dakota borders. The city is located in an extremely marshy and watery environment, surrounded by hundreds of small bodies of water. Wascana Creek is located in the southeast corner of the city and flows toward the southeast.

On October 10, 1950, three-year-old Irene Rempel was playing with her four-year-old friend Annie Klain of 2444 McAra Street in Regina. It's completely unclear how or why the girls decided to take a walk from the yard, but they did. It wasn't long after they vanished at 2 p.m. that law enforcement authorities were called, and the search started for both girls. Volunteers and Royal Canadian Mounted Police (RCMP) started to comb the entire neighborhoods of both girls without having any success.

At 5:25 p.m., a motorist saw Annie walking in Douglas Park and gave the girl a ride back to her home. Irene wasn't with Annie. Searchers had no idea where she was, and Annie couldn't offer any clarity other than where she was walking. The park is located in the southeast corner of Regina and several blocks from the girl's residence but just two blocks from Wascana Lake, which empties into Wascana Creek.

At approximately 8 p.m., Irene still had not been found. The local RCMP commander went back to the barracks and emptied it of all twenty-five men and ordered them into the field to search. The call was also made for all canine search teams.

As the night got later, the temperature dropped, and it was getting quite cold. At just after 10 p.m., a canine team was one and a half miles outside the city limit of Regina, in a prairie near Wascana Creek, when they made a discovery. An October 11, 1950, article in the *Leader Post* had the following description of the find: "When I walked up to the girl she didn't say anything but she whimpered a little. She was sitting in the pasture but quite close to the creek. She must have walked into it before because her feet were wet. She had her hands crossed in front of her and her head was hanging down. She had taken off her coat and overalls and she must have taken off her shoes earlier because they weren't around." Irene was taken to a local hospital, where she was determined to have a mild case of exposure. She spent one night in the hospital and was released the following morning in good condition.

Rescuers tried to question Irene about her excursion, but she didn't say anything. It was later learned that Irene came to Canada from Germany just two years earlier and only spoke German. Irene's mom did state that the girl said that she "ran and ran" and was never afraid.

Summary

This incident occurred on a cold October night in a creek. Irene's feet were wet, and her shoes were missing. She had removed her coat and overalls. She was over one and a half miles from the city limits of Regina in the middle of the prairie. How Irene got from a neighborhood in Regina to a creek setting in the prairie of Saskatchewan is the million-dollar question. This was quite a journey for any three-year-old.

The article reviewed for the incident did state that Irene was found shivering and cold. Why wasn't she wearing her coat and overalls? Where were Irene's clothing and shoes?

Irene was found heading out of the city along a creek line. This is a highly unusual incident for the "Missing 411" books. This girl goes missing near the center of the city and heads directly to its outskirts and then continues along a creek. The fact of following a creek seems to be something that is consistent with other cases. It is unusual that searchers found Irene's feet wet, and she was shivering. Why would Irene voluntarily go into the creek if it was cold outside? She was in a prairie, an easy location to walk. The creek bed offers good cover if you were trying to hide because of the foliage along most creek banks, and the creek itself conceals footprints. I doubt that a three-year-old girl has the intellect to understand the concealment facts associated with a creek.

Irene was found with her head down and not saying anything. It didn't sound like she was happy to see searchers, or maybe she was in a semiconscious state.

Richard Spyglass
Missing: 08/05/64, 7:00 p.m., Mosquito Indian Reserve, Saskatchewan, Ontario
Age at disappearance: 5
Disability• Berries• Disability

On August 5, 1964, Richard Spyglass was with a group of family members who were bailing hay on the Mosquito Indian Reserve approximately seventy miles northwest of Saskatoon. It was early evening when the group realized that Richard had disappeared. The men searched the fields and then expanded into the bogs and sloughs of the area. After a short time, local law enforcement was notified and they responded with twenty officers and search dogs.

The exact area of the search is twenty miles south of North Battleford. The area is swampy, with many lakes and dams. This area is one of the last in the region that hasn't been fully developed into a farming area. Searchers didn't believe Richard could have traveled far because of the thick brush and his young age.

Dozens of people searched for Richard and knew he couldn't speak; he was mute since birth. The searchers decided that since the boy could hear, they would constantly blast a message calling for him. Unfortunately, this didn't work.

Almost twenty-four hours after Richard disappeared, Ted Menssa was working his farm 8½ miles to the north. Ted stated that there was a very old street near where he was working, and he saw the boy standing in the road, not saying anything. The boy was carrying a bottle of freshly picked berries. The farmer offered the boy some food but he refused it.

Ted said the boy had a few scratches on his face, and he didn't say anything. Ted was later informed that the boy was a mute. Richard was found far outside the confines of the search area, and this shocked many of the searchers.

Case Summary

The first puzzling aspect of this case is that Richard was found carrying a bottle of freshly picked berries. The area where he went missing is extremely wild (without many residents). Where did he get the bottle and the berries? There isn't one SAR book anywhere that states that a five-year-old boy could wander 8½ miles through swamps and bush in a twenty-four-hour period. How did Richard manage to accomplish this? In the book *Lost Person Behavior* by Robert Koester, he states that a child between the ages of four and six will be found 95 percent of the time in less than a 5.1 mile radius from the point last seen.

In my humble opinion, there appears to be an inordinate amount of young children who go missing under the circumstances described in this book in which the children are suffering from some type of disability and cannot speak or are too young to describe what happened to them. Is this merely a coincidence?

Ashley Krestianson
Missing: 07/14/94, Tisdale, Saskatchewan
Age at disappearance: 8
Point of Separation• Water• Weather• Missing Clothing• Twins

Kelly Krestianson had taken her twin eight-year-old girls, Lindsay and Ashley, to the Barrier Chaparrel Vacation Ranch on the outskirts of Tisdale, Saskatchewan. Here is the description that the vacation ranch had on their Web site: "At Barrier Chaparral, a prairie ranch vacation combines wide open spaces with great natural beauty and physical activities that range from challenging to exhilarating. Guests enjoy the pristine prairie air and tranquil rural lifestyle as they join in trail rides, canoeing, fishing and trapshooting, plus rodeos and paw wows."

The ranch leverages the area history in regards to First Nations People.

On July 14, 1994, Kelly had to leave the ranch for a few hours to deliver Avon products to local farmers' and ranchers' wives. Lindsay and Ashley stayed at the ranch and visited with a local friend. The girls decided they would go horseback riding and would have a footrace back to the stables. Ashley told the girls that she knew a shortcut and raced off down another trail. Lindsay and their friend took the main trail and arrived at the stables. Ashley never arrived.

Lindsay quickly became worried and notified the ranch authorities. The ranch started a quick search and then notified local authorities and Ashley's dad, Buddy. Buddy worked for the Canadian Highway Authority in Tisdale and was quickly on the scene.

The RCMP responded immediately and in force. Within hours after arriving, RCMP officials had called for four additional cities to respond with their detachments. Within three days there were four airplanes, four canine teams, one army helicopter equipped with FLIR, and over five hundred searchers scouring the ranch for the young girl. The helicopter pilot conducted low flyovers through the area looking for a heat signature on the ground, but nothing was found after several days in the air.

The area around the ranch is very swampy, grassy, and at points, extremely thick with vegetation. It would be hard to imagine any young person making great progress through such a diverse and tough environment. One of the main issues hampering search efforts the first three days was that the area was hit by heavy rains, which obliterated tracks and reduced the scent in the air. The shortcut that Ashley had taken was a clear path, and a person would not be confused about which direction to take, this was a baffling point to investigators.

After two weeks of not finding any evidence of Ashley, the government called off their search. The termination of the search angered many residents, and a few continued with the SAR despite the government pulling all resources. The government's theory was that Ashley could not have survived in the elements for over two weeks.

It was during the second week in September, more than two months after Ashley disappeared, that a hunter stumbled upon the young girl's skeleton 3.125 miles east and 4.375 miles south of the guest ranch. The bones were found in a very rugged area of high grass and swamps.

The RCMP reported to the press that at the scene of the skeleton they found a pair of girl's shorts and one shoe. No shirt or other shoe was found, even though the RCMP did an extensive search of the area for evidence.

The RCMP also made a statement about the location of Ashley's remains. They hadn't searched the area on the ground because they never believed that Ashley could have gotten that far in those rugged conditions.

The search for Ashley Krestianson was described as the largest at the time in the history of Alberta. The province threw every available resource into this effort and still couldn't find the girl before it was too late. The province utilized the best search information and still didn't search far enough out to find Ashley.

The location of Ashley's body and the rationale behind why it was found there does not make sense. The circumstances are similar to the Kory Kelly case in Minnesota (See Missing-411 Eastern United States).

Yukon

Population: 40,962
Capital City: Whitehorse

Yukon is the northwestern-most province in Canada, bordering the Beaufort Sea to the north, Alaska to the west, British Columbia to the south and the Northwest Territories to the east. The northernmost area of the territory is in the Arctic Circle. This is an ideal location to travel and view one of the most beautiful sites that nature offers us, the Aurora Borealis.

Whitehorse is the largest city in the Yukon with a population of 28,000. The town is approximately 50 miles north of the British Columbia border and sits on the Yukon River, the largest river in the region. Don't expect a large metropolitan city with hundreds of shops and restaurants. It does have a great theater that has a play from the 1800s that's memorable and worth attending.

The climate in this area in Canada can vary widely. I've seen days with 90-degree temperatures at 3 P.M. and into the thirties at night. The topography also is quite divergent, from lowlands to vast mountain ranges above the tree line. I have personally seen Grizzly bear, Caribou, Moose, and Dall Sheep, all in one day. There was a time in my life when I was working for a British Columbian Company. I was fortunate that we had business meetings at Inconnu Lodge in the Yukon. You can only take a floatplane or helicopter into the facility. It sits adjacent to a pristine lake surrounded by high mountains. The beauty of flying into the lodge cannot be described accurately.

If you like sports, Yukon offers many for all season. In the winter you can ski, snowshoe and play hockey in the outdoors. The summer provides fantastic fishing, hunting, river rafting, and even gold panning. Dawson City sprang onto the map in the 1870s when gold was discovered in the tributaries of the Yukon River. The gold rush took off in a big way on the 1890s and is still booming today at a different level. Instead of small gold panning operations of the 1800s, there are now multi-million dollar facilities that mine 24 hours a day during the summer months. The winters are too harsh to mine, and the operations close.

The Yukon needs to have the vast majority of their food and supplies transported into the area. The transportation fees mean that many items that you need for everyday living are expensive. Proportionately, wages in the Yukon are higher than provinces in the southern areas of Canada.

If you are thinking about moving to the Yukon, you better have a hardened soul. The average temperatures from November to March are far below freezing. I was there for the first time many years ago, and there were very few paved roads. Today, the economy is good, and the government has paved many roads that were not in years past.

Yukon will always hold a special place in my heart for its hundreds and hundreds of miles of unspoiled wilderness. The Yukon River has a gorgeous turquoise color of pure beauty, coupled with the Aurora Borealis, will leave you memories that will last a lifetime.

Yukon List of missing people by date.

Missing Person	Date, Missing• Age • Sex
Gertrude Duquette	07/07/64• 30•F
James Miller	09/22/74• 42• M
Bart Schleyer	09/14/04•49•M

Gertrude Duquette
Missing: 07/07/64, Dawson City, Yukon
Age at disappearance: 30 years
Water• Canine

Dawson City sits in the far western side Yukon just thirty miles from the Alaska border. The area has notoriety for mining and the Yukon River that flows through the city. The region around Dawson is famous today for a variety of gold mining television shows that proliferate in the area. If you ever get to this city, you have to go to the Sourdough Saloon and order the world-famous Sour toe Cocktail. The bartender puts a very old amputated toe in your drink as you guzzle the liquor.

In July 1964, Dawson City had a disappearance that made international headlines and is explained in this July 27 article in the

Nanaimo Daily News, "Miss Duquette recently returned to Dawson City from Calgary. She was believed to have gone for a walk with her mongrel dog before she was reported missing. Her dog returned home July 11 with porcupine quills in his muzzle. Forty men later combed the hillside near Dawson with no results."

Gertrude Duquette's disappearance puzzled the city of 1,375 permanent residents. A witness did come forward indicating that Gertrude had been seen in the afternoon of July 7 near the cemetery just outside of Dawson. The "Paddle Wheel" graveyard is outside the northern edge of town off a dirt road. The area around the cemetery is very thick with foliage and gets remote quickly. Highway 92 ends on the northwest side of the Yukon River and is the closest paved road to the location.

The RCMP committed 40 officers and search and rescue personnel along with a helicopter and two fixed-wing aircraft for ten days in their effort to locate Gertrude. The search effort found nothing.

After the official search ended for Gertrude, her friends and family continued the SAR for an additional week covering a twelve square mile area. The family also took Gertrude's dog out into the countryside trying to see if they showed any interest in tracking the scent. Nothing was ever found of Gertrude Duquette.

James Miller
Missing: 09/22/74, Dendel Lake, Yukon Territory, Canada
Age at disappearance: 42 years
Weather• Canines• Weather

I think that any outdoorsman dreams of a trip of a lifetime to an exotic location to bag a giant fish, hunt for big game and deal with the conflicts that always surface on a trip off the grid. This is a story about a hunter that lived the dream, and nightmare.

Richboro Pennsylvania is a northern suburb of Philadelphia and the hometown for 42-year-old James Miller. He was an outdoorsman, husband to Dianne and dad to his three sons, Jim, Richard, and Jeff. His business was successful, and he was able to save money for a trip to the Yukon Territory in far northwestern Canada. James would not be traveling alone; he was going with his friend, Glen Bierman.

In mid-September of 1974, James and Glen made the lengthy trip with multiple flights to eventually arrive in the small city of Watson Lake, Yukon Territory. Once they arrived, an outfitter had arranged for the pair to meet two guides and a cook for the excursion.

On September 15, the five men boarded a float plane and flew 145 miles to Dendel Lake where they made a temporary camp. They hunted for a few days and then traveled by horseback ten miles further north into the wilderness. They had directions that the plane would pick them up at Dendel on September 30.

By every account I could locate, James and Glen had the hunt of a lifetime. One man had shot a grizzly, both got a caribou, and they were last going for Bighorn sheep. They were hunting the La-Biche (Several different spellings) Mountains, noted for their height and ruggedness. Miller was on a mountain with the other guys, saw a sheep down the hillside 75 yards away, shot and killed it. The group went down, dressed out the animal and started carrying the remains back to camp. This October 21, 1974 article in the *Morning Call* had details, "After the second kill, Glen Bierman, 25, Penns Park, Bucks County who also made the trip, two guides and Miller decided to head back to their mountain camp. Bierman led the way followed by Miller and two guides together at the rear of a stretched outline. But Miller never returned to camp. No one knows how he was separated. Shots were fired in the area and the three who returned believed Miller fired his gun in response. Searches by the three failed. "We were sure he'd return," they told his wife." He was very experienced." But Miller was not to be found. After several days of problems with a radio, authorities were finally contacted. That was on September 27." What I find highly unusual about the previous statement was the failure of the radio to work. Was there some electronic interference or just a bad radio?

The RCMP eventually got to the scene and dropped in two officers, a canine unit and support equipment. The search lasted for at least nine days. This October 8, 1974 article in the *Edmonton Journal* had additional details, "An RCMP spokesman said Monday that weather had prevented a helicopter from going into the area to pick up a tracking dog and its handler."

I have been to the Yukon at least six times. I've flown the back-country in helicopters and float planes, some for business and other times for pleasure. I can tell you that the area is remote and not populated. Miller and Bierman were in some of the most desolate country in North America. If you have an emergency in this area, you are on your own for several days, more if there are weather issues.

On October 20, the RCMP announced that the search for Miller was over. The seasons were starting to change and with it the weather.

In early November, Diane Miller, James' wife flew to Watson Lake and met with the RCMP. She needed to see the location where her husband vanished and understand why the search was over. Police flew Mrs. Miller in a twin-engine Otter to the search area and adjacent mountain, and I can only guess that she was stunned at the vastness and lack of humanity. She returned to RCMP headquarters, thanked them for the diligence and commitment to finding her husband and returned to Pennsylvania.

This story has a factor to it that makes the disappearance challenging to understand. Even the story told directly by the guides on scene, they don't know how James got separated from three other people when he was hiking between them. People who don't read my work don't seem to understand how unusual the cases are and how unmistakably unusual the surrounding facts. I have no doubt the six-day delay in getting RCMP to the scene did not help in the search. The inoperable radio and weather played a significant role in this case.

Bart Schleyer
Missing 09/14/04, Reid Lakes, Yukon Territory, Canada
Age at disappearance: 49

If there ever was an outdoorsman who would be considered a man's man, it was Bart Schleyer. Bart was born in Cheyenne, Wyoming, in 1954. Due to the location of his birth and the fact that his father, a physician named Otis, was an avid hunter, Bart's life was destined to be lived outdoors. His father took him around the world on hunting adventures, and this had the boy hooked on the hunt, but not the kill.

Bart graduated in 1979 from Montana State University (MSU) with a master's degree in wildlife biology. He wrote his thesis on bear activity in Yellowstone National Park and attempted to understand how the bear reacted when confronted by humans. Bart later worked for the Interagency Grizzly Bear Study at MSU and learned live bear trapping

Bart Schleyer

skills. Later in life he became the world master of luring bears into traps. Many professionals stated that Bart knew more about bear behavior, tracking, and luring than anyone in the world.

Bart worked for a variety of groups after he graduated from college. At one point he was employed by the Montana Fish and Game Department, where he would set bear trap lines in some of the toughest terrain in the Bob Marshall Wilderness. Once the bears were trapped, Bart would install collars and follow the bears throughout the summer to study their behavior.

One of the many stories about Bart's athletic prowess tells of days he spent hiking the mountains, tracking and walking for some twelve hours—where there were no trails—before heading back to his cabin. Once home, Bart would start an exercise regime of push-ups, squats (using logs he had crafted for the task), and a variety of other exercises that would cripple the average man. Remember, Bart was doing these exercises after a full day in the mountains!

He moved to Alaska for a short period and studied taxidermy while enjoying the Alaskan outdoors. For Bart's next adventure, he was recruited by a friend to travel to the Russian Far East to study and trap Siberian tigers. Bart was again the optimum expert for trapping, collaring, and studying the tigers. It was also in Russia that he developed a relationship with a beautiful Russian woman, Tatiana. Bart and Tatiana had a son, Artyom. This was the first time he had dedicated time to a relationship and family.

In 2002 Bart moved to the Yukon Territory and called White-horse home. He developed a keen interest in the Yukon wildlife and was specifically interested in bowhunting sheep and moose. As a hunter, Bart had conquered almost every continent and most big game with his bow. He felt it offered a bigger challenge than hunting with a rifle. It should be clear to all readers that bowhunting is a skill that can take years to perfect. You must be stealthy, patient, and committed to be a successful bowhunter. Bowhunting is much more dangerous than using a firearm because you must get very close to your game. You will read about bowhunters in this book that disappeared and were never found.

On September 14, 2004, Bart arranged for a floatplane to fly him to Reid Lakes. The lakes sit approximately 110 miles east of the Alaska border, five miles west of the Klondike Highway, and ten miles south of McQuesten, Yukon. There are four major lakes in the Reid Lakes chain, with the largest being 1¼ miles long and about the same distance wide. The lakes are isolated from the highway by a river, and travelers cannot get to the lakes unless they fly in.

Bart's plane successfully landed at the largest of the Reid Lakes and dropped him and his gear on the shoreline. Bart not only took a tent and supplies but also an inflatable raft to meander around the lake.

I have spent many weeks in the Yukon and developed a few contacts. Warren Lafave is the owner of Inconnu Lodge in the eastern side of the province. When I asked Warren for a provincial wildlife contact to discuss the region around Reid Lakes, he sent me to Rick Fernel.

Rick spent twenty-five years as a wildlife biologist for the Yukon Territory before retiring in 2008. I asked Rick about the Reid Lakes area because I wanted to understand what type of wildlife and habitat it offers. Rick immediately stated that he knew about the Bart Schleyer incident and could never understand why he went to Reid Lakes. He said the fishing wasn't good at the lakes, and there wasn't much wildlife in the area. Rick made it clear that there were many other locations with better fishing and outstanding wildlife opportunities that put Reid Lakes to shame.

Bart had scheduled his floatplane to pick him up at Reid Lakes on September 28. The pilot arrived at the lake, pulled up to Bart's camp, and was confused by what he found.

Bart's tent was found knocked down, but the pilot was not sure by what. Near the tent, he found Bart's backpack with bear spray, along with his VHF radio and a knife. The pilot yelled for Bart but did not get a response. He imagined that if Bart had left, he would have taken his backpack and supplies. The pilot left the area and contacted RCMP, who later contacted friends.

The RCMP initially had a very limited role in the search for Bart. After he was reported missing, the RCMP did a flyby over Reid Lakes. That was it. Bart's friends arrived at the area and immediately went across the lake from his tent. Here they found his inflatable boat. Sixty feet inland from the boat, the team found a bag full of gear. Leaning next to the bag on an adjacent tree was Bart's bow and arrows. The bag of supplies had not been touched, and it was obvious to his friends that he had been sitting on it. They said it appeared as though Bart had been calling moose from the location, so they continued to scour the area. A short distance away, they found a camouflage facemask with a small amount of blood on it. They then decided to call the RCMP back to the scene.

On October 3, 2004, Yukon RCMP and conservation officers went to Reid Lakes in mass and set a grid search pattern in an attempt to find Bart Schleyer. Sixty yards from the bow, searchers found a skull and a few teeth. They also found a pair of camouflage pants, a camera, and a few small bones. The teeth were later positively identified as Bart's. Most investigators would stop the investigation at this point and claim a grizzly killed the wildlife biologist. But there were too many strange circumstances to claim a grizzly had killed a man who lured grizzly bears for a living.

For starters, there was significant bear and wolf scat at the scene. Many samples of scat were recovered and sent to a lab for testing. One issue that completely baffled investigators: there was no clothing found in any of the bear scat. When bears eat people, they eat everything—clothing, jewelry, anything you are wearing goes in and eventually comes out. It was also odd that Bart's pants were lying on the ground near the scene, almost as though he had removed them, or they had somehow come off. Most of the clothing that Bart would have been wearing was never found, even after a wide and comprehensive search of the area.

Conservation officers at the scene knew that bears usually cache their kills, burying them for a later meal. A thorough search of the Reid Lakes area didn't produce any evidence of a cache or any bloody ground from a body being dragged or wounded. The other troubling issue is that there was no sign of a struggle anywhere in the Reid Lakes camp where Bart was staying or near his bow. No moss, tundra, or branches were disturbed; it was a very calm site.

Several investigators made statements that his death is a mystery, and the idea that a bear killed him does not make any sense. People who worked with Bart all claimed that he would have gone down with a struggle. His friends said Bart was in outstanding shape and would have fought for his life. They do not believe a bear could have attacked Bart by surprise.

One of the last items that investigators found sixty yards from the bow was Bart's cap and a balaclava he was wearing. There was no damage to the cap or the balaclava, no blood, nothing to indicate something dreadful had happened. Investigators also found it very strange that Bart's balaclava was found with no punctures or bite marks in it, which is unusual because bears normally bite the head and neck. The coroner would later make a supporting statement that the skull did not have punctures or bite marks that would be associated with a bear attack.

Investigators find it difficult to believe that animals would have killed Bart and then left his bag completely undisturbed. Investigators also don't understand why a predator would kill and consume Bart and not travel the half mile to his camp to consume his food. Based on what they found at Bart's campsite, investigators believe that he had been alive at Reid Lakes just one night.

Coroner Sharon Hanley examined the little remains of Bart Schleyer and stated that with no tissue to examine it was difficult to draw conclusions. The coroner also stated that the bones that were recovered were "gnawed on by an animal." She did not specify what type of animal.

I asked Rick Fernel to share his thoughts about the scene where Bart was found. He said if I were to ask him about the strangest case in almost thirty years in the Yukon, it would be the Bart Schleyer disappearance. Rick stated that in all his years in the Yukon, it was his expert belief that "bears don't consume people up here." He stated that the largest of the Reid Lakes is shallow, with lots of bugs. It's a place where people don't travel. He said it appeared that Bart had taken his inflatable boat across the lake to hunt. Maybe he heard or saw something, but it was obvious from the scene that he was sitting and calling moose when something terrible happened.

One of the last statements Rick made about the disappearance of Bart was in regard to bears. He said it did appear that a bear had eaten a portion of Bart, but he didn't believe it killed or consumed all of him because there was no clothing in the scat and his pants were found in the bush. Rick stated that if Yukon Conservation Officers find any carnivorous bear in the area, they form a team to hunt and kill the bear. They never did this in Bart's case, and there was never any follow-up. Rick's closing statement on the Bert Schleyer case: "This was really, really an odd case."

Case Summary

Bart was a man that was very much in touch with the environment. He knew how to stalk and hunt game and how to attract, trap, and collar bears. The man even made his own bow and arrows with which he hunted—he was that in touch with nature. Everyone who made a statement about Bart called the man extremely humble, not your typical wildlife biologist.

Bart was sixty feet from the lake, sitting on a bag and calling for moose. He was keenly aware of every sound around the lakes. He felt he was not in any imminent danger, as his bow was found leaning against a tree (unless, of course, someone put that bow in that position after his death).

Bart was attacked and killed. His pants were off his body but not torn to shreds, although they did sustain some damage. The idea that Bart removed his own pants in an area known for significant bug activity and clouds of mosquitoes is quite doubtful. Whatever took Bart was very fast, very powerful, and had no interest in any of his food or tools. It does appear that something took Bart's clothes but left his pants. Something felt that Bart was a threat, but why?

Investigators believe that Bart had spent one complete night at his camp (based on the supplies used and garbage found at the scene). If Bart had been there one night, the odors that emanate from cooking would have been apparent miles away in a desolate region like Reid Lakes. It might have been these smells that brought Bart's predator to his location.

Bart Schleyer was the optimum man to be bowhunting in the Yukon Territory. If Bart could become a victim, any of us could be a victim. A recurring theme in this book is that many of these stories have never had significant press coverage and the vast majority of North Americans have never heard of these victims. I would hope that making the reader aware of the dangers that exist in the wilds of North America would elevate their senses and take additional precautionary measures when enjoying the wild.

Cases Similar to the Schleyer Disappearance

Bart's strange disappearance shares similarities with others, including the cases of Charles McCullar and Robert Winters from Crater Lake (OR), Atadero, Colorado, and Geraldine Huggan in Minaki, Ontario. Three men, one boy, and one girl disappeared into a very desolate region. When their remains were found, only their skulls and small pieces of bone were located.

In the Charles McCullar case, they found his pants and socks. That's it. Just like in Bart's case, they never found the majority of his other supplies, his shirt, or his coat. Also, one major item was missing in both cases: boots. Both of these men's boots were missing from the scene, yet in both cases their pants were left. There are no grizzly bears in Oregon, and yet Charles was completely consumed.

In the Geraldine Huggan case, investigators found one of her pant legs pulled inside out. American Indian trackers found human footprints in the area, although RCMP discounted their statements. They also found threads and bits of cloth from Geraldine's shirt. The physician who examined the clothing and the few remnants of Geraldine stated there was no blood on any clothing found, same as the other two incidents. There were a few tufts of hair found in the area where it is believed Geraldine died.

Canadian List of Missing by Date

**The first letter(s) in the list indicates location of disappearance.
A= Alberta
B= British Columbia
M= Manitoba
NB= New Brunswick
NF= Newfoundland & Labrador
NS= Nova Scotia
NT= Northwest Territory
O= Ontario
Q= Quebec
S= Saskatchewan
Y= Yukon

Name	Date/ Time Missing • Age • Sex • Location
NS• Son of John Henderson	11/15/1826• 4 • M
Q• Daughter of Belliveau	1865 • 5 • F
Q• Grace Cooper	08/08/13-1:00 p.m. • 5 •F
O• Edward Boreham	10/11/26 at 9:00 a.m. • 2 •M
Q• Emile Erazola	05/25/27•4•M
S• Allen Anderson	06/24/27-10:00 a.m.•2•M
S• Eddie Hamilton	07/06/28• 2• M
O• Ralph McKay	10/27/28-2:15 a.m.•21•M
O• Eva Hall	08/15/32–PM•13•F
M• T.H. Vigfusson	05/04/34-1:00 A.M.• 70• F
M• Betty Wolfrum	05/15/34•4•F
A• Evelyn Rauch	07/15/34–9 a.m. •2 • F
M• Florence Spence	08/05/34 at 3:00 p.m.•3•F
M• Frank Goy	08/07/34 •7•M
M• George Wanke	07/27/35•58•M
M• Jack Pike	09/05/35•5•M
B• Danny Schlicter	10/17/35-AM• 3• M
S• Freddie Mollenbeck	05/22/37-p.m.•2•M
S• Hazel Scraba	05/23/37-Unk •11•F

S• Ludvina Machishyn   05/23/37-Unk •10•F
A• Edward Schnaknacht   09/01/37–PM •4 •M
M• Simon Skogan   07/02/40•9•M
M• James McAmmond   10/05/41•19•M
B• Eric Catchpole   10/22/41- noon• 2 1/2• M
B• Kenneth Duncan   11/27/43-3:00 p.m.• 21• M
B• Leslie Heal   11/05/44-1:30 p.m.• 26•M
B• Frank Johnson   09/06/45• 65•M
B• Louis Majers   11/03/45•39•M
Q• Dominique Danis   11/23/47-12 :30 p.m.• 52•M
NT• Paul Robert   05/07/49• 21• M
A• Cathleen Whitlock   07/22/49-P.M.• 62• F
A• Helen Bogen   08/07/50-10:00 A.M.• 2½ •F
A• Lorraine Smith   09/02/50•2•F
S• Irene Rempel   10/10/50–2 p.m.•3•F
B• Alma Hall   06/09/51• 28• F
B• Raymond Hall   06/09/51•6•M
B• Leo Gaspard   07/31/51-Unk • 60 •M
B• David Anderson   05/20/53-10:00 A.M.• 3 1/2• M
O• Geraldine Huggan   07/05/53•5•F
B• Arthur Tibbett   11/09/53•29•M
B• Helena Jackson   04/11/54•46•F
B• John Last   09/26/54•24•M
NS• Howard Newell   01/22/55-Noon •6 •M
O• Eugene Loughlin   11/12/55- 4:00 p.m.• 62•M
O• Jack Ostrom   05/29/57 •74 •M
B• Herman Jungerhuis   11/10/57• 55• M
B• Cindy Lou Maclane   09/09/58-9:00 A.M.• 2• F
B• Tony Richard Beauchamp   09/16/58-3:00 P.M.• 2• M
M• Alex Thorne   10/04/58–Unk•44•M
O• Meryl Newcombe   10/29/59• 50•M
O• George Weeden   10/29/59• 63•M
B• Betty Jean Masters   07/03/60- 8:00 P.M.• 20 MOS• F
B• Gezo Peczeli   09/18/60• 21• M
NT• Herbert Lafferty   10/08/60-Noon•12•M
O• Sander Lingman   11/01/60•35•M
B• Wallace Marr   11/19/62• 30•M

Y• Gertrude Duquette   07/07/64• 30•F
S• Richard Spyglass   08/05/64•5•M
B• Leslie Evans   06/11/66•39•M
B• John Evans   06/11/66•14•M
B• Clancy O'Brien   08/20/66 P.M.• 9• M
B• Roger Olds   08/25/66•19•M
O• Diane Prevost   09/17/66•2•F
B• Myron Shutty   07/09/67-2:30 P.M.• 5• M
B• Kenneth Vanderleest   07/14/67–PM • 3 • M
B• Alphonse Boudreault   11/09/70•22•M
B• Michael Bryant   11/14/70-5:00 p.m.•32•M
O• Adrian McNaughton   06/12/72-PM•5•M
A• Paul Schroeder   07/06/72- 6:30 P.M.• 72• M
O• Elizabeth Kant   10/16/72• 45•F
B• Richard Wenegast   10/27/73- 1:30 p.m.• 31• M
O• Brian Henry   05/05/74•21•M
NB• Robert Comeau   06/28/74• 42•M
B• Margaret Andersen   07/06/74- 7:00 p.m.•59•F
Y• James Miller   09/22/74• 42• M
B• Yehudi Prior   09/23/74• 2• M
O• Jane Smith   08/09/75•20•F
B• Henry Hansen   09/22/75• Unk• M
O• Raymond Juranitich   10/08/75•48•M
NF• Anne Abraham   08/05/76 at 3:00 p.m. • 22 •F
NT• Fred Van Duffelen   12/17/78, 4:00 a.m.• 26•M
A• Kevin Reimer   06/29/79–Noon •9•M
A• James Caraley   07/18/79•22•M
O• Foster Bezanson   10/25/80• 64• M
A• Steve Maclaren   06/30/81•25•M
B• Wendy Riley   02/11/83-PM• 29• F
A• Shelly Bacsu   05/03/83•16•F
B• Nicholas Vanderbilt   08/22/84• 25• M
B• Francis Glenhill   08/22/84• 29• M
A• Sharel Haresym   09/04/84•35•F
O• Toivo Reinikanen   09/26/84•36•M
O• Jessica Azzopardi   07/24/85–3:30 p.m.•20 MOS• F
B• Janice Pedlar   02/08/86- P.M., 37• F

M• Madeline Grisdale   07/06/86•49•F
B• Lynn Hillier   07/24/86• 2• F
O• Clayton McFaul   08/15/86•50•M
A• Jesse Rinker   05/04/87–4:30 p.m.•2•M
B• Charlie Musso   09/07/87-5:00 p.m.•61•M
B• Emerson Dobroskay   10/28/88-p.m.•21•M
B• Wally Finnegan   11/04/89• 51•M
A• Brian Adrian   02/04/91• 37•M
A• Lillian Owens   06/28/91•46•F
B• Raymond Krieger   08/28/92-9:00 p.m.• 48•M
Q• Glen Moquin   08/09/93-Noon• 22• M
B• Steven Eby   11/14/93-3:00 p.m.•29•M
O• Michael McIntyre   04/07/94•37•M
B• Richard Grey   04/14/94•22•M
S• Ashley Krestianson   07/14/94•8•F
A• Donald Belliveau   01/27/95•28•M
A• Rhonda Runningbird   03/26/95•25•F
B• Samuel Wright   06/03/95- 6:00 P.M.• M
O• William Reed   08/01/95•69•M
A• Knut Thielemann   08/04/95•22•M
Q• Chris Brown   11/11/95- 2:00 P.M.•26•M
B• Ian Ralph Sutherland   08/15/96•30•M
O• Frank Szpak   09/23/96• 69•M
A• Melvin Hoel   03/12/97•64•M
B• Karl Walter   06/28/97-5:00 p.m.•65•M
O• Bernard Champagne   07/10/97• 80• M
Q• Guy Ouellet   07/18/98-2:00 P.M.• 42• M
M• Marcus McKay   07/15/00–PM•8•M
B• Brian Douglas Faughnan   07/12/02 • 35 • M
O• Raymond Tunnicliffe   08/26/02•72•M
Q• Jimmy Rambone Jr.   09/03/03–3 p.m. • 51 • M
B• Richard Milner   09/29/03•43•M
O• Joseph Grozelle   10/22/03-5:00 a.m.•21•M
B• Juaqueline Bob   07/06/04• 41•F
Y• Bart Schleyer   09/14/04•49•M
B• Jared Stanley   01/10/05•25•M
B• David Koch   05/25/05 at 8:00 p.m.•36•M

Q• Mark Kraynak 08/22/05-3:32 a.m.•23•M
Q• Steven Wright 08/22/05-3:32 a.m.•20•M
A• Tom Howell 09/12/05•46•M
A• Wai Fan 09/28/05•43•M
B• Tom Leonard 10/02/05• 40•M
NF• Andrew Sexton 02/25/06•21•M
A• Robert Leigh 08/13/06 •20•M
A• Stephanie Stewart 08/26/06•70•F
NB• Matthew Sloan 09/17/06-11:30 p.m.•26•M
A• Robert Neale 05/02/07•77•M
O• Christine Calayca 08/06/07•20•F
B• John Kahler 11/04/07-4:00 A.M.• 29• M
B• William Pilkenton 02/15/08• 7•M
B• Michael Raster 08/08/08• 43• M
O• Lachlan Cranswick 01/23/10 •41•M
B• Tyler Wright 08/10/10–Unk • 35 • M
B• Rachael Bagnall 09/08/10-Unk • 25•F
B• Jonathan Jette 09/08/10-Unk • 34•M
NS• Harris Hill 11/10/10-1:00 P.M. • 87•M
NF• Cleon Smith 04/02/11-p.m•30•M
B• Darcy Brian Turner 06/20/11 • 55 • M
A• Kevin Kennedy 08/21/11•59•M
NF• William Oberkiser 10/09/11• 65•M
O• Daniel Trask 11/03/11–Unk•28•M
B• Matthew Huszar 12/16/11-p.m.•25• M
B• David Christian 03/27/12-11:30 p.m.•27• M
A• Rhonda Cardinal 07/13/12–Unk•42•F
B• Raymond Salmen 05/28/13• 65•M
O• Jeffery Boucher 01/13/14-7:00 a.m.•52•M
O• Douglas Queen 03/17/14-Noon •48•M
NS• Marty Leger 05/29/14-4:00 p.m.•30•M
B• Sylvia Apps 07/13/14 at 4:00 P.M. • 69 • F
O• Ethan Stokes 01/25/15-1:45 a.m.•20•M
B• Sukhjeet Saggu 06/05/15 at 4:00 P.M. • 20 • M
B• Neville Jewell 09/12/15-6:00 p.m.•52•M
B• Deanna Wertz 07/19/16 • 46 • F
B• Gordon Sagoo 08/14/16 at 2:00 p.m. • 50 • M

B• Debbie Blair   09/29/16 at noon • 65 • F
M• Mark McKelvey   07/24/17-8:30 A.M.• 36• M
O• Paul Yelland   10/23/17-12:30 p.m.• 66• M
B• Alison Raspa   11/23/17- 1:15 A.M.• 25• F
B• Travis Thomas   08/07/18•40•M

172   Total
129   Males (66%)
43   Females (33%)
Average Age= 32 years

Victims Found= 45%
Victims Never Found= 55%

Disappearances by Location

Location	Males	Females	Total
Alberta	15	10	25
British Columbia	55	14	69
Manitoba	8	4	12
New Brunswick	2	2	4
Newfoundland	3	1	4
Nova Scotia	4	0	4
Northwest Territory	3	0	3
Ontario	25	7	32
Quebec	8	2	10
Saskatchewan	4	4	8
Yukon	2	1	3
Totals	129	43	172

Years with Most Disappearances:
2005- 7 Disappearances
2011- 6
1995- 6
1934- 5
1966- 5
1974- 5
2010- 5

1937- 4
1960- 4
1974- 4
1984- 4
1986- 4
2006- 4
2014- 4

The most common time for someone to disappear in North America is 4:00 P.M.

Multiple Disappearances in a short time period:

Two disappearances in a short time span:

M• Florence Spence	08/05/34 at 3:00 p.m.•3•F	
M• Frank Goy	08/07/34 •7•M	
B• Cindy Lou Maclane	09/09/58-9:00 A.M.• 2• F	
B• Tony Richard Beauchamp	09/16/58-3:00 P.M.• 2• M	
O• Meryl Newcombe	10/29/59• 50•M	
O• George Weeden	10/29/59• 63•M	
B• Leslie Evans	06/11/66•39•M	
B• John Evans	06/11/66•14•M	
B• Clancy O'Brien	08/20/66 P.M.• 9• M	
B• Roger Olds	08/25/66•19•M	
B• Myron Shutty	07/09/67-2:30 P.M.• 5• M	
B• Kenneth Vanderleest	07/14/67–PM • 3 • M	
B• Alphonse Boudreault	11/09/70•22•M	
B• Michael Bryant	11/14/70-5:00 p.m.•32•M	

Y• James Miller   09/22/74• 42• M
B• Yehudi Prior   09/23/74• 2• M

B• Nicholas Vanderbilt   08/22/84• 25• M
B• Francis Glenhill   08/22/84• 29• M

O• Michael McIntyre   04/07/94•37•M
B• Richard Grey   04/14/94•22•M

O• William Reed   08/01/95•69•M
A• Knut Thielemann   08/04/95•22•M

B• Rachael Bagnall   09/08/10-Unk • 25•F
B• Jonathan Jette   09/08/10-Unk • 34•M

Three disappearances in two days, all in the same province.
S• Freddie Mollenbeck   05/22/37-p.m.•2•M
S• Hazel Scraba   05/23/37-Unk •11•F
S• Ludvina Machishyn   05/23/37-Unk •10•F

Notable Cases and Quotes

In past books, I have included a section that highlighted notable cases that should be at the forefront of the reader's mind. Every disappearance in this book is unusual, but the cases cited in this section should cause you to pause to understand the ramifications of what was revealed.

Emile Erazola
Missing: 05/25/27, Montreal, Quebec
Age at disappearance: 4 years
A child disappearing in a large city may not impact many as strange or unusual. Children were out walking in the town with their aunt. In past books, I have noted that many disappearances occur when not in the presence of the parents. As they were out, severe weather struck (weather issue), and the aunt had a memory lapse (lack of memory of the incident). During the time that the aunt cannot recall what happened, Emile disappeared.

It is the facts surrounding the discovery of the body that should be placed in your memory bank. Here was the quote, "When the body was found yesterday afternoon, examination of the bushes surrounding the vacant field failed to show how the boy managed to get into the field." The same article went on to say the boy did not have any scratches or bruises. It's evident that the investigating officer saw the strangeness of this incident when they tried to look for tracks, etc., showing the boy walked into the field or was carried by someone. If no tracks are going into the field or bushes, and the boy did not have any scratches, how did Emile get into the position he was found? Where was he for the twelve hours that he was not with his family?

**Pay close attention to the dates of the following four cases.
Betty Wolfrum- 4 years
Missing: 05/15/34
Moosehorn, Manitoba
Betty was a German-speaking four-year-old that vanished from her rural farm for 110 hours. During the time she was missing, the area was inundated by a heavy rainstorm (weather issue). A local

farmer went to an isolated area and recovered the missing girl. Here was the farmer's statement following his discovery, "I did not expect to come back alive, or, if I did come back, I would be all broken up." Other farmers made the statement that their cows had been coming back milked by someone. The area of this disappearance was extremely remote; everyone who lived in the region knew who resided in the area.

What was the farmer afraid of when he recovered, Betty? What had been milking the cows?

Evelyn Rauch- 2 years
Missing: 07/15/34
Rocky Mountain House, Alberta
This little girl disappeared from her parent's rural property and was found hours later unable to explain where she had been or how she vanished (memory loss).

Florence Spence-3 years
Missing: 08/05/34
Beresford Lake, Manitoba
Florence was with her family and was taking a hike to an abandoned mine in the far eastern section of Manitoba near Beresford Lake. Somehow, Florence, got separated from her family and was lost. A friend of the family had a dream about the girl, awoke the following day, and walked straight into a remote and desolate region of the bush and recovered the girl. The fact that some people have these unusual dreams and can find people has been presented several times in my past books. Who or what is telling these people where the children can be located? Past readers have stated that it appears that something takes the children and when they are done, notifies a person on the periphery that they can retrieve them.

Frank Goy- 7 years
Missing: 08/07/34
Dallas, Manitoba
The Goy family lived on the outskirts of Dallas, Manitoba, in a rural region. Their seven-year-old son disappeared and was found

328 | Missing 411 Canada

three days later, thirteen miles (Distance Traveled) away. Traveling thirteen miles through wild bushland in three days is quite an accomplishment for an adult, let alone a seven-year-old boy.

I've just presented four cases of young children disappearing in less than three months. This run of missing cases of young children is phenomenal. Even more perplexing is that three of these incidents are in Manitoba.

5/5/34- Wolfrum- Disappeared 40 miles southwest of Frank Goy.
8/5/34- Spence - Disappeared 100 miles southeast of Betty Wolfrum. Are these four cases all just a coincidence of dates and locations? Are all of these disappearances just a coincidence that they happened close to each other in Manitoba? There were no other disappearances that formed a cluster anywhere in Canada during this time.

Jack Pike- 5 years
Missing: 09/05/35
Norbert, Manitoba
If the previous four Manitoba cases weren't enough to tweak your interest, how about the Jack Pike case? This incident happened just one month after the Florence Spence case.

The Pike family was picking berries, Jack wandered off, and the parents heard him scream. The boy disappeared and was eventually located on the opposite side of an adjacent river. How did the boy get across the water?

Simon Skogan- 9 years
Missing: 07/02/40
55 Miles north of Winnipeg, Manitoba
Simon disappeared berry picking and was never found. This was another search and rescue where local farmers stated that their cows were coming back milked. I know some readers will think that vagrants, etc. are probably doing this. In the Skogan case, there were eighty soldiers and hundreds of locals that searched for the boy. They never found any evidence of people camping in the region. These remote areas of the Canadian north have the local farmers and ranchers knowing their property like you know your backyard. The

residents would know anyone who came into the region and made an encampment. What or who is milking these cows? Is there a relationship between the cows being milked and the disappearances?

Geraldine Huggan- 5 years
Missing: 07/05/53
Minaki, Ontario

The Huggan family were at a rural cabin when Geraldine went missing. The search for the girl included First Nations, tracking experts. She was eventually found consumed by something. There were very few remains left to identify. The trackers did locate her pants with one leg inside out. The searchers were adamant that there was no blood on the clothing, an important point. Bears and wolves do not care about clothing; they will eat right through the cloth. Experts on the scene stated that there were wolf tracks in the area, but they did not consume the girl (their statement). One additional piece of controversy in this incident was that trackers found what they thought was an adult-sized footprint in the moss.

Who or what made the footprint in the moss? I do not believe that these First Nation Trackers would make a mistake between a bear and a human print.

What consumed Geraldine? This case is very close in facts to the disappearance I chronicled of the of a young boy, page 224, Missing 411 Western United States. This was another incident where a pant leg was found inside out, and the facts surrounding the disappearance are unexplained to this day.

Cindy Lou MacLane
Missing: 09/09/58, Willow River, BC
Age at disappearance: 2 years

Residents of the rural Canadian bush know the wildlife in their area and subsequently know the sounds they make. When you get five men together and they all hear a sound they can't identify, I'm paying attention. This is exactly what happened when five locals stayed out in the bush overnight and all heard a whimpering sound that imitated a young child's whimper. A massive search the following day found nothing.

There was also a very strange behavior exhibited by a tracking dog on this case. It ran in circles near a river bank. The handler stated the dog had found 4 of 5 missing people in the past and had never acted in this way before. The handler stated they didn't know what to make of the behavior. If the behavior was near the river edge, well, maybe the child went into the water, exhibiting this near the bank, makes no sense.

Marcus McKay- 8 years
Missing: 07/15/00
Waterhen Lake, Manitoba

Little Marcus was hunting with his father, got separated, and was lost. In this incident, the boy's grandmother had an unusual dream, here is the quote, "The little boy was lying down beside a bear to be warm." What is fascinating about this quote is that young children who have disappeared and returned alive have stated doing the same thing. The stories are in my past books.

Was the grandmother correct, was Marcus Marcus keeping warm with the assistance of a bear?

Leo Gaspard
Missing 07/31/51
Pitt Lake, British Columbia

There are strange stories associated with this area of British Columbia. The following quote exemplifies the unusual things seen in the night sky, "Strange lights recently have been flickering in the skies above the Pitt Lake Mountains in the icy wilderness of British Columbia. The aged Indians of the district say the weird illumination is caused by the spirits of the 11 murdered squaws of Slummack, a strange Indian killer who disposed of women to protect the secret of his fabulously rich Lost Creek mine." The lights described in the quote would be called something else today. There is always an ounce of truth in all myths, what is a Slummack?

Rhonda Cardinal- 42 years
Missing: 07/31/12
Calling Lake, Alberta

This disappearance is centered on a remote hunting cabin. Rhonda disappeared, and her recollection of the incident is described in this quote," Ms. Cardinal can't explain why she left the first cabin, she 'blacked out,' woke up lost and started wandering through the bush."

This lack of memory has been described in many cases in the eight other Missing 411 books. What is happening to these people in remote areas? Could "blacking out" be one of the reasons people are lost and disappear? What did she do while she has no memory?

Jessica Azzopardi- 20 months
Missing: 07/24/85
Lake Saint Clair, Ontario

Lake Saint Clair sits between Lake Erie and Lake Huron. The Azzopardi's owned a residence on the Ontario side of the lake.

In Missing 411: Law, I wrote extensively about the unusual nature of disappearances throughout the Great Lakes region. Land, water, and air disappearances in this area are profoundly strange.

Jessica vanished from her backyard that led to the lake. Her body was found in the water 14 hours after she disappeared six miles from her residents. The Coast Guard stated they didn't believe it is possible for a body to float that distance in that time frame. The big kicker, in this case, the coroner stated that Jessica had drowned just 90 minutes before she was found.

The possibility that another boater dumped the body in the lake is not realistic. The lake was full of law enforcement and Coast Guard boats searching for the girl. Why would any criminal risk being seen under these circumstances? They could easily dump the body on a remote shore in the woods.

Where was Jessica for the 14 hours she was missing? It's a fact that she wasn't in the water that entire time as she would've drowned earlier, or she would have suffered hypothermia.

In Missing 411: A Sobering Coincidence, I described a series of people who vanished and were later found in water. Many of these victims were young men who had been drinking. In several of these cases, the coroner could not determine the cause of death. Jessica's case adds many facts that are not typically found in cases on land.

332 | Missing 411 Canada

The fact we know how long she had been dead is essential. We also know precisely how long she had been in the water, 90 minutes.

How did Jessica enter the water? How was she removed from her backyard without anyone see or hearing anything? Where was she prior to entering the water?

Sukhjeet Saggu- 20 years
Missing: 06/05/15
Lindeman Lake, British Columbia

I have made a clear finding in my past books that many of the missing either disappear in or near a boulder field or are found in boulder fields. This incident is a profound example of the association of boulder fields and missing people.

Sukhjeet jogged ahead of his friends on a trail and vanished. His friends called local search and rescue to look for their friend. I encourage people to look at this region from Google Earth to understand the topography of the land.

The victim's body was located far from the trail and in a very isolated location. Read the words of the SAR personnel, they are concerned and confused by what they found, "An RCMP helicopter spotted the man's body within a boulder field Saturday afternoon. At this time, the cause of death has not been released, but circumstances of the disappearance have been deemed highly unusual as he was found away from the meeting point with his friends- far away from the lake and any trail." The SAR commander made the following statement, "It was very, very strange and difficult to explain why he ended up where he did,' said Fraser, adding that the boulder field is quite a bit of elevation above the lake, and a fair distance from the trail."

How would Sukhjeet get to that location? Why would he be there? The incline of the boulder field is slight; did he fall, or was he dropped?

These are obviously not all of the intriguing cases, but we wanted to pick out a few that you can concentrate on.

Best Safety Practices When Entering the Wilderness

- Always notify a friend or relative exactly where you are going, when you are entering and exiting. Be comfortable in knowing that this person will call for SAR if they do not hear from you at an agreed upon time.
- Carry a hard copy map of the area you are visiting.
- Check the weather before you enter the wilderness.
- Carry extra water and energy bars
- Purchase and carry a lightweight orange emergency blanket
- Have a whistle with you at all times.
- Carry a personal Locator Beacon and/or a Satellite Phone.
- If you feel comfortable and are trained, coupled with it is legal, carry a firearm and extra ammunition. If lost, stay in your position and fire 3 round in rapid succession, this indicates you are lost. Repeat the three round bursts every hour.

Thank you for taking the time to read one of our nine books in the series that has dealt with issues that the majority of the family's highlighted inside will never forget.

Contact me anytime at: missing411@yahoo.com

David Paulides

MISSING 411 OVERVIEW

Missing 411 (The Movie)
This was our first documentary.
This 4K 91-minute documentary chronicles the disappearances of five children from the wilds of North America. Les Stroud is one of the stars of the show and plays an integral role of explaining the possibilities of a young child traversing miles in the outdoors. Former *Los Angeles Magazine* and NBC movie critic John Barbour rated this the #1 documentary of 2017
Released: June 2017
Executive Producer: David Paulides
Directors: Ben Paulides, Mike Degrazier
Starring: George Knapp, Les Stroud, David Paulides
Available in Blu-ray and HD DVD

Missing 411: The Hunted
Documentary #2
A 97 minute movie based on the unusual disappearances of a series of hunters with common profile points. There are a series of interviews with search and rescue commanders and law enforcement authorities. The movie ends with two different stories of unexplained circumstances that hunters have faced in the woods, supported with scientific evidence. This movie reached #1 in the world on iTunes.
Released: June 2019
Executive Producer: David Paulides
Director: Mike Degrazier
Starring: David Paulides
Available in HD DVD

Missing 411: Western United States
The eastern and western books were originally one book. I split and published them as two books, which I released one month apart.
Published: February 2, 2012
367 pages
Covers the western United States and Canada

Missing 411: Eastern United States
Published: March 5, 2012
358 pages
Covers the eastern United States

Missing 411: North America and Beyond
Published: February 28, 2013
488 pages
New stories of missing people from the United States, Canada, Australia, England, France, Iceland, and Indonesia

Missing 411: The Devil's in the Detail
Published: April 18, 2014
446 pages
New stories from the United States, Canada, Australia, Borneo, Ecuador, United Kingdom, New Zealand, Switzerland, and Austria. There is an extensive analysis in the back of the book of cases from the first four books, including statistics.

Missing 411: A Sobering Coincidence
Published: July 22, 2015
398 pages
This book exposes an entirely new set of unusual disappearances with young men found in bodies of water. Cases are documented from the United States, Canada, France, Spain, and the United Kingdom.

Missing 411: Hunters
Published: June 21, 2016
362 pages
These are stories of armed hunters who disappeared under very unusual circumstances. Cases are documented from the United States, Canada, Australia, and Azerbaijan.

Missing 411: Off the Grid
Published: September 16, 2017
401 Pages
Entirely new stories from the United States, Canada, and six other countries. Tables, lists, and analysis from past books are in the conclusions. Statements from SAR personnel are highlighted.

Missing 411: LAW
Published: September 2018
375 Pages
This is a new spoke in the investigative wheel that presents a series of aircraft disappearances United States, Scotland and Australia. The book also presents recently released studies of land based vanishing in the United States, Canada, Italy, Norway and the United Kingdom. The manuscript ends covering geographical triangles and water related disappearances.

All items are available online from our website. We *do not* sell on Amazon or any other online service. All books are $24.95 plus shipping and handling directly from our website store. We do ship internationally.

www.canammissing.com

INDEX